Stunning

CSS3

A PROJECT-BASED GUIDE
TO THE LATEST IN CSS

Zoe Mickley Gillenwater

New
Riders

Stunning CSS3: A project-based guide to the latest in CSS
Zoe Mickley Gillenwater

New Riders
1249 Eighth Street
Berkeley, CA 94710
(510) 524-2178
Fax: (510) 524-2221

Find us on the Web at www.newriders.com
To report errors, please send a note to errata@peachpit.com
New Riders is an imprint of Peachpit, a division of Pearson Education
Copyright © 2011 by Zoe Gillenwater

Acquisitions Editor: Wendy Sharp
Production Editor: Hilal Sala
Project/Copy Editor: Wendy Katz
Technical Editor: Chris Mills
Cover design: Charlene Charles-Will
Interior design: Mimi Heft, Charlene Charles-Will
Compositor: Danielle Foster
Indexer: Emily Glossbrenner

ISBN 13: 978-0-321-72213-3
ISBN 10:   0-321-72213-2

9 8 7 6 5 4 3 2 1

Printed and bound in the United States of America

To Mr. Butkus,
for teaching me HTML and Photoshop 4
at Downers Grove North High School

Acknowledgments

I want to thank everyone whose assistance has made writing this book possible and painless.

Immense thanks go to my copy editor Wendy Katz for ensuring my writing was clear, precise, and polished. It was wonderful to work with you again. Thank you for your guidance, advice, and revisions, particularly your continual correction of my placement of the word "only." Someday I'll learn its mysteries.

My writing also owes a lot to the tremendous work of Chris Mills, my technical editor. Thank you for painstakingly checking my code, offering helpful suggestions, answering my technical questions, and pointing out areas to correct or clarify.

I'm grateful to my acquisitions editor at Peachpit, Wendy Sharp, for making the book a reality. Thanks also to all the other staff at Peachpit/New Riders who have been involved in producing this book. I don't know your names, but I know how hard you've worked on this and how talented you are, and I'm grateful.

Thanks to David Fugate, my literary agent, for his guidance and advocacy.

There are many people who weren't directly involved in the writing of the book but to whom I owe so much of my knowledge. Thanks to Zoltan Hawryluk, Paul Irish, and Richard Fink for answering my technical questions and providing great tools for working with CSS3. I'm grateful to my high school teacher Mr. Butkus for starting me down this path by teaching me HTML and Photoshop 4. Thanks also to my former boss Lamar Heyward for putting the crazy idea of using CSS for all style and layout into my head. I've also learned so much from the work of John Allsopp, Dan Cederholm, Andy Clarke, Chris Coyier, Roger Johansson, Eric Meyer, Trent Walton, Estelle Weyl, and many others. Thanks for being so brilliant and sharing it with the rest of us.

Finally, thanks to my fantastic family. Cary, I'm so thankful for your loving support through this second book-writing expedition. You've been incredibly patient with my long hours and listening to me complain about browser bugs and confusing W3C specs, and you've taken such good care of Asha while I've toiled away. Mom, Dad, and Faith, you also watched Asha a good bit during this process, and I'm very grateful for your help. Asha, thanks also to you for letting Mama work and coming to visit me with hug breaks every once in a while. I love you all.

Table of Contents

Introduction

CSS3, the newest version of the style sheet language of the web, is less about creating new effects and more about accomplishing the beautiful web design effects you're familiar with in fantastic new ways—ways that are more efficient and produce more usable and flexible results than the techniques we've been using for the last decade.

CSS3 is still changing and evolving, as are browsers to support it and web designers to figure out how best to use it. CSS3 can create some stunningly beautiful and cool effects, as you'll see throughout this book. But if these effects aren't practical for real-world sites right now, what's the point? In this book, I'll focus on teaching you the cutting-edge CSS techniques that can truly improve your sites and are ready to be used in your work right away.

This book is not an encyclopedia or reference guide to CSS3; it won't teach you every single property, selector, and value that's new to CSS since version 2.1. Instead, it will teach you the most popular, useful, and well-supported pieces of CSS3 through a series of practical but innovative projects. Each chapter (after Chapter 1) walks you through one or more exercises involving the new techniques of CSS3 to produce a finished web page or section of a page. You can adapt these exercises to your own projects, or use them as inspiration for completely different ways to creatively use the new properties, selectors, and values you've learned.

In some ways, CSS3 is a new way of thinking as much as a new way of developing your pages. It can be hard to think of how to use the new border-image property, for instance, when you've been making web sites for years and aren't used to having the option of using an image for the border of a box. Because of this, I've included a list of ideas for how to use each CSS3 property, selector, and value I cover, beyond just the single way we use it in the exercise. I hope to provide you with plenty of inspiration for how to put the CSS3 techniques you're learning to work in your own projects, plus the technical know-how to make sure you can use CSS3 comfortably and efficiently.

Who Should Read this Book

This book is meant for anyone who already has experience using CSS, but wants to take their sites and skills to the next level. I assume that you know HTML and CSS syntax and terminology, but you don't need to be a CSS expert, and you certainly don't need to have any experience using anything that's new to CSS3. Whether you've just started using CSS or have been developing sites with it for years, this book will teach you powerful new techniques to add to your CSS toolkit.

Exercise Files

Each of the chapters is made up of at least one exercise where you will have the opportunity to implement the techniques in a real page, step by step. You can download the files for these exercises at the book's companion site at www.stunningcss3.com and work along in them as you go through the steps of each exercise. I've provided both a starter file and final file for each exercise, as well as a few intermediate steps for the longer exercises, so you can check in periodically and make sure you've made the correct changes to your own files.

You can use whatever code editor you like when working with the exercise files. There are no tools in particular that you must have in order to work with and create CSS. I personally use Adobe Dreamweaver, but do all of my CSS development in code view by hand. If you're using Dreamweaver or a similar editor, I recommend you too work on the CSS by hand.

Although a great deal of effort has been made to check the code in this book, there are bound to be a few errors. Please report any errors to me through the email form on the book's web site, and I'll be sure to note them on the site and update the exercise files if needed.

Links

Each chapter contains several links to related resources, articles, tutorials, tools, and examples that I think would be useful for you. And it's certainly easier to click on a live link than painstakingly type out a URL that you're copying from a printed book, so I've provided a compendium of all the links from each chapter on www.stunningcss3.com.

CSS3 is a rapidly changing topic, so in a few cases, I'll be updating these link lists as new resources come out. You'll see a note in the book every time one of these continually updated lists of resources is present, pointing you to the book site to find the latest information.

Browsers

The exercises in this book have been tested in the latest versions of the major browsers. At the time of this writing, these browser versions are Chrome 6, Firefox 3.6, Internet Explorer 8, Opera 10.6, and Safari 5. The exercises were also tested in the beta versions of Internet Explorer 9 and Firefox 4 available at the time of this writing, but behavior may be different from what's described in the book by the time these browsers are finalized and released.

The exercises have also been tested in older browser versions that are still in significant use today (such as Internet Explorer 7 and 6). In many cases, the CSS3 effects we'll be adding that work in the newest browsers also work in older versions of those same browsers; even when they don't, the pages still work, are always perfectly usable, and look fine. We'll always go over possible ways to provide workarounds or fallbacks for non-supporting browsers for each technique.

For information on which browsers a given technique works in, I've provided a table of browser-support information for each property or selector introduced in each chapter. Each browser is set to "yes," "partial," or "no." A value of "yes" means the browser supports all of the syntax and behavior; it may have very minor bugs or inconsistencies with the spec, but overall it's compliant. A value of "partial" means the browser supports some of the syntax and behavior, but not all, or not without significant bugs or inconsistencies.

Some CSS3 properties work only using a vendor-specific prefixed version of the property (you'll learn about these prefixed properties in Chapter 1). I've indicated which browsers require the prefixes on a given property in the browser support tables.

In cases where support in a given browser is relatively new and there's a chance that some users of the older, non-supporting versions of that browser are still out there, I've provided the version number of the browser in the browser support table, indicating which version was the earliest to support the property or selector. If the browser has supported the property or selector for the last few versions and

NOTE: On the flip side, I've also occasionally included the browser version number in the support table when it's particularly notable how early the property or selector was supported—for instance, the fact that IE 4 supports `@font-face`!

it's unlikely that there's any significant number of users of the non-supporting versions, I have not included the earliest version number in the support table; you can feel safe that all versions of that browser in use support it.

Conventions Used Throughout this Book

This book uses a few terms that are worth noting at the outset.

- *W3C* refers to the World Wide Web Consortium, the organization that creates the official standards and specifications of the web, including CSS3.

- *IE* refers to the Windows Internet Explorer browser. IE 8 and earlier means IE 8, 7, and 6.

- *Webkit-based browsers* means Safari (both on desktop and on mobile devices), Chrome, and any other browsers that use a recent version of the Webkit browser-rendering engine.

- Occasionally, you'll see a reference to "all browsers." This means all browsers that are in significant use today, not literally every single obscure browser that may have a fractional piece of market share.

All of the exercises in this book are written in HTML5 markup. However, all that means in this case is that I've used the short and sweet HTML5 doctype, `<!DOCTYPE html>`, as well as the shorter `meta` character encoding, `style`, and `script` tags. I haven't included any of the new elements that HTML5 introduces, such as `section` or `article`, so the pages will work without any trouble in IE 8 and earlier, but you're welcome to change the markup for your own pages in whatever way you like. All the exercises will also work in HTML 4.01 or XHTML 1.

All CSS examples shown should be placed in an external style sheet or in the head of an HTML or XHTML document. The exercise files have their CSS contained in the head of the page, for ease of editing, but it's best to move that CSS to an external style sheet for actual production files.

Some code examples will contain characters or lines colored teal-blue. This indicates that content has been added or changed since the last time you saw that same code snippet, or, in a new code snippet, that there is a particular part that you need to focus on. In some cases. you'll see a ¬ character at the beginning of a line of code, indicating that the text has had to wrap to a new line within the confines of the layout of this book—but this doesn't mean you have to break the line there.

Each property or selector introduced in this book has a "lowdown" sidebar providing a brief overview of its syntax, behavior, and use cases. Not every detail of syntax could be included, of course, but the most essential information you need is there for quick reference. I've also provided a link to whichever CSS3 module the property or selector is a part of on the W3C site so you can refer to the full specification when needed.

The CSS3 Lowdown

Before you start using CSS3, you should have a grasp of the what, why, and how behind it. In this chapter, you'll learn how CSS3 is different from CSS 2.1 and get an overview on where browser support currently stands. For those browsers that don't support CSS3 as fully as we would like, we'll go over a number of ways to provide workarounds and CSS3 emulation. You'll also learn about all the practical benefits that can come from using CSS3 right away in your projects, including a number of reasons (let's not call them "arguments") you can use to convince skeptical clients or bosses. Finally, we'll go over how CSS3 fits into a progressive enhancement design methodology and best practices for using CSS3 to make it as robust and future-proof as possible.

What is CSS3?

CSS3 is an extension of CSS 2.1 that adds powerful new functionality, but it's no longer a single specification. Instead, it's been divided up into several *modules*. Each module is a standalone specification for a subsection of CSS, like selectors, text, or backgrounds. Every module has its own set of authors and its own timetable. The advantage of this is that the entire CSS3 specification doesn't have to be held up waiting for one little bit to get worked out—the module that that little bit is in can wait, while the rest moves forward.

You can see a list of all the modules, plus their current status on the path towards being finalized, at www.w3.org/Style/CSS/current-work. We'll discuss the status of these modules later in this chapter, but for now let's get right into what's new and exciting in CSS3.

Overview of What's New

Much of CSS3 is a repeat of CSS 2.1, of course. But there are many additions and revisions. What follows isn't an exhaustive list of differences—there are far too many changes to list here—but an overview of the best-supported, popular, and useful changes to CSS from level 2.1 to level 3.

- **Image-free visual effects.** CSS3 contains a lot of new properties that allow you to create visual effects that previously could be accomplished only with images (or sometimes scripting), such as rounded corners, drop shadows, semitransparent backgrounds, gradients, and images for borders. Many of these new properties are in the Backgrounds and Borders module; others are in the Colors and Image Values modules. We'll go over many of these effects in Chapter 2, and use them again in later chapters.

- **Box transformations.** Another category of visual effects that CSS3 makes possible are those that manipulate the box's position and shape in two- or three-dimensional space, such as rotating, scaling, or skewing it. These effects are called transforms, and are covered in the 2D Transforms and 3D Transforms modules. You'll learn about transforms in Chapter 2.

◆ **Unique fonts.** The Fonts module introduces the `@font-face` rule that allows you to link to a font file on your server and use it to display the text on your page, instead of being limited to the fonts on your users' machines. This makes beautiful typography so much more attainable. You'll learn about `@font-face` in Chapter 3.

◆ **Powerful selectors.** CSS3 introduces over a dozen new selectors, mostly pseudo-classes and attribute selectors. They allow you to target specific pieces of your HTML without needing to add IDs or classes, streamlining your code and making it more error-proof. These selectors are included in the Selectors module, naturally. You'll learn about some of them in Chapters 4 and 5.

◆ **Transitions and animations.** CSS3 transitions, covered in a module of the same name, are a simple type of animation that allow you to ease the change from one style on an element to another, such as gradually and smoothly changing the color of a button when you hover over it. Full-fledged CSS3 animations, again covered in a module of the same name, can make more complicated style changes and movements possible without needing Flash or JavaScript. Both are covered in Chapter 5.

◆ **Media queries.** The Media Queries module introduces syntax for feeding styles based on the capabilities of the user's display or device, such as the viewport width, screen resolution, and how many colors it can display. Media queries are a great tool for creating mobile-optimized web sites. You'll learn about them in Chapter 6.

◆ **Multiple-column layouts.** CSS3 introduces a few new modules that make multi-column layouts easier to create. The Multi-column Layout module deals with flowing the text of a single block into multiple columns, similar to newspaper layout; we'll cover this in Chapter 6. The Flexible Box Layout module deals with making blocks align horizontally or vertically with each other and making them more flexible to the available space than floats or positioning can be. There are also more experimental layout modules called Template Layout and Grid Positioning. We'll cover these last three layout systems in Chapter 7.

Where CSS3 Stands

So just how soon is all this cool new CSS3 stuff going to be finalized so we can use it??, I can hear you asking. As I mentioned before, each module is on its own timetable, and you can see the status of each at www.w3.org/Style/CSS/current-work (**Figure 1.1**). The table lists the status, usually called a *maturity level* but sometimes called a *stability status* by the W3C, of the current version of the module as well as the next version, with links to each document.

FIGURE 1.1 All of the current CSS3 modules and their statuses

High Priority	Current	Upcoming
CSS Level 2 Revision 1	Candidate Recommendation	Proposed Recommendation
Selectors	Proposed Recommendation	Recommendation
CSS Mobile Profile 2.0	Candidate Recommendation	Proposed Recommendation
CSS Marquee	Candidate Recommendation	Proposed Recommendation
Medium Priority	**Current**	**Upcoming**
CSS Snapshot 2007	Last Call	Candidate Recommendation
CSS Namespaces	Candidate Recommendation	Proposed Recommendation
CSS Paged Media	Last Call	Last Call
CSS Print Profile	Last Call	Candidate Recommendation
CSS Values and Units	Working Draft	Working Draft
CSS Cascading and Inheritance	Working Draft	Working Draft
CSS Text	Working Draft	Working Draft
CSS Text Layout		Working Draft
CSS Line Grid		Working Draft
CSS Ruby	Candidate Recommendation	Working Draft
CSS Generated Content for Paged Media	Working Draft	Working Draft
CSS Backgrounds and Borders Level 3	Last Call	Candidate Recommendation
CSS Fonts	Working Draft	Last Call
CSS Basic Box Model	Working Draft	Working Draft
CSS Multi-column Layout	Candidate Recommendation	Proposed Recommendation
CSS Template Layout	Working Draft	Working Draft
Media Queries	Candidate Recommendation	Proposed Recommendation
CSS Speech	Working Draft	Working Draft
CSS Color	Last Call	Proposed Recommendation
CSS Basic User Interface	Candidate Recommendation	Test Suite
CSS Scoping		Working Draft
CSS Grid Positioning	Working Draft	Working Draft
CSS Flexible Box Layout	Working Draft	Working Draft
CSS Image Values	Working Draft	Working Draft
CSS 2D Transformations	Working Draft	Working Draft
CSS 3D Transformations	Working Draft	Working Draft
CSS Transitions	Working Draft	Working Draft
CSS Animations	Working Draft	Working Draft
Low Priority	**Current**	**Upcoming**
CSSOM View	Working Draft	Working Draft
CSS Extended Box Model		Working Draft
CSS Object Model		Working Draft
CSS Syntax	Working Draft	Working Draft
CSS Lists	Working Draft	Working Draft
CSS Tables		Working Draft
CSS Reader Media Type	Working Draft	-
CSS Positioning		Working Draft
CSS Generated and Replaced Content	Working Draft	Working Draft
CSS Line Layout	Working Draft	Working Draft
CSS Hyperlink Presentation	Working Draft	Working Draft
CSS style Attribute Syntax	Last Call	Candidate Recommendation
CSS Math		Working Draft
CSS Presentation Levels	Working Draft	Working Draft
CSS Aural Style Sheets		Working Draft
CSS TV Profile 1.0	Candidate Recommendation	Proposed Recommendation
Behavioral Extensions to CSS	Working Draft	Working Draft
CSS Introduction	Working Draft	Working Draft
Other	**Current**	**Upcoming**
SVG	Recommendation	Recommendation

The levels the W3C uses are, from least mature to most mature:

1. **Working Draft.** The first publicly available version of the specification, published for review by the community, in order to solicit further changes. A module or specification can go through several working drafts.

2. **Last Call.** A working draft with a deadline for final comments. It indicates the working group thinks the module does what it should—though it usually receives significant changes after this point—and is probably planning to advance it to the next level.

3. **Candidate Recommendation.** The working group believes the module meets requirements, is stable, and should be implemented by browsers and put into everyday use by web developers, in order to see how implementable it is. Browsers are allowed to drop their vendor prefixes. Changes are still possible after this point, but not many and not major.

4. **Proposed Recommendation.** A mature, well-reviewed document that has been sent to the W3C Advisory Committee for final endorsement. There are rarely changes after this point.

5. **Recommendation.** Complete and finalized. Normally referred to as a "standard."

Hopefully it's clear from this list that we web developers are not only *allowed* to use W3C specifications long before they are complete and finalized Recommendations, but that we are *expected* to. In fact, if you look at the list on the W3C site, shown in Figure 1.1, you may notice that only the SVG module, at the very bottom of the list, is at Recommendation status (at the time of this writing). Even CSS 2.1, which we've been using for many, many years, is still a Candidate Recommendation, not even a Proposed Recommendation. Thus, even though it is not a finalized standard, we can use much of CSS3 now.

Use CSS3 Now

A couple of CSS3 modules are at Candidate Recommendation status, indicating they should be used, but it's also fine to use some pieces that are still in Working Draft status. While you should wait to use properties and techniques that are still undergoing change and have poor browser support, there's no need to wait to use the better-supported and stable parts of CSS3 in appropriate situations.

Not until new CSS techniques get put to work can we discover the real-world challenges of using them so that the W3C can address these challenges. Using new CSS techniques now in real situations helps the web development community uncover shortcomings, discrepancies, and holes in the specification, and introduces new ideas for how the specification can be improved, extended, or clarified. We can help CSS3 become better by testing it out while we still have a chance to change it, rather than waiting until the specification is finalized and missing our chance.

Using these somewhat cutting-edge techniques also shows the browser vendors which pieces of CSS3 are the most popular and useful to web developers. In effect, it pressures those vendors to support the new pieces of CSS and move forward.

So, using new CSS early is an essential part of the process towards getting that new CSS to be standard CSS. It will never get finalized if it never gets used.

I'm not saying that everything that's listed on the W3C site is fair game to use right now. Not all new properties and techniques are ready to be used now, or to be used on every project. You should use only those pieces of CSS3 that are fairly stable and won't harm non-supporting browsers by their lack. And you should use them wisely! Don't add CSS3 just because you can—decide if it makes sense for the site's goals and its users, and add it where appropriate.

Some pieces of CSS3 are not at Candidate Recommendation level yet, but have stable syntax that has not changed for a long time and probably won't change in the future. Unfortunately, there's no way to know what these pieces are by looking at the W3C site alone. Instead, you have to rely on other articles and books to fill you in on the history and stability of a particular property or technique. In this book, we'll deal almost entirely with pieces of CSS3 that are stable and practical to use now; in the rare exceptions when we do delve into the more experimental, I'll always give you a heads-up.

The State of Browser Support

Another consideration that will usually go into whether or not you use a piece of CSS3 is how well-supported it is by major browsers, or the browsers of your particular users. While there are times when you may add more experimental and poorly supported CSS, perhaps as a little Easter egg for a particular browser, usually it's not practical to spend time adding CSS that will be seen by only a tiny sliver of your audience.

But in order to know which pieces of CSS3 are going to be seen by a good chunk of your audience, you need to know what browsers are currently in wide use.

Browser Market Share

Browser usage is always changing and hard to establish with certainty, but **Figure 1.2** shows the most used browsers in October 2010, rounded to the nearest percentage. These figures come from the well-trusted and broadly-sourced statistics from Net Applications (http://marketshare.hitslink.com/browser-market-share.aspx? qprid=0). For statistics from many other sources, visit the Wikipedia page "Usage share of web browsers" at http://en.wikipedia.org/wiki/Usage_share_of_web_browsers.

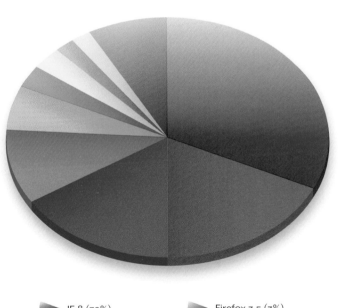

FIGURE 1.2 Browser usage share for October 2010

IE 8 (32%)

Firefox 3.6 (18%)

IE 6 (16%)

IE 7 (10%)

Chrome 6 (6%)

Firefox 3.5 (3%)

Safari 5 (3%)

Chrome 7 (2%)

Opera 10.x (2%)

Other (8%)

Note how small IE 6's portion of the pie has become (compared to its peak near the start of 2006, when it had roughly 85 percent of the market, and IE 5.x had roughly 5 percent). While it's certainly not insignificant, now there are a few more Firefox 3.6 users than IE 6 users; when other versions of Firefox, Chrome, Safari, and Opera are thrown in, IE 6 actually has far fewer users than more modern and standards-compliant browsers do. Often, the first question asked when a blogger shows a cool CSS technique is "But how does it look in IE 6?" However, given current browser statistics, it's just as relevant to ask how it looks in Firefox.

That's not to say you should ignore testing in IE 6 or block its users from your sites. I believe your content should be accessible in all browsers, and it's not hard to make a web page that looks decent and is easy to use in IE 6. But it's becoming increasingly impractical to spend a ton of time agonizing over making your page look spectacular for a decreasing segment of the audience. Of course, if your particular audience is heavy on the IE 6 users, do what you need to do. As I mentioned earlier, you have to decide what and how much CSS3 makes sense for your own site. Tailor it to the project and users, not to generic overall browser-share statistics.

But unless your own site's statistics are very different from the overall population, we can no longer use the excuse that non-IE users are a fringe group that doesn't need special attention. All the time spent making your page look great in IE 6 and 7 might be just as well spent on making it look great in non-IE browsers. And using CSS3 is one of the easiest ways to make your sites look great in non-IE browsers—and even occasionally IE too—as you'll learn throughout this book.

How the Major Players Stack Up

NOTE: Browser support information will also be summarized in Appendix A.

Luckily, the most stable pieces of CSS3 that we'd want to use do have good browser support already. I'll go over detailed browser-support information in each chapter when I explain each property, technique, or selector, but it's helpful to get a big-picture view of where the browsers stand. I've given each a letter grade that I feel sums up their overall support of properties, selectors, and values new to CSS3.

♦ **Safari 5, Safari for iOS4, and Chrome 5: B+.** While Safari and Chrome are not the same browser and do have differences in how they render some CSS3 properties, they do share the same Webkit rendering engine and have a nearly identical level of CSS3 support.

They support most of what is new to CSS3. Their edge comes from supporting animations, which no other browsers do. Safari 5 is also the only browser to support 3D transforms. Their main failings are that their gradient syntax is non-standard and their implementations of the multi-columns and flexible box layout modules are buggy and incomplete. They also don't support the template layout or grid positioning modules, but no browsers do yet.

◆ **Safari 4 and Safari for iOS3: B.** Apple's mobile operating system, called iOS, is currently at version 3 on iPads and original versions of iPhone and iPod Touch, as well as newer versions of iPhone and iPod Touch whose users have not yet updated. The version of Safari on iOS3 matches up to the desktop version of Safari 4. Safari 4 has mostly the same level of CSS3 support as Safari 5, just no 3D transforms and some minor syntax problems with a few properties.

◆ **Firefox 4: B+.** Firefox 4 supports all of the same things as Safari 5, except animations and 3D transforms. It makes up for that "lack" with a more standards-compliant gradients syntax, a slightly better implementation of the multi-columns layout module, and support for the `calc` function, which no other browser supports. It too has a buggy and incomplete implementation of the flexible box layout module.

◆ **Firefox 3.6: B.** Firefox 3.6 supports generally the same things as Firefox 4, except transitions and `calc`.

◆ **Opera 10.6: B.** Opera 10.6 supports mostly the same things as Firefox 3.6, but not gradients or flexible box layout. It supports transitions, which Firefox 3.6 does not.

◆ **Opera 10.5 and Opera Mobile 10.1: B-.** Opera Mobile 10.1 corresponds to the 10.5 version of the desktop version. These versions of Opera support generally the same things as Opera 10.6, but are a little bit more buggy on a few properties.

◆ **IE 9: C+.** IE 9 is still a beta as I write this, but for now, it supports roughly half of what the other major browsers so. The upside is that the pieces it supports, it supports well, and without a browser prefix. (You'll learn about browser-specific prefixes later in the chapter.)

◆ **IE 8, 7, and 6: D-.** Unsurprisingly, since these browsers were released far before CSS3 was well developed, IE 8, 7, and 6 support almost no CSS3. They all support `@font-face` and the `word-wrap` property. IE 7 and 8 also support CSS3 attribute selectors. IE 8 also supports `box-sizing`.

OTHER BROWSER SUPPORT SOURCES

While I provide detailed browser support information throughout this book, CSS3 browser support is continually changing. Also, since this book doesn't act as a comprehensive encyclopedia of CSS3 properties, values, functions, rules, and selectors, you'll need to look elsewhere to find which browsers support some pieces of CSS3.

Mozilla, Opera, and Safari quite helpfully maintain their own lists of what they support:

◆ https://developer.mozilla.org/en/Mozilla_CSS_support_chart

◆ www.opera.com/docs/specs

◆ http://developer.apple.com/safari/library/documentation/AppleApplications/Reference/SafariCSSRef

Other browser support sites include:

◆ Wikipedia's "Comparison of layout engines (Cascading Style Sheets)" (http://en.wikipedia.org/wiki/Comparison_of_layout_engines_(CSS)) is as comprehensive and detailed as you would guess a Wikipedia page to be.

◆ FindMeByIP (www.findmebyip.com/litmus) lists support for the major CSS3 properties and selectors, as well as HTML5 features, in many browsers.

◆ "When can I use…" (http://caniuse.com/#cats=CSS3) lists support for several popular CSS3 properties and techniques in current, older, and upcoming versions of the big-five browsers.

◆ Standardista (www.standardista.com/css3) currently includes detailed support charts for borders, backgrounds, columns, @font-face, and selectors. More modules are added periodically.

◆ QuirksMode's "CSS contents and browser compatibility" (www.quirksmode.org/css/contents.html) lists support for a variety of CSS3 and 2.1 selectors and properties. Each has its own page with details of how it should work and how browsers handle it.

◆ The site CSS Infos maintains lists of -moz- and -webkit- properties, showing which version of the browser each property appeared in. See http://css-infos.net/properties/firefox.php and http://css-infos.net/properties/webkit.php.

◆ Campaign Monitor provides a guide on email clients' CSS support, with CSS3 properties indicated, at www.campaignmonitor.com/css, so you know what you can and can't use in HTML email newsletters.

These varying levels of browser support mean that your pages will look different in different browsers. This is OK, and frankly unavoidable, whether you use CSS3 or not. Web pages have never been able to look identical everywhere because of the user-controlled nature of the medium. And today, there's an even wider variety of devices, monitors, browsers, and settings that people use to browse the web, so you're even less likely to create a page that looks identical everywhere.

As long as you focus on making pages that are usable and accessible for everyone, the cosmetic differences shouldn't matter much. That's part of the philosophy behind progressive enhancement.

Progressive Enhancement

Progressive enhancement is a method of developing web pages where you first make them work and look decent in base-level browsers and devices, and then layer on non-essential, more advanced CSS and JavaScript enhancements for current and future browsers with better support. For example, you may build a form in plain, semantic HTML that looks fine without CSS available and works without JavaScript enabled, and then enhance its appearance with CSS and its usability with JavaScript client-side validation, adding to server-side validation you already have in place. The goal is to create the richest experience possible for everyone by taking advantage of the capabilities of modern browsers while still making sites that are completely usable for everyone. The book *Designing with Progressive Enhancement* (www.filamentgroup.com/dwpe) sums it up nicely:

> *Progressive enhancement...aims to deliver the best possible experience to the widest possible audience—whether your users are viewing your sites on an iPhone, a high-end desktop system, a Kindle, or hearing them on a screen-reader, their experience should be as fully featured and functional as possible.*

Advantages

While this noble goal of giving as many people as possible the best experience possible sounds great, you might be able to achieve it without using progressive enhancement techniques. You could provide workarounds for older browsers to make them match the

appearance and behavior of the site in newer ones as closely as possible. But this isn't usually wise. Using progressive enhancement
instead, where the site's visual richness increases in ever more modern browsers, is usually better both for your users and for yourself.

GRACEFUL DEGRADATION

You may be familiar with the term *graceful degradation* and think it's
the same as progressive enhancement. It's actually an opposite way
of working, though both often have the same outcome. When you
develop with a graceful degradation methodology, you build your
site completely, with all of the features and enhancements you want
to include. Then you add in fallbacks for browsers that can't support
the fully featured version, making the site degrade in a way that won't
break in older browsers.

In progressive enhancement, you're not reverse-engineering a completed site to work with older browsers. You start out with clean,
semantic HTML and good content, which will work in all devices and
browsers, and then layer on extra styling and features in an unobtrusive
way that won't harm the base-level browsers, and which will automatically work as browsers improve. You'll see how this works with the exercises in this book; each page starts out working and looking fine, and
then we'll layer on the CSS3 to enhance it.

For one thing, it takes a lot of work and time to add hacks, workarounds, emulation scripts, and other techniques to try to get an
identical appearance in less capable browsers. Even if you do finally
achieve a near identical appearance—at least with the limited set of
user settings you test with—what's the gain for the user? All that time
you spent trying to make IE act like a browser that's 10 years newer
could have been spent adding accessibility techniques, performing usability testing, or making other site enhancements that would
actually help the users, instead of just making things look a little
bit prettier.

Besides, as I mentioned before, it's impossible to make your site look
identical everywhere, so even if you work hard at this goal, you're still
going to come up short. So if the site is going to look somewhat different no matter what, why not use CSS3 to make that difference look

stunning in the latest browsers? Some CSS3 techniques are simply not "emulatable" in non-supporting browsers. By using progressive enhancement, you don't have to leave out these techniques, dumbing the site down for everyone. There's no reason users of newer browsers should have to miss out on some of the really great techniques CSS3 has to offer, simply because some people can't or won't upgrade their browser. Instead, get older browsers as far as you can, and then keep on improving and pushing the boundaries of the site for newer browsers. This way, everyone gets the best possible site. As time goes by and users upgrade and browser support improves, more of your visitors will see more of your enhancements, effectively making your site better over time without your doing a thing. You just build it once, and it gets better and better over time.

Most people will never know that your site looks different in different browsers and devices, as regular people don't go around scrutinizing the details of a design in multiple browsers like we obsessive web designers do. Even if they do use multiple browsers to view your site, it's unlikely they'll give the visual differences much thought if those differences don't affect how easily they can use the site (which they shouldn't, if you're doing your job right). After all, someone who is viewing your web site on IE 8 at work, Chrome on his home laptop, Safari on his iPhone, and Opera on his Wii is probably pretty used to seeing some differences pop up between all these devices.

Let Me Put it This Way...

I'm a big fan of metaphors, not only in everyday life, but in my work. I find they're a good way to explain a technical concept to clients or convince them of the importance of some usability change I want to make. So, even if you're already on board with progressive enhancement, perhaps you can use one of the following metaphors on a hesitating client or boss.

Let's say you ask your selfless spouse to make you a cheeseburger for dinner. When he or she brings the cheeseburger to the table, it has all the components it needs to earn its name: a bun, a juicy hamburger patty, gooey melted cheese, maybe even some ketchup and mustard. It tastes good and gets the job done.

You have no reason to suspect that your next-door neighbor serves cheeseburgers that come not only with all the same components as your own, but also with lettuce, tomato, bacon, caramelized onions, and a fried egg. None of these are necessary parts of a cheeseburger, but they're delicious enhancements.

It can work similarly with web sites. A bare-bones but functional and clean-looking web site in IE 6 is like a basic cheeseburger. The web site does what visitors expect it to and has the content they need. An IE 6 user has no reason to suspect that Firefox users are seeing something more fancy, enhanced with CSS3. Unless something looks truly broken or incomplete in a less-capable browser (like if your burger got served up with no patty)—in which case you should fix it—your users are not likely to ever know that things could look better if they were using a more advanced browser.

If you're a vegetarian and the cheeseburger metaphor doesn't do it for you, just think about a cup of high-quality but plain ice cream versus one with whipped cream, hot fudge, and sprinkles added. Or perhaps electronics is more your thing. Whether you watch TV with a small, old tube TV or with a flat-screen, high-definition LCD screen, you're getting the same programming. It just looks a lot better on the LCD TV. It's silly to expect it to look the same on a device that is very old—like IE 6, released in 2001.

Another thing that is silly to expect is for a Blu-ray disc to play in a VCR. It was never meant to, as VCRs came out way before Blu-ray discs were developed. It uses newer technology to add better quality and more features than VHS tapes offered. You still get the movie on the VHS, as you wanted, but the movie looks better and you get extra bonuses on the Blu-ray version. Everyone gets the movie they wanted, and owners of newer technology get a little something extra now instead of being forced to wait until all the VCRs die out.

Similarly, when someone presents a CSS3 technique, it doesn't make sense to ask if it works in IE 6, which came out long before CSS3 was developed. As long as the web developer is providing the same content to IE 6, and the CSS3 technique doesn't actually make the site worse in IE 6, it's fine to use a design technique that not everyone can see.

Benefits of CSS3

I hope it's now clear why progressive enhancement as a general development methodology is not only acceptable but good, but we haven't really talked about the benefits of CSS3 in particular. The advantages of using CSS3 over alternative, older techniques extends far beyond just how cool CSS3 can make your pages look—though that's certainly not a benefit to be ignored. As you'll learn throughout this book, CSS3 allows you to create some really beautiful effects, adding a layer of polish and richness to your web designs.

But most of the visual effects that CSS3 allows you to create can be accomplished without CSS3, using alternative tools such as images, JavaScript, or Flash. So there needs to be some other reason beyond that "it looks cool" to use CSS3.

And there *is* another reason. Lots of them, actually. It basically comes down to this: using CSS3, you can decrease not only the time you spend developing and maintaining pages, but also the time spent in loading those pages. Simultaneously, you can increase usability and accessibility, make your pages more adaptable across devices, and even enhance your search engine placement. Let's look at each of these benefits in more detail.

MORE ON PROGRESSIVE ENHANCEMENT

There's a lot more that could be said about progressive enhancement—in fact, there's a whole book about it called *Designing with Progressive Enhancement* (www.filamentgroup.com/dwpe). Although I think I've made the point well enough, you may need a more in-depth explanation of what progressive enhancement is and why it matters in order to convince your teammates, boss, or clients. So here are links to a few excellent articles on the subject:

◆ "The Case for Designing with Progressive Enhancement," by Todd Parker, Maggie Costello Wachs, Scott Jehl, and Patty Toland (www.peachpit.com/articles/article.aspx?p=1586457)

◆ "Progressive Enhancement: What It Is, And How To Use It?," by Sam Dwyer (www.smashing magazine.com/2009/04/22/progressive-enhancement-what-it-is-and-how-to-use-it)

◆ "Progressive Enhancement: Paving the Way for Future Web Design," by Steven Champeon (www.hesketh.com/publications/articles/progressive-enhancement-paving-the-way-for)

◆ "Graceful degradation versus progressive enhancement," by Christian Heilman (http://dev.opera.com/articles/view/graceful-degradation-progressive-enhance)

Reduced Development and Maintenance Time

By providing the same visual effects, many CSS3 techniques can be a replacement for "called" images. For instance, to create a drop shadow behind a box, you no longer need to create one or more images to use as backgrounds on that box. Instead, just use the CSS3 box-shadow property to generate a shadow. This frees you from having to spend the time creating, slicing, and optimizing those images.

You can also tweak CSS more quickly than images if you need to make changes down the road, or simply test out different variations. If your client wants to see how that drop shadow looks if it was blurrier, or a little farther displaced from the box, or red instead of gray, you can create each of these variations in a matter of seconds using CSS3, rather than having to fire up Photoshop to modify and re-export images.

Some CSS3 techniques also allow you to do away with scripts or Flash—a nice efficiency boost, as you don't need to spend time hunting for the perfect script, configuring it for your site, and testing it.

Finally, many CSS3 techniques can streamline your markup by requiring fewer nested divs and classes, and this also can translate into a little less work time for you. For instance, it's now possible to put multiple background images on a single element, so you don't have to add extra nested elements in just the right configuration and style them all separately. Also, you can use CSS3 selectors to target elements in the HTML based on their position in the document tree, so you don't have to take the time to create a set of classes, apply them to all the necessary elements, and then make sure they're used correctly on new content down the road.

Increased Page Performance

Less markup and fewer images means fewer kilobytes for users to download, resulting in faster-loading pages. Fewer images, scripts, and Flash files also mean fewer HTTP requests, which is one of the best ways to speed up your pages. In fact, the Yahoo! Exceptional Performance Team called reducing HTTP requests "the most important guideline for improving performance for first time visitors" (http://developer.yahoo.com/performance/rules.html).

THE RIGHT TOOLS IN THE RIGHT PLACES

At various points throughout this book, I'm going to tout how a CSS3 technique can replace an image, JavaScript file, Flash file, class, or nested `div`. But I want to make clear right now that I don't believe that any of these things are inherently bad. I'm certainly not advocating doing away with all images online, for example—that's ridiculous. All of these things are spectacular tools that have appropriate uses. It's not wise to use CSS in place of one of these technologies if the other is better suited to the job, such as using CSS to power drop-down menus when JavaScript works so much better, just because CSS is "cooler." But if CSS3 can do something more efficiently or produce better usability, with an equally or better appearance, I think it's the wise choice.

When the browser fetches your page from the host server, it's making an HTTP request. Every time the browser finds another file used in that web page—a style sheet, image file, script, and so forth—it has to go back to the server to get this file. This trip takes time and has a much bigger impact on page loading speed than simply how many total kilobytes all of the components take up. What this means is that, in general, a page with 10 images at 10 kilobytes each, for a total of 100 kilobytes to download, is going to take a lot longer to load than a page with one 100-kilobyte image—or probably even one 200-kilobyte image.

Using CSS3, it's quite possible to make a graphically rich site that uses not a single image, drastically cutting the number of HTTP requests and increasing how fast your pages load.

Now, I'm not saying that *every* bit of CSS3 you add will make your pages faster; it depends on what you'd be using instead of CSS3, if anything, as well as on exactly how you implement the CSS3 version.

For instance, a font file that's linked to with the `@font-face` rule, which you'll learn about in Chapter 3, is another HTTP request and another thing the user has to download, and font files can sometimes be very large. So, in some cases, using `@font-face` could slow your pages down. On the other hand, if you were going to be using dozens or hundreds of images of text instead of `@font-face`, having users download one font file is often much faster. It may also be faster than a JavaScript or Flash-based text replacement method. This is one of those instances where the loss or gain in speed depends on what you're comparing the CSS3 version against, as well as which fonts you're using, if you're subsetting the characters within them, and other factors of your particular implementation of @font-face.

Some graphically rich CSS3 techniques, such as gradients, can reduce HTTP requests but may also make the browser processor work very hard to render the effects, making the browser sluggish and decreasing usability. Don't overuse complex effects, and test thoroughly those that you do implement.

But the point is that many CSS3 techniques can greatly improve your page performance in almost all instances. This alone is a great reason to start using CSS3, because users really care about page loading speed. Recently, both Bing and Google ran similar experiments in which they deliberately delayed their server response time by different amounts of milliseconds to see how it would affect user experience. They found that the longer users wait, the less engaged they are with a page, evidenced by making fewer search queries and clicking on fewer results, and the more likely they are to leave. Even delays of under half a second have an impact. For more details on the business implications of slow pages, see "The performance business pitch" by Stoyan Stefanov (www.phpied.com/the-performance-business-pitch).

Better Search Engine Placement

Fast pages are not only good for your users, but they make Google happy—and don't we all want to be on Google's good side? In March 2010, Google started rewarding fast pages by making speed a ranking factor, so pages that load faster can appear a little higher in the search results than their slower competitors.

Even if Google wasn't using speed as a ranking factor and no other search engines ever will, you may still get a bit of a boost in search engine placement if you replace images of text or Flash files of text with real text styled with CSS3. While search engines can read text in images' alt attributes and some Flash files, regular text in heading tags is usually going to be given more weight by the search engines.

Increased Usability and Accessibility

An even bigger benefit of real text instead of images of text is that real text is more usable for everyone, and particularly for people with disabilities. Real text can be resized or recolored by users to make it easier to read, selected to copy and paste, searched for with the browser's Find function, indexed by search engines and other tools, and translated into other languages.

That said, CSS3 isn't a magic bullet for readability; as with any CSS or design technique, it can be abused, and can harm legibility instead of aiding it. But when used wisely, using `@font-face`, `text-shadow`, transforms, and other CSS3 effects on real text instead of resorting to images for these effects can make your pages more usable.

Another way to improve usability with CSS3 is to use media queries. I already mentioned how media queries let you customize styles based on the characteristics of the user's display, allowing you to tailor styles to the user's device and settings. This technique can ensure your design is making the best use of space and is as readable as possible for the user's browsing scenario. You'll learn about media queries in Chapter 6.

Staying at the Front of the Pack

There's one other benefit to learning and using CSS3 that is exclusive to you: it keeps you at the top of the web designer pile. CSS3 is not going away. This is how we're all going to be building sites in the future. Knowing CSS3 is an increasingly important and marketable career skill. Right now, it's something that sets you apart as a top-notch designer or developer. Sooner than later, it will be something that's expected of you. Start using it now, at least on personal projects, and keep moving your skills and career forward.

Case Study: The Highway Safety Research Center

To get a better sense of many of these CSS3 benefits, let's look at how a real site could be tangibly improved by using CSS3 in place of older web design techniques. Instead of picking on some stranger's site, I thought I would critique one of my own.

Before CSS3

I designed and developed the CSS and HTML for the UNC Highway Safety Research Center's site (www.hsrc.unc.edu) back in 2006. **Figure 1.3** shows the HSRC home page. It hasn't changed much since I originally built it, and isn't nearly as complex as some of the inner pages, or certainly as many other web pages out there, but even so, it has a lot of images for such a simple page. You can see that it uses lots of rounded corners, subtle gradients, and shadows.

I wanted to see how the current page would perform with all these images. So I downloaded it and tested it in Firefox 3.6, IE 8, and IE 6. Table 1.1 shows how many HTTP requests occurred and the average page loading time in each browser.

FIGURE 1.3 The home page for the Highway Safety Research Center

TABLE 1.1 Performance in original page

	FIREFOX 3.6	IE 8	IE 6
HTTP requests	36	37	47
Page loading time (in seconds)	1.5	1.3	3

These loading times aren't horrible, I suppose, but they could certainly be better. Especially in IE 6—the poor thing is getting a pretty long wait. If I could get the number of HTTP requests down, that alone would make a big dent in loading times across the board.

A lot of these HTTP requests were coming from the tabbed navigation bar. Every tab is a separate image that contains three states: the inactive state, the rollover state, and the current page indicator (**Figure 1.4**). When I originally made this page, I was using the background image technique called "CSS sprites" where you combine multiple images into one and move around the visible portion using the background-position property. But I wasn't using sprites as aggressively as I could have.

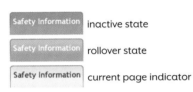 inactive state

rollover state

current page indicator

FIGURE 1.4 Each tab image is made up of three states of the link.

I didn't want to compare the new CSS3 version I was going to make against this poorly optimized version, so I combined all the tabs into one big image, modified the CSS to use this new image, and tested this revised version of the page. Table 1.2 shows the results.

TABLE 1.2 Performance in revised page

	FIREFOX 3.6	IE 8	IE 6
HTTP requests	29	30	33
Page loading time (in seconds)	1.3	1.15	2
Decrease in loading time	13%	11%	33%

Taking a chunk out of the HTTP requests definitely improved the page loading times, especially in the case of IE 6. But keep in mind that this one big sprite image with all the tabs in it is was more difficult to make and will be harder to maintain than individual images; it also made the CSS more complicated than before. That's the tradeoff that you get any time you use sprites. But this page was a better comparison for a CSS3-enhanced version of the page.

After CSS3

To create the CSS3 version of the page, I removed nine images and replaced them with pure CSS equivalents (**Figure 1.5**). Despite the changes, the page looks almost identical to the "before" version when viewed in modern browsers.

FIGURE 1.5
CSS3 abilities over-rode the need for nine images, previously used in the numbered spots shown. The overall page looks about the same as it did in Figure 1.3.

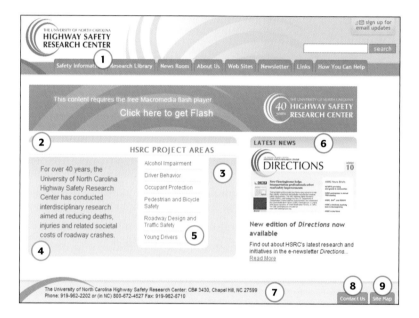

I removed the sprite image used for the tabs, and remade the tabs without using a single image by using border-radius and CSS3-generated gradients (**Figure 1.6**). With these changes to the tabs, they're now using real text, instead of an image of text, making them more accessible.

FIGURE 1.6 The image tabs (left) look almost identical to the tabs made with CSS3 (right).

I used this same technique for the two tabs in the footer, and replaced the footer's gradient background image with a CSS3 gradient. I also used a CSS3 gradient to replace the background image in the proj-ect areas box and behind the "Latest News" text. Then I replaced the small gradient at the bottom of the header with a box-shadow on the navigation bar.

I used border-radius to remove the rounded corner images from the top and bottom of the project areas box, the bottom of the list inside it, and the "Latest News" heading block. For both the "HSRC Project Areas" and "Latest News" heading text, I got rid of the images and instead used @font-face on real text. The font I chose isn't identical to that used in the images, but the one used in the image doesn't allow @font-face embedding in its license, and the new one is pretty close. For the three bottom borders under the "HSRC Project Areas" text, I used box-shadow, which can create the appearance of multiple borders without having to use an image.

This isn't every single instance where CSS3 could be added on this page, but it does take care of the ones most easily and quickly fixed without causing much trouble to non-supporting browsers. The CSS file size has increased slightly due to all the new CSS3, but not by too much, because most of it replaces long background declarations. The HTML is identical, except for changes to what's linked to in the head.

Table 1.3 shows how this page performed. Even though using @font-face added two HTTP requests, the overall number still decreased significantly because I got rid of nine images. I also got rid of the JavaScript I was using in IE 6 to support alpha-transparent PNGs; it was no longer needed since there are no longer any alpha-transparent PNGs.

TABLE 1.3 Performance in CSS3 page

	FIREFOX 3.6	IE 8	IE 6
HTTP requests	22	23	24
Page loading time (in seconds)	1.1	1	1.5
Decrease in loading time	15%	13%	25%

The decrease in loading time that I measured was compared to the optimized "before" version that used the one big sprite image. On average, loading time went down by 15 percent in Firefox 3.6, 13 percent in IE 8, and 25 percent in IE 6. This is a limited example, of course; this decrease could be further magnified by replacing more images, and it could be much larger on larger or more complex sites, where it's not uncommon to find several dozen or more "interface" images (as opposed to content images, like photos) on a single page. But the point is that CSS3 alone was able to make the page load significantly faster, as well as improve its usability and accessibility a bit.

This can translate into happier site users, and happy users are always good for the people behind the site too.

Ironically, even though IE 6 can't see a bit of the changes we've made, its users benefit most from the addition of CSS3 to the page. IE 6 users get to enjoy much faster loading pages, thanks to these CSS3 effects replacing images.

NOTE: The beta of IE 9 available at the time of this writing does show most of CSS3 effects I added. It may show even more by the time it's actually released.

But how does it *look* in IE? Is it a horrible train wreck? See for yourself in **Figure 1.7**, showing IE 8, and take my word for it that IE 6 is practically identical. IE simply sees rectangular corners instead of round ones, and no subtle gradients. Does it look just as good? No, I don't think so. Does it look horrible? Again, I don't think so. Is there any reason IE users will know that they're missing out on these visual effects? Not likely. And even if they did, do you think they would choose rounded corners over faster page loading speeds?

FIGURE 1.7 The page looks fine in IE 8 and earlier, even though these browsers don't understand the CSS3 I added.

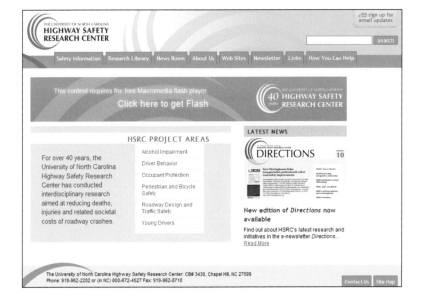

You could work around IE's failure to see some of the visual effects by feeding it the rounded corner images and so forth, but is it really worth it? It's a lot of extra work for you, and it takes away all the great gains we've made in page performance for IE users. It depends on the project; there are lots of times where it makes sense, and we'll add IE workarounds several times and in several ways throughout this book. I'm not saying you should never provide workarounds for IE or other browsers, but you have to consider the tradeoffs.

Using CSS3 Wisely

Now that you've seen how useful and beneficial CSS3 can be, can you just plop it into your style sheets and get going? Well, yes, but I wouldn't recommend it without learning some best practices first. Just as with CSS 2.1, CSS3 has its own special considerations that should go into how you craft your style sheets to make them more organized, efficient, and future-proof. You also need to know how to implement CSS3 in a way that won't harm non-supporting browsers, and how to provide workarounds for those browsers when you so choose.

Browser Prefixes

When a browser implements a new property, value, or selector that is not yet at Candidate Recommendation status, it adds a prefix onto the front of the property with a code for its rendering engine. For instance, `-moz-border-radius` is the version of the `border-radius` property currently used by Mozilla-based browsers, like Firefox. Table 1.4 provides a list of the available prefixes.

TABLE 1.4   Browser-specific prefixes for CSS properties

PREFIX	RENDERING ENGINE	POPULAR BROWSERS USING THIS RENDERING ENGINE
`-khtml-`	KHTML	Konqueror
`-ms-`	Trident	Internet Explorer
`-moz-`	Mozilla	Firefox, Camino, Flock
`-o-*`	Presto	Opera, Opera Mobile, Opera Mini, Nintendo Wii browser
`-webkit-`	Webkit	Safari, Safari on iOS, Chrome, Android browser

* In the Presto rendering engine, speech-related properties are prefixed with -xv- instead of -o-.

In this book, we'll be sticking with the `-moz-`, `-o-`, and `-webkit-` prefixes. The others aren't as often-used in general and weren't needed for the techniques we'll be covering.

WHY THEY EXIST

Vendor prefixes allow browsers to try out new properties, values, and selectors before they are finalized—a good way for them to be tested in the wild, and then corrected and refined if necessary. If the browser were to jump straight to the unprefixed, standard property, they would be locked into whatever behavior they originally use.

Developers would start using the unprefixed property immediately, and would expect it to continue producing the same behavior from that point onward. If the browser changed the property after this point, either because its implementation was buggy or the specification itself had changed, it would risk breaking all the existing sites that had already started using the property. Not only does it lock the browser into its first, buggy implementation, it pressures the other browsers and W3C to follow suit. Eric Meyer gives two real examples of how this unfortunate cycle has happened in the past in his excellent article "Prefix or Posthack" (www.alistapart.com/articles/prefix-or-posthack).

Even if the browser didn't change its implementation so as not to break existing sites, what if the W3C changed the specification? And what if other browsers started using the new behavior described in the updated specification? Now you have different browsers displaying one single, standard property in different ways. That's exactly how it used to be in the days of Netscape 4, Mac IE 5, and Windows IE 6. Complicated and unstable hacks, based on bugs completely unrelated to the actual properties they meant to fix, proliferated because non-standard browser behaviors weren't quarantined in browser-specific properties.

A prefixed property indicates to developers that the property is somewhat experimental and subject to change. It gives the browsers flexibility to continue making changes if necessary, which allows the browsers to release and refine new properties more quickly. This, in turn, gives developers the opportunity to use new properties sooner and participate in the refinement process through testing in real-world scenarios.

Once the specification has become more stable and the browser has achieved a correct implementation of the property, it can drop the vendor prefix. If the developer also had the non-prefixed version of the property in her styles—which is wise for future compatibility—her pages would now be able to automatically take advantage of the finalized behavior of the property. If she didn't have the non-prefixed property, there's no harm done—the old prefixed property will continue to work in the same way as before. None of the sites using the prefixed version of the property will break.

PROBLEMS WITH PREFIXES

Browser prefixes do have a few disadvantages, though. The chief complaint leveled against them is that you often end up with a few lines of CSS that all accomplish the same thing, such as:

```
div {
    -moz-transform: rotate(45deg);
    -o-transform: rotate(45deg);
    -webkit-transform: rotate(45deg);
    transform: rotate(45deg);
}
```

This repetition adds to the file size of your style sheets and can be just plain annoying. It would be so much cleaner and nicer to have a single line using the standard property. Many CSS preprocessor scripts allow you to do this, actually—just write the non-prefixed property and it creates the browser-specific CSS for you. Tools that can do this for you include Sass (http://sass-lang.com), LESS (http://lesscss.org), and eCSStender (www.alistapart.com/articles/stop-forking-with-css3), to name a few. But using scripting to remove the prefixes has a number of disadvantages itself. If a browser has a buggy implementation of a property, you can't choose not to use that browser's prefix but keep using the other ones. Nor can you use different values for various browsers to accommodate their slightly different renderings of the same property. Also, adding scripts may slow your pages down. Eric Meyer (www.alistapart.com/articles/prefix-or-posthack) explains what might be most risky about this method:

> By hiding the prefixed properties behind a processor, authors may forget that what they're using is experimental and subject to change. Cognitively, they may start to treat what they're using as settled and stable when it may be nothing of the kind.

Although the repetition of browser prefixes is cumbersome, the alternative of one standard property producing different behaviors in each browser as they develop their implementations, resulting in convoluted hacks to work around the inconsistencies, is far more annoying. Plus, as time goes on and support improves, you can remove the prefixed properties, making your style sheets cleaner, instead of having to maintain hacks in your sheets for years because of a non-standard browser behavior that has snuck into a non-prefixed property. Let me quote Eric Meyer's article once more, where he talks about how the "pain" of prefixes is temporary:

It's a little like a vaccine—the shot hurts now, true, but it's really not that bad in comparison to the disease it prevents. And in this case, you're being vaccinated against a bad case of multi-year parser hacking and browser sniffing. We suffered through that long plague once already. Prefixes will, if used properly, ward off another outbreak for a long time to come.

TIP: When you're ready to remove certain prefixes from your CSS, you can use regular expressions to help you with the task; see www.venturelab.co .uk/devblog/2010/07/ vendor-prefixes-what-happens-next.

Another problem with prefixes is that they don't validate. This isn't a problem in and of itself—validation is just a troubleshooting tool, so if you know why you are getting an error for a prefixed property, you can just ignore that error and move on. But having a whole bunch of "benign" errors for prefixed properties mixed in with the others can make it harder to spot the errors you're really concerned about.

To ease both of these problems—the repetition and the lack of validation—some people separate out the prefixed properties into their own sheet. That way, the main style sheet is kept pristine and will validate (or at least expose only the "real" validation errors when you check it). But many CSS people (including me) are not fans of this solution. First, it adds another HTTP request; this impacts performance far more than the few extra bytes that the prefixed properties would add to the main sheet. Second, it makes it easy to forget you are using the prefixed properties; since they're to be used with more caution than regular properties, paying attention to them is essential. If a browser changes the behavior of one of its prefixed properties, you may neglect to update your rules accordingly. Or if you're simply trying to figure out why something is behaving in a certain way, it make take you a long time to remember that old prefix style sheet and track down the culprit. So I'm sorry to say that filtering through the validation errors caused by prefixes is probably the lesser evil compared with keeping a separate style sheet for prefixed properties.

Despite these disadvantages, most CSS developers are glad that prefixed properties are available and agree that their benefits, explained earlier, make them worthwhile to use in appropriate situations.

THE PROPER WAY TO USE BROWSER-SPECIFIC PROPERTIES

When you use prefixed properties, you should always include the non-prefixed property as well, and always *after* all the prefixed versions. This ensures that when the browser supports the non-prefixed property, it will use it, overriding the prefixed property listed earlier and using the newer, more correct behavior.

For instance, until the release of Safari 5, Safari used the `-webkit-border-radius` property. And it was a good thing it did—its implementation was incorrect in a couple ways (or rather, it became incorrect as the W3C refined the spec). For one thing, Safari 4 and earlier didn't allow you to round each corner independently in the `-webkit-border-radius` property, as the specification says you should be able to. It also used incorrect syntax for specifying the curve of elliptical instead of perfectly rounded corners.

But this was OK. You could keep the incorrect syntax contained in the `-webkit-border-radius` property, unseen by any non-Webkit browsers. And by including the standard `border-radius` property last, containing the correct syntax, you could take advantage of the improved implementation of Safari 5 as soon as it was available, without having to make a single change to your style sheets. The standard property was already there, just waiting to be used.

While including the standard property last is almost always advisable, there are some rare times when I think you should leave it off entirely, and just use the browser-specific versions. If it looks like the syntax is still going through significant changes, I would advise waiting to include the standard property until it becomes more stable. There's no point in including it if it's just going to be ignored or break when the specification is finally firmed up and browsers start using the standard property.

A great example of this is CSS3-generated gradients. In Chapter 2, you'll learn about how their W3C syntax is still young and that Firefox and Webkit use radically different syntax in their prefixed properties. This may make you decide against using gradients entirely—but on the other hand, it's a purely visual effect that degrades without a hitch in non-supporting browsers, and perhaps you're going to use it only on an experimental, personal, or single-browser site like an iPhone app. If you do decide to use gradients despite the possibility of later syntax changes, the safest course of action is to use the prefixed versions only. But these cases are rare, partially because browsers don't usually make a prefixed version of a property until the syntax is pretty well fleshed out, and also because even in those cases where they do, you'll usually want to wait for more stable syntax.

Another optional guideline to follow when using browser prefixes is to always preemptively include all possible prefixed versions, even if some are not being used, on the chance that later they will be. I'm

NOTE: There's a handy table of the prefixed properties in the four major rendering engines at http://peter.sh/experiments/vendor-prefixed-css-property-overview. Use it to compare which browsers are currently using a prefixed property versus a non-prefixed property versus no property at all.

neither absolutely for nor against this policy—for me, it depends on the situation. If I'm working on a site that I'll have to hand off completely and never touch again, I may think it best to include all possible vendor-prefixed properties. But if I'm going to be working on the site continually, I may find it most efficient to include only the prefixed properties I need now, and add others later if browsers start supporting them. You can do it either way.

No matter which prefixed properties you choose to include, it's a good idea to put comments in your CSS indicating which property is used by which browser. It's not always as obvious as you might think. For instance, here's how a group of border-radius properties might look with comments:

```
-moz-border-radius: 20px; /* Firefox */
-webkit-border-radius: 20px; /* Safari 4 and earlier */
border-radius: 20px; /* Opera, Chrome, Safari 5, IE 9 */
```

By including these comments, it makes it easy to later remove the properties you no longer need when you decide to drop support for a particular browser.

Dealing with Non-supporting Browsers

There's no single way that you ought to handle browsers that don't support the CSS3 you're adding. Again, the route you take depends on what's best for the site, your users, your client, your own personal preference, and CSS3 technique itself. We'll discuss a few different routes you can take with non-supporting browsers, and throughout the book we'll use them all at various points, each when appropriate.

ACCEPTING THE DIFFERENCE

In many cases, the best way to deal with browsers not supporting some of your CSS3 is to just accept the different visual appearance. That's what progressive enhancement is all about, after all, and in a few cases, you have no choice, as there's really no replacement for the CSS3 version. But even in those cases where you do have a choice, you have to ask yourself if the time you take creating a fallback method for non-supporting browsers is really worth it. Will it really help the users? Will it improve sales or newsletter signups or whatever the goal of the site is? In some cases, the answer will be yes—so go ahead and use an appropriate workaround. But in many cases, the answer is no, as the CSS3 effect is a non-essential, cosmetic enhancement. And in some cases, adding the workaround will actually make things worse for your visitors, as adding back images in older browsers may slow the page down, for instance.

Most CSS3 effects will not harm non-supporting browsers if they're not seen. An example of this is the Twitter site (www.twitter.com). Twitter's site uses `border-radius` to create rounded corners at various places throughout the design, as well as other CSS3 effects that aren't seen in IE 8 and earlier. In up-to-date, non-IE browsers, the "What's happening?" box, where you type your tweets, has rounded corners, plus a blue glow around it when you place your cursor inside it (**Figure 1.8**). In IE 8 and earlier, the box simply has straight corners and no glow (**Figure 1.9**). There's nothing broken or wrong about this appearance—it's just different. That difference isn't harming IE users at all, so there was no need for Twitter to provide workaround techniques to emulate the same appearance.

FIGURE 1.8 Twitter's tweet box has rounded corners and a blue glow in Firefox.

FIGURE 1.9 IE 8 doesn't see the rounded corners or glow, but there's nothing broken-looking or ugly in its alternative appearance.

But there are times when failing to provide a fallback *can* make things worse for non-supporting browsers. For instance, if you make a background color semitransparent using HSLA or RGBA—two new ways of declaring color in CSS3—browsers that don't understand these types of color values will have no color to display, and will make the background completely transparent. Depending on the text color and the color of whatever is now showing through that transparent box, the text may be completely unreadable (**Figure 1.10**). This is not one of the situations where you can just accept the difference. You need to provide a workaround.

FIGURE 1.10 **In Firefox (left), the box has a semitransparent background, but in IE 8 (right), no background appears, making the text unreadable.**

So, as with lots of things in CSS, it requires testing in multiple browsers to determine what the best course of action is. Often you can be all zen and accept the difference, but sometimes you can't.

PROVIDING A NON-CSS3 AND CSS3 VALUE FOR A PROPERTY

In cases where you want to or must provide a fallback, you can sometimes do so simply by providing more than one value for a property in the same rule: the first one for non-supporting browsers, and the second, CSS3 one for more advanced browsers. Non-supporting browsers will ignore the rules they don't understand, and CSS3-capable browsers will override the older values with the newer values.

For instance, in the case of the nonexistent background color mentioned above, you can provide a solid fallback color in hex notation first, then the HSLA or RGBA version, like so:

```
div {
    background: #CC0000;
    background: hsla(0, 100%, 40%, .5);
}
```

Note that a method like this rarely actually emulates the appearance or behavior of the CSS3 property—the fallback color here is solid, not semitransparent. But it provides an acceptable second-choice appearance when doing nothing at all would make the page unusable for users of non-supporting browsers.

USING MODERNIZR TO DETECT CSS3 SUPPORT

When you want to use two different values to target non-CSS3 and CSS3-supporting browsers, it's not always possible to include both values in the same rule, as I was able to do with the background color above. There are times when the two values would clash. Or maybe the two values don't clash, but you want to provide completely different and more extensive fallback styles for the older browsers, and you don't want the CSS3 browsers to read and use them.

You could get into browser sniffing, where you use programming to detect which browser a visitor is using, to create different rules for different browsers, but that's unreliable and messy. A better solution is the script called Modernizr, available at www.modernizr.com. It detects whether the user's browser supports a number of CSS3 and HTML5 features. Modernizr then adds classes to the html element that indicate which it does and doesn't support, such as "no-multiplebgs" if the browser doesn't support having multiple background images on a single element and "multiplebgs" if it does.

With these classes in place, you can easily write styles for each class and be sure that each rule will be seen only by browsers that do (or don't) support the piece of CSS3 or HTML5 you're concerned about. The following rules could be used to apply different background colors or images to browsers based on whether or not they support multiple background images:

```
#wrapper {
    background-color: #ccc;
    background-image: url(one.png), url(two.png),
                      url(three.png);
}
.no-multiplebgs #wrapper {
    background-image: url(alternate.gif);
}
```

The first rule is seen by all browsers, whether or not JavaScript is enabled and whether or not they support CSS3. Browsers that don't support multiple backgrounds will use the background color, and browsers that do will use the three background images. The next rule is seen only by browsers that don't support multiple backgrounds and do have JavaScript enabled. It feeds these browsers a single alternative background image in place of the three separate ones it wasn't able to use. So no matter what level of CSS support the browser has, and whether JavaScript is available or not, each browser gets a background on the wrapper div.

For the most part, Modernizr is best for providing alternative (rather than emulating) styles to non-supporting browsers. But there are times when you could use it to emulate the CSS3 behavior or appearance. For instance, if you wanted to round the corners of a box, you could use border-radius for some browsers, and then use a background image of rounded corners for browsers that don't support border-radius:

NOTE: The CSS for
the no-borderradius
rules would actually be
more complicated than
what is shown here, as
you'd need to position
each corner image
independently, possibly
on more than one
HTML element. But I've
simplified the CSS shown
in order to just focus on
how Modernizr works for
this example.

```
div {
    -moz-border-radius: 10px;
    -webkit-border-radius: 10px;
    border-radius: 10px;
}
.no-borderradius div {
    background: url(corners.gif);
}
```

Modernizr can be a very powerful resource. I recommend the article
"Taking Advantage of HTML5 and CSS3 with Modernizr," by Faruk
Ateş (www.alistapart.com/articles/taking-advantage-of-html5-and-
css3-with-modernizr) to see more examples of how Modernizr can be
harnessed to customize the styles to the capabilities of the browsers.

USING JAVASCRIPT TO EMULATE CSS3

So far, the workarounds we've gone over mostly provide an alternative
style to the non-supporting browsers, instead of emulating the CSS3
behavior. In most cases, alternatives are fine. But if you need to have a
more consistent appearance between the two, you need to emulate.

JavaScript can often be put to work to make non-supporting browsers
do the same thing that CSS3 makes more advanced browsers do. For
instance, for years now there have been scripts available for creating
rounded corners.

In each chapter of this book, we'll go over appropriate scripts for the
technique we're covering, but here are a few popular scripts that aren't
"uni-taskers"—they each can handle a variety of CSS3 emulation tasks:

◆   IE7, by Dean Edwards (http://code.google.com/p/ie7-js). Makes
    CSS3 pseudo-classes and attribute selectors work in IE 6 through
    8. Also makes the CSS3 properties box-sizing and opacity work,
    along with a bunch of CSS 2.1 properties and selectors that old
    versions of IE don't support.

◆   Selectivizr, by Keith Clark (http://selectivizr.com). Makes CSS3
    pseudo-classes and attribute selectors work in IE 6 through 8.
    Must be used in conjunction with another JavaScript library.

◆   cssSandpaper, by Zoltan Hawryluk (www.useragentman.com/blog/
    csssandpaper-a-css3-javascript-library). Makes 2D transforms,
    box-shadow, gradients, opacity, RGBA, and HSLA work in IE and
    other non-supporting browsers.

◆ PIE, by Jason Johnston (http://css3pie.com). Makes `border-radius`, `box-shadow`, multiple backgrounds, `background-origin`, background-clip, and linear gradients work in IE 6 through 8. It also enables limited support for `border-image` and RGBA.

IE FILTERS

Another way to emulate CSS3 without using JavaScript is to use Microsoft's *filters* in your CSS to create a variety of visual effects. These only work in IE, of course, and they're applied via its proprietary `filter` or `-ms-filter` property. The syntax for the value of the `filter` property partially depends on the specific filter being used, but the basic format is `filter: progid:DXImageTransform.Microsoft.filtername(sProperties)`, where "filtername" is the name of the filter and "sProperties" is its value. In IE 8, the syntax was updated to `-ms-filter` as the property name, and you're supposed to put quotation marks around its value. You'll see examples of filters in use in Chapter 2.

You can see a full list of available filters at http://msdn.microsoft.com/en-us/library/ms532853%28v=VS.85%29.aspx, but here are the ones that can be used to emulate CSS3 effects:

◆ The DropShadow, Shadow, Glow, and Blur filters can emulate `box-shadow` and `text-shadow`.

◆ The Gradient filter can emulate RGBA, HSLA, and linear gradients.

◆ The Alpha and BasicImage filters can emulate `opacity`.

◆ The Matrix and BasicImage filters can emulate 2D transforms.

The nice thing about filters is that they work without JavaScript and only in IE, without any need to hide them from other browsers, making them simple to apply. But they do have several disadvantages to be aware of:

◆ **Length.** It takes a lot of characters to write a filter. If you use a lot of filters in a single sheet, you could increase its file size significantly. To combat this, you could place the filters in an IE-only style sheet, fed to IE with conditional comments, as you'll learn about in a moment. That way, at least the browsers that don't need them don't have to download the extra bytes.

◆ **Invalid CSS.** Your style sheets won't validate if they contain filters. This isn't really a problem as long as you understand why they're not validating. But if it bothers you, you can place the filters in an IE-only style sheet so that at least your main style sheets validate.

NOTE: New scripts will likely continue to be released after this book has gone to print. To see the most up-to-date list of CSS3 emulation scripts, go to www.stunningcss3.com/resources.

♦ **Performance.** Filters can make the page load slowly and use up a lot of memory.

♦ **Jagged text.** Filters can turn off ClearType rendering in Windows so that text is no longer anti-aliased, making it look jagged.

♦ **Other bugs.** Occasionally, filters will trigger other bugs in IE. For instance, in Chapter 2, you'll see how a filter makes CSS-generated content disappear.

Because of these problems, I recommend you use filters only when you really have to. When you do use them, do so sparingly, and test thoroughly.

Filtering IE with Conditional Comments

Often, the only browsers for which you need to provide workarounds are IE 6 through 8. In these cases, you'll need some good ways to feed rules or scripts to IE only (or hide them from IE). You're probably already adept at doing this—providing IE with its own care and feeding is nothing new to CSS3. But just in case you need a refresher, this section offers a few ways you can target IE and IE alone.

Hacks that take advantage of CSS bugs in IE are the oldest way of targeting IE, and many people still use them. The most popular and useful IE hacks are the star html hack (http://css-discuss.incutio.com/wiki/Star_Html_Hack) and the underscore hack (http://wellstyled.com/css-underscore-hack.html). The nice thing about hacks is that they're right there in your main style sheet—they're easy to spot when you need to make changes or track down where some style is coming from, and they don't add another HTTP request. But some hacks are invalid CSS, and using many of them adds to the file size of *all* browsers, not just the ones that need them. Plus, unless you have the hacks memorized, you can't tell at a glance which browser is getting which value, and this can make it harder for other developers on your team to maintain your code.

Because of these problems, most CSS developers now use *conditional comments* when they want to target IE. Conditional comments are a special form of HTML comment that only IE can read. They're valid HTML, so they don't harm any other browsers—all non-IE browsers just skip over them, just like any other HTML comment. They allow you to write HTML that only IE will use, or that only certain versions of IE will use.

But don't we want to feed IE its own CSS, not HTML? Yes, but conditional comments allow us to do this, in a few different ways.

PROVIDING IE-ONLY STYLE SHEETS

The first conditional-comment option is to place a `link` or `@import` directive for an IE-only style sheet inside a conditional comment that targets all versions of IE, like this:

```
<!--[if IE]>
<link rel="stylesheet" href="ie_all.css" type="text/css">
<![endif]-->
```

Within this style sheet you can then use hacks to feed rules to different versions of IE, if necessary. However, with IE 9 coming out soon and having much better standards support, you probably want to make sure that version doesn't use your IE hack sheet. To avoid this, structure your conditional comment so that it targets only IE 8 and earlier, using this syntax:

```
<!--[if lte IE 8]>
<link rel="stylesheet" href="ie_lte8.css" type="text/css">
<![endif]-->
```

The `lte` part of the conditional comment stands for "less than or equal to." Other possible values are `lt` for "less than," `gte` for "greater than or equal to," and `gt` for "greater than."

Instead of using just one IE sheet, another option is to use multiple conditional comments to feed a different style sheet to each version of IE you need to fix, like this:

```
<!--[if IE 6]>
<link rel="stylesheet" href="ie_6.css" type="text/css">
<![endif]-->
<!--[if IE 7]>
<link rel="stylesheet" href="ie_7.css" type="text/css">
<![endif]-->
<!--[if IE 8]>
<link rel="stylesheet" href="ie_8.css" type="text/css">
<![endif]-->
```

This avoids the need for having hacks in any of the style sheets, but it may be a little harder to maintain.

TIP: It's also a good idea to use conditional comments to feed scripts that fix IE, such as the ones listed above, to IE only. That way, no other browser will download a script it doesn't need.

DISADVANTAGES OF CONDITIONAL COMMENTS

While conditional comments are great because of how reliably they filter IE, using them to feed IE-only style sheets is not without its disadvantages:

* **Extra HTTP requests.** Every extra sheet you create is another resource the browser has to get from the server, and each of those trips slows your pages.

* **Rules for single-object split between two or more places.** This can increase the time (and frustration) it takes to debug a problem on an object, as it may take you a while to remember that you have another sheet with rules for the same object hidden away in it. It's also easy to forget the IE rules if you later change something in your main sheet that ought to be changed in the IE sheet as well.

* **Block parallel downloading in IE 8.** Having a conditional comment in your HTML blocks IE 8 from downloading other resources on the page until the main CSS file has been downloaded. It doesn't matter what version of IE you're targeting with your conditional comment, and it doesn't matter if the conditional comment is being used to serve CSS or not—this bug is always there in IE 8. And it's a pretty bad one—it can add significantly to the loading time of your pages. The only fix is to add an empty conditional comment above the main CSS file, or to use conditional comments around the html tag instead of elsewhere. We'll go over this latter solution in a moment. Find out more about this bug at www.phpied.com/conditional-comments-block-downloads.

HIDING FROM IE

Conditional comments can also be used to hide content from IE, not just feed it content. These are called downlevel-revealed conditional comments (though it's not a very helpful name). The syntax looks like this:

```
<!--[if !IE]>-->
<link rel="stylesheet" href="not_ie.css" type="text/css">
<!--<![endif]-->
```

The exclamation mark in front of IE tells all versions of IE that they're not to use anything until they see <![endif], which closes the conditional comment.

This time, all other non-IE browsers do see the HTML between the conditional comments, because the beginning and closing conditional comments are actually each a standalone, regular HTML comment. Here's what non-IE browsers essentially see:

```
<!-- stuff that doesn't concern me, and now the comment is
over and I should start parsing again -->
<link rel="stylesheet" href="not_ie.css" type="text/css">
<!-- more stuff that doesn't concern me, and now this
comment is over -->
```

See how each comment is a standalone comment that opens and closes itself on the same line? There's no reason for browsers to ignore the HTML outside of the comments. IE ignores it only because it's been programmed to do so with its special syntax.

You can also use downlevel-revealed conditional comments on specific versions of IE, like this:

```
<!--[if !IE 6]>-->
<link rel="stylesheet" href="not_ie6.css" type="text/css">
<!--<![endif]-->
```

NOTE: For more on complex and clever conditional comment syntax, see "Things You Might Not Know About Conditional Comments" by Louis Lazaris (www.impressivewebs.com/conditional-comments).

ADDING IE-VERSION CLASSES ON THE html TAG

Another method of using conditional comments is not to use them to feed IE its own style sheets, but to add classes to the html tag that indicate what version of IE is in use. Then, you simply write rules for each of these classes in your main style sheet. This technique isn't as common as other conditional comment methods, but it's been gaining in popularity since Paul Irish blogged about it in 2008 (http://paulirish.com/2008/conditional-stylesheets-vs-css-hacks-answer-neither).

Here's what the HTML could look like:

```
<!--[if lt IE 7]> <html class="ie6" lang="en"> <![endif]-->
<!--[if IE 7]>    <html class="ie7" lang="en"> <![endif]-->
<!--[if IE 8]>    <html class="ie8" lang="en"> <![endif]-->
<!--[if IE 9]>    <html class="ie9" lang="en"> <![endif]-->
<!--[if gt IE 9]> <html lang="en"> <![endif]-->
<!--[if !IE]>--> <html lang="en"> <!--<![endif]-->
```

NOTE: The spaces between the tags in this code are simply there to make it easier to read. You can remove them in your real pages if you like.

WHY THE html TAG?

If you prefer, you could just as easily use this trick to apply classes to the body tag or a wrapper div instead of the html tag—just so long as it's some element that's around all the other elements on the page.

But the html element does have an advantage over other wrapper tags: it doesn't block parallel downloading of style sheets in IE 8 (as explained earlier in "Disadvantages of conditional comments"). Adding conditional comments around the body tag or a wrapper div doesn't fix this IE 8 bug; in these cases, you'd need to add an empty conditional comment above your main CSS file to stop the bug.

It's worth mentioning that in HTML 4 and XHTML 1, class attributes weren't allowed on the html tag, so this technique would make your page's markup invalid. But they are allowed now in HTML5—and, luckily, that's the doctype we're using throughout this book!

I know this looks rather overwhelming, but it's really quite simple if you walk through it line by line. Each line is simply being read by a different version of IE and spitting out a different html tag. For instance, when IE 6 loads the page, it sees the conditional comment for lt IE 7, says "Hey, I'm less than 7! I'm going to apply the stuff inside this conditional comment!" and spits out the HTML <html class="ie6" lang="en">. IE 6 then gets to the next conditional comment and sees that it doesn't apply to itself, so it skips it. And so on down the page. This happens in every version of IE, so each gets only one html tag, and each html tag has a class on it that identifies which version of IE is in use.

Non-IE browsers ignore all conditional comments, so they ignore the first five lines. The sixth line uses a downlevel-revealed conditional comment, so IE doesn't use it and non-IE browsers do. Thus, non-IE browsers apply only the last line with a plain, class-less html tag.

Once you have this HTML in place, you can create rules for any version of IE you wish directly in your main style sheet, removing an HTTP request and keeping your rules all in one place for easier debugging and maintenance. You don't have to use hacks, and you don't have to worry that non-IE browsers might see something they shouldn't. For instance, if you wanted to feed IE 6 a height value to make up for its lack of min-height support, you could simply do this:

```
div { min-height: 100px; }
.ie6 div { height: 100px; }
```

While including IE-specific rules in your main style sheet does add to its size, the increase should be minimal—hopefully, you are writing CSS that avoids IE bugs in the first place instead of getting littered with hacks. Plus, remember that HTTP requests are far more expensive in terms of page performance than an extra kilobyte or two, so overall this technique should be more efficient, both in terms of page performance and of your development and maintenance process.

Because of these advantages, I like this last option for filtering IE the best, so it's the method we'll be using in this book. Feel free to skip the html classes and separate IE rules out into their own sheets instead if that's your preference.

Dealing with Unsupportive Clients or Bosses

Sometimes the obstacle to using CSS3 successfully isn't so much the lack of support in *browsers*, but rather from your client or boss. If you're concerned about getting pushback from the people paying the bills, here are a few strategies that I hope will help you get CSS3 accepted at your workplace.

Don't Tell Them Everything

Let's start off with what might be the easiest "buy-in" strategy of all— call it the anti-strategy, if you will. I'll say it bluntly: maybe your client or boss need not know at all that you're even using CSS3. Think of it this way: if you hire someone to build you a house, you don't need or want to know the names of every tool, material, and technique the contractor is going to use along the way. You care about some of the technical details, but for the most part you're more concerned with the bigger picture and making sure your goals are met—in whatever way that contractor thinks is best.

Sometimes web design is a bit like this. While there are plenty of technical details you *do* need to run by your client or boss before implementing them, there comes a point where you just need to decide what the best tool for the job is, and use it. For instance, it's probably best to discuss whether you'll be using CSS3 animations or Flash for a particular animation on the site, but you don't necessarily need to ask your client whether he wants to use HSLA or an alpha-transparent PNG for a semitransparent background. Nor do you need to ask if it's OK if you add a subtle `text-shadow` to a heading to make it stand out a bit more. If you're going to be using CSS3 in limited amounts for small visual details, you can probably quietly decide that on your own, and then just implement it.

Educate Them About Progressive Enhancement Up Front

When you're still in the sales-pitch phase of a new project, be sure to always include some discussion of progressive enhancement. Before starting work, make sure your client understands the basic idea behind progressive enhancement and how it will affect her own site. You'll probably need to show visual examples in multiple devices and browsers, preferably from real sites, to make the point clear. Discuss which browsers you will enhance and which browsers will get the more bare-bones version. Find out which browsers matter most to your particular client based on usage statistics for her current site or the planned audience of a new site.

When discussing progressive enhancement with your client or boss, you don't need to go into technical details, but talk about how designs looking different in different browsers is inevitable and even good. To convince them it's good, you'll probably need to play to one or all of these three angles: saved money, happier users, and better search engine placement.

Tell them how designing using progressive enhancement, and CSS3 in particular, can reduce initial development time as well as mainte-nance time over the entire life of the project, costing them less. Also tell them how they can save money on bandwidth costs because CSS3 reduces the need for so many external resources like images, and often reduces file sizes. Remind your client that performing compli-cated workarounds for IE is billable time, and question what the ROI of that choice will be.

Talk about the ways that CSS3 can improve usability and how this can translate into happier users who stay on the site longer, which in turn can translate into more sales, signups, or whatever goal the site is aiming for.

Impress them with your knowledge of Google's search algorithm by explaining that Google now rewards fast sites, and go on to explain how CSS3 can make their sites faster.

In short, emphasize to your client or boss that progressive enhancement is in his or her best interest—because it truly is. It may not get accepted overnight, but keep working on helping your clients understand the reasoning behind web design and development best practices like progressive enhancement. Some day—pretty soon, we hope—these practices will be mainstream, and assumed, and then you'll already be ahead of the pack in providing better benefit to all users.

Manage Expectations from Design Mockups

One of the ways designers most frequently get into trouble is by showing their clients something in a design comp, otherwise known as a mockup, and then having the client expect the final product to look exactly like that in all browsers at all times. Even if you intended for the appearance shown in the mockup to display only in up-to-date, advanced browsers, you'll often end up forced to add in workarounds and hacks to try to make it look the same everywhere. There are a few ways you can avoid getting stuck in this trap.

DESIGN IN THE BROWSER

The best way to avoid setting unrealistic expectations based on your design comps is to never create any comps at all—or at least never show them to your client. Instead of using Photoshop or Fireworks to mock up your design as a static image, go straight to HTML and CSS to create the design mockup in its real, final medium. Show the client a working page that he can play with. As long as you make sure to show it to him in his own browser, he'll be able to see only what his browser is capable of, and no more.

Although this method of going straight to the CSS may seem like it would be a lot more work, given the fact that if the client doesn't like the site you might have to rebuild it entirely, it shouldn't be more work if done wisely. In fact, working in HTML and CSS should save you time.

You'll need to make sure that you get a lot of information up front from the client about what he expects from the design and what his tastes are. Don't settle for "I'll know it when I see it." Push him to give you detailed answers.

MORE ON DESIGNING WITHOUT A GRAPHICS PROGRAM

For more on the rationale and process behind designing in a browser, see:

◆ "Make Your Mockup in Markup," by Meagan Fisher (http://24ways.org/2009/make-your-mockup-in-markup)

◆ "Walls Come Tumbling Down presentation slides and transcript," by Andy Clarke (http://forabeautifulweb.com/blog/about/walls_come_tumbling_down_presentation_slides_and_transcript)

Also, work out the overall page structure and layout, using simple wireframes, before delving into any CSS work. That way, even if the client doesn't like the images, colors, or fonts you used, at least everything will be in the right place, or close to it, making changes to the design at this point much less time-consuming.

In fact, being able to change the appearance by editing CSS in a single file is often much faster than editing graphic comps. In the time it takes you to get the anti-aliasing and line-height and text wrapping just the way you want them in a graphics program, you could have probably done the same thing twice in CSS, and had a more accurate representation of how it would really look in the browser to boot. Also, being able to play with the design in a browser allows you to spot problems in the design that would only occur in a live page. You can fix these problems as soon as you spot them, instead of placing problematic design elements into a comp that your client might then fall in love with, forcing you to spend hours agonizing over how to actually implement them in a real page.

You can still use a graphics program for generating your own ideas in the early stages of creating a design, and for laying out small areas of the page that do need complex graphics that CSS alone can't handle. But overall, using the real tool that web pages are styled with—CSS—to build your designs will lead to fewer headaches down the road.

Despite these benefits, I know that designing in the browser is a huge shift from how most web designers work and what most clients expect. I admit that I have not been able to do it myself very often. Plus, you may have no control over the comps—they may be created by separate designers and simply handed over to you with instructions to build exactly what is shown. If it's not possible to design in the browser in your situation, read on for other ways you can avoid setting your clients up for disappointment.

EXPLAIN THE LIMITATIONS OF COMPS

If you're going to present your clients with traditional design comps, showing only one view of each page, be sure to explain to them that they're just mockups, not true representations of what everyone will see. Before ever showing them a comp, make sure they understand that static images can never be completely accurate because it's impossible to show all the variations in browsers, screen sizes, available fonts, and more. Explain that not every visual detail they see in the mockup will be available to every viewer—including possibly themselves—in the browser. Some people will see slightly less attractive variations based on what their browsers can and can't handle, but you'll use the best features of each browser to give a good experience to everyone.

SHOW POSSIBLE VARIATIONS

If you have the time, it's well worth it to create variations of each comp, to show some of the possible variations that users in different scenarios will see. For instance, you might create a comp of the home page at three different widths: 480 pixels for mobile phones, 750 pixels for small monitors, 1200 pixels for wide monitors. You might also create a comp to emulate IE 8's expected appearance, showing, perhaps, that this browser won't see the rounded corners and translucent backgrounds shown in the main comp.

Yes, this is more work up front. But if it keeps you from having to jump through hoops to try to make the page look just as gorgeous in IE as it does elsewhere, and if it allows you to use CSS3 and enjoy all of its time-saving benefits, then in the long run it will probably be less work. And you'll have a better finished web site to show for it.

2

Speech Bubbles

One of the most fun and easy uses of CSS3 is for layering on visual "frosting"—non-essential visual flair and little details that can push your design from adequate to alluring. We'll use some of the most straightforward and well-supported CSS3 properties to create the appearance of three-dimensional speech bubbles that can be used to style blog comments, pull quotes, and more.

WHAT YOU'LL LEARN

We'll create the appearance of speech bubbles without using any images, just these pieces of pure CSS:

- The `word-wrap` property to contain overflowing text
- The `border-radius` property to create rounded corners
- HSLA to create semitransparent backgrounds
- The `linear-gradient` function to create gradient backgrounds
- The `box-shadow` property to create drop shadows behind objects
- The `text-shadow` property to create drop shadows behind (you guessed it) text
- The `transform` property to rotate objects

The Base Page

Let's say you're working on styling a blog's comments section. Before delving into any CSS3 fanciness, you'd want to get some basic styles in place to take care of older, non-CSS3-supporting browsers. As I mentioned in Chapter 1, it's important to make sure your pages are functional and at least decent-looking in browsers that don't support CSS3 before you add on CSS3 as part of progressive enhancement.

FIGURE 2.1 The comments area before any CSS3 is applied.

Figure 2.1 shows a blog's comments section with some basic styles applied. The text, avatar image, commenter's name, and date for each comment have been laid out neatly, the text is formatted, and we even have some basic backgrounds and borders in place. There's nothing wrong with this comments area; it's usable, it's clean, it's attractive. Anyone seeing it in an older browser would not think they were missing something or that the page was "broken."

But there's a lot we can do with CSS3, without adding a single image or touching the markup, to jazz up the page's appearance. To get started, download the exercise files for this chapter at www.stunningcss3.com, and open speech-bubble_start.html in your code editor of choice. Its CSS is contained in a `style` element in the head of the page, for ease of editing.

Corralling Long Text

OK, I know I just said we were going to jazz up the comments' appearance. But before we get into the actual speech bubble styles, let's quickly take care of an old, frustrating text-formatting problem that can be solved with the simplest bit of CSS3 you can imagine.

It's not uncommon for people to include URLs in comments and forum posts, and these URLs often overflow their containers due to their length (**Figure 2.2**). If the URLs have dashes (-) in them, all the major browsers can wrap the text of the URLs just fine. But Webkit-based browsers and IE will not wrap at the forward-slash (/) character, and none of the major browsers will wrap at underscores (_).

NOTE: Here's a pleasant surprise: the word-wrap property works in IE, as far back as version 5.5! The property was actually created by Microsoft and later adopted by W3C.

I really enjoy reading your blog, but what happens when I put a long URL in my comment text, like this one:
http://forabeautifulweb.com
/blog/about
/what_does_browser_testing_mean_today/

Asha Gillenwater
March 10, 2010

FIGURE 2.2 Long URLs often overflow their containers, especially if they contain underscores.

In CSS3, there's finally an easy way to tell the browser to wrap text within words and stop it from overflowing. All you have to do is give the word-wrap property a value of break-word, and the browser will wrap text within a word if it has to in order to keep it from overflowing.

THE LOWDOWN ON THE word-wrap PROPERTY

The word-wrap property is part of the Text module found at www.w3.org/TR/css3-text. It controls whether or not text is allowed to break within "words." (The separate text-wrap property controls how lines break between words.) The word-wrap property can be set either to normal (the default) or break-word.

Other than breaking long URLs, you might want to use word-wrap for:

◆ Keeping data tables from becoming too wide and overflowing or breaking your layout; see www.456bereastreet.com/archive/200704/how_to_prevent_html_tables_from_becoming_too_wide

◆ Wrapping displayed code snippets in pre elements; see www.longren.org/2006/09/27/wrapping-text-inside-pre-tags

TABLE 2.1 word-wrap **browser support**

IE	FIREFOX	OPERA	SAFARI	CHROME
Yes, 5.5+	Yes, 3.5+	Yes	Yes	Yes

In speech-bubble_start.html, find the blockquote rule in the CSS in the head of the page, and add the word-wrap property:

```
blockquote {
    margin: 0 0 0 112px;
    padding: 10px 15px 5px 15px;
    border-top: 1px solid #fff;
    background-color: #A6DADC;
    word-wrap: break-word;
}
```

Save the page and check it in a very narrow browser window. Ah, much better. The browser will still try to wrap first at normal breakpoints, but if it has to, it will now wrap the text at underscores or even within a word (**Figure 2.3**). Obviously, placing a break within a word is not ideal, but I think in this case it's preferable to the text overflowing and will probably only occur on long URLs, not regular text.

Now that we've taken care of that little annoyance, let's start making these comments look like speech bubbles!

I really enjoy reading your blog, but what happens when I put a long URL in my comment text, like this one: http://forabeautifulweb.com /blog/about /what_does_browser_testing_mea n_today/

Asha Gillenwater
March 10, 2010

FIGURE 2.3 The browser will now break text between any two characters.

Graphic Effects Sans Graphics

You can create very graphic-looking speech bubbles without using any actual graphics. Avoiding graphics has many benefits beyond just being able to amaze your designer friends. You benefit by saving all the time and effort spent creating, slicing, and optimizing graphics, and then redoing them when your client inevitably wants to make one small change. Your visitors benefit from the increase in page speed that comes from having less data to download and fewer HTTP requests to the server.

NOTE: There's more in-depth information on the benefits of reducing images in Chapter 1, as well as a real-world case study.

Rounding the Corners

Those sharp, rectangular-cornered comments don't look very bubble-y, do they? Let's round the corners to start getting more of a speech-bubble look.

Rounded corners are a simple, common visual effect that used to be surprisingly hard to create in an actual web page. Creating the rounded-corner images in a graphics program was time-consuming, as was creating the actual HTML and CSS. You'd often have to add a bunch of extra nested divs to place each corner image separately, since CSS 2.1 allows only one background image per box, and the CSS used to actually control the placement of the images could get complicated. The images, along with the bloated markup and CSS, bulked up the amount that each visitor had to download, slowing down page-loading speeds. Even if you used a script to dynamically create the rounded corners instead of manually creating and applying images, you were still adding to the number of files that users had to download and decreasing your pages' performance. All this trouble for some simple-looking little rounded corners!

CREATING OVALS AND CIRCLES WITH border-radius

If you want your speech bubbles to be complete ovals instead of rounded rectangles, you'll need to use elliptical-shaped corners instead of perfectly round ones. *Elliptical* just means that the curve of each corner is somewhat flattened out—just like an oval. To specify an elliptical corner, you write two measurements, separated by a slash, such as this: border-radius: 50px/20px. (Safari 3 and 4 use the non-standard syntax of no slash, just a space.) This means that the curve will extend horizontally 50 pixels but vertically only 20 pixels, making a flattened, elliptical curve. You can make each corner have different angles; find out how at http://css-tricks.com/snippets/css/rounded-corners.

To create circles, first give your box the same width and height; use ems as the unit of measurement instead of pixels to ensure it can grow with its text. Then set each corner's border-radius to one-half the width/height value. For instance, if you have a box that is 10 ems wide and tall, use border-radius: 5em. See http://blog.creativityden.com/the-hidden-power-of-border-radius-2 for more examples.

In CSS3, creating rounded corners can be as simple as border-radius: 10px on a single div. No extra markup, no images, no JavaScript.

Of course, while CSS3 continues to be developed and gain browser support, it's a little more complicated in real-world usage. But it's still really, really easy.

In your page, modify the blockquote rule to match the following:

```
blockquote {
    margin: 0 0 0 112px;
    padding: 10px 15px 5px 15px;
    -moz-border-radius: 20px;
    -webkit-border-radius: 20px;
    border-radius: 20px;
    border-top: 1px solid #fff;
    background-color: #A6DADC;
    word-wrap: break-word;
}
```

The `border-radius: 20px;` declaration is the W3C standard syntax for rounded corners, specifying that all four corners should be rounded by 20 pixels. This syntax is currently supported by Opera, Chrome, Safari 5, and IE 9. Firefox and Safari 4 and earlier use the `-moz-border-radius` and `-webkit-border-radius` properties, respectively. As explained in Chapter 1, browser vendors use these browser-specific prefixes when the specification is still being worked out and they think it may change. The non-prefixed version of the property (in this case, plain `border-radius`) should always come last, so that when browsers *do* support the non-prefixed property, it overrides the earlier rules, which may use non-standard behavior from an older version of the spec.

> **NOTE:** You don't have to actually declare a border when using `border-radius`. If there is no border, the browser just rounds the background area.

THE LOWDOWN ON THE `border-radius` PROPERTY

The `border-radius` property is part of the Backgrounds and Borders module found at www.w3.org/TR/css3-background. It's shorthand for the properties specifying the rounding amount of each of the four corners, in this order: `border-top-left-radius`, `border-top-right-radius`, `border-bottom-right-radius`, `border-bottom-left-radius`. Mozilla's properties for individual corners have the non-standard syntax of `-moz-border-radius-topleft` and so forth.

You can write out all four values, with spaces in between, in one `border-radius` property, or just use one value to round all four corners the same amount. Safari 4 and Safari on iOS 3 and earlier don't allow you to specify multiple corners in the shorthand `border-radius` property, other than writing one value to specify all four at once.

See the "Creating ovals and circles with `border-radius`" sidebar for the syntax for elliptical curves on corners. Also see www.owlfolio.org/htmletc/border-radius and http://muddledramblings.com/table-of-css3-border-radius-compliance for more `border-radius` syntax details and examples.

Other than speech bubbles, you might want to use `border-radius` for:

- Buttons; see http://blogfreakz.com/button/css3-button-tutorials and http://css-tricks.com/examples/ButtonMaker
- Tabs
- Dialog boxes
- Circular badges
- Bar charts; seewww.marcofolio.net/css/animated_wicked_css3_3d_bar_chart.html
- Smiley faces; see http://ryanroberts.co.uk/_dev/experiments/css-border-faces

TABLE 2.2 border-radius **browser support**

IE	FIREFOX	OPERA	SAFARI	CHROME
Yes, 9+	Yes with -moz-	Yes	Yes, 5+; 4+ with -webkit-	Yes

NOTE: See how I keep referring back to Chapter 1? If you skipped it, please go back and read it now. There's some important stuff there.

With these three lines added, the corners are now rounded in all browsers except IE 8 and earlier (**Figure 2.4**). These versions of IE simply ignore the properties and keep the corners straight—no harm done. This is a great example of progressive enhancement, as explained in Chapter 1. Since this is a purely decorative effect, I see no harm in IE users missing it. If you do, read on.

FIGURE 2.4 The border-radius **property applied**

WORKAROUNDS FOR IE

If you really must have rounded corners in IE 8 and earlier, you can use one of these scripts:

◆ "PIE," by Jason Johnston (http://css3pie.com), reads the border-radius properties that are already present in your CSS and makes them work in IE 6 and later. It also adds several other CSS3 effects to IE.

◆ "curved-corner," by Remiz Rahnas (http://code.google.com/p/curved-corner), also reads the border-radius properties out of your CSS, but works only when all four corners have the same border-radius.

- "IE-CSS3," by Nick Fetchak (http://fetchak.com/ie-css3), is based off of curved-corner but also adds drop shadows in IE.

- "DD_roundies," by Drew Diller (http://dillerdesign.com/experi-ment/DD_roundies), lets you round corners individually, but it doesn't read the values from your CSS; you have to manually set the IE values separately.

Besides these IE-specific scripts, there are a number of rounded-corner scripts and image-based techniques out there that were developed before the `border-radius` property gained support, so you could always go back to one of these older techniques for IE. You can choose between dozens of options at www.smileycat.com/miaow/archives/000044.php and http://css-discuss.incutio.com/wiki/Rounded_Corners.

If you do use a script or images for IE, make sure to hide them from other browsers by placing the script references or IE styles within conditional comments, or by using Modernizr, both of which are explained in Chapter 1. That way, only IE users get the performance hit of using an old-school rounded-corner method, and non-IE users get the faster, pure CSS version. You'll have to decide if the extra work and performance hit is worth having IE users see rounded instead of straight corners.

Adding the Bubble's Tail

With rounded corners, each comment box now looks more like a bubble, but a speech bubble isn't complete without a pointer or arrow, commonly called a "tail," pointing to the speaker. We can add that tail without using any graphics. In fact, we can add it without using any CSS3—the technique only uses properties and selectors from CSS 2.

CREATING TRIANGLES OUT OF BORDERS

All we need to create a tail is a triangle, and you can create triangles with pure CSS by using regular old borders. When two borders of a box meet at a corner, the browser draws their meeting point at an angle (**Figure 2.5**). If you reduce that box's `width` and `height` to zero, and give every border a thick width and a different color, you'll end up with the appearance of four triangles pushed together, each point-ing in a different direction (**Figure 2.6**).

FIGURE 2.5 **By making the top border a differ-ent color, you can see that borders meet at corners at an angle.**

FIGURE 2.6 **When a box has no width or height, each border creates the appear-ance of a triangle.**

TIP: Remember, in CSS, when you have four values in a single property, like in the `border-color` property shown in the code here, the first value is for the top, the second for the right, the third for the bottom, and the fourth for the left. Think of going around a clock clockwise.

Here's what the HTML and CSS used to create Figure 2.6 look like:

```
<div class="triangles"></div>

.triangles {
  border-color: red green blue orange;
  border-style: solid;
  border-width: 20px;
  width: 0;
  height: 0;
}
```

What would happen if you made the top, left, and bottom borders transparent instead of colored? Only the right border would show, leaving the appearance of a left-pointing triangle (**Figure 2.7**):

FIGURE 2.7 Making all but one of the borders transparent creates the appearance of a single triangle.

```
<div class="triangle-left"></div>

.triangle-left {
  border-color: transparent green transparent transparent;
  border-style: solid;
  border-width: 20px;
  width: 0;
  height: 0;
}
```

So, to sum that up, all you need to do to create a triangle using CSS is give an element zero `width` and `height`, give it thick borders, and make all but one of those borders transparent. You can vary the angle of the triangle by making the widths of the borders different on different sides.

GENERATING THE TAIL

Now that you know how to make an image-free triangle, let's add a left-pointing triangle to the left side of each comment, pointing to the commenter's avatar. To do this, we could nest a `span` or `div` inside each comment, and then transform this element into our triangle, but let's leave the HTML pristine and use CSS-generated content to make the element we need appear.

Generated content is a CSS 2.1 technique where you place content into your CSS to have it appear in your HTML. It's useful for adding things that you don't want to manually hard-code into the HTML, like numbers before headings or icons after links. It shouldn't be used for essential content that would be missed if the user couldn't access the CSS file.

To create generated content, you need to specify *where* the content is to be inserted, using either the ::before or ::after pseudo-elements (also written as :before and :after), and specify *what* content to insert, using the content property.

WHAT'S WITH THE DOUBLE COLONS?

You may have noticed that I wrote the ::before and ::after pseudo-elements with double colons instead of the single colons you may be used to seeing. No, it's not a typo. CSS3 changed the syntax for pseudo-elements to use double colons, while pseudo-classes retain the single colons.

You can continue to use the single colon versions if you wish; they still work just fine. In fact, since IE 8 and earlier don't support the double-colon versions, we'll stick with the single colon versions in this book. You could also use both as a grouped selector, such as .caption:before, .caption::before { content: "Figure: ";}.

For instance, to insert the word "Figure" before every image caption on your page, you could use the following CSS:

```
.caption:before {
    content: "Figure: ";
}
```

This CSS would turn the HTML <p class="caption">Isn't my cat cute?</p> into this text when seen on the page:

Figure: Isn't my cat cute?

In the case of the speech-bubble tail we want to generate, all we want to see are the *borders* of the generated content, not the content itself. So, let's generate a piece of invisible content: a non-breaking space.

The HTML entity for a non-breaking space is , but you can't use HTML entities within the content property. Instead, you need to use the hexadecimal part of the character's Unicode code point (or reference). That may sound really confusing and difficult and science-y, but don't be scared—there are lots of handy charts online that allow you to look up this kind of stuff.

For instance, at www.digitalmediaminute.com/reference/entity you can see 252 little boxes, each showing one of the allowed entities in (X)HTML. In the "Filter entities by keyword" box, type "non-breaking

TIP: Another useful tool is the Unicode Code Converter at http://rishida.net/tools/conversion, where you can put in the character or its HTML entity name and convert it into a bunch of different formats, including its hexadecimal code point.

space." 251 of the boxes will disappear, leaving you with one box showing , the HTML entity name. Position your cursor over the box (**Figure 2.8**). Two other codes will appear: its numerical code (in this case,) and its Unicode code (u00A0). You just want the hexadecimal part of the Unicode code, which is the part after the "u." Copy the text "00A0" onto your clipboard.

FIGURE 2.8 **Use the XHTML Character Entity Reference to look up the Unicode code points of various entities.**

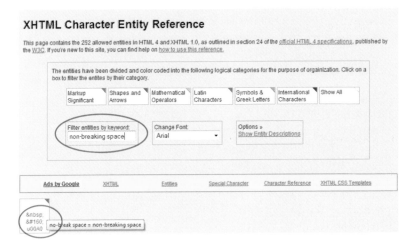

NOTE: Unicode code points are often written with a prefix of "U+" instead of just "u." In either of these cases, the part you want to include in the content property is just the four-digit hexadecimal part that comes after the prefix.

Now we're almost there; but even though we now have the Unicode code we need, we can't put it straight into the content property, like so:

```
blockquote:after {
    content:"00A0";
}
```

If we did this, the browser would quite logically make the text "00A0" show up, instead of the non-breaking space. To tell the browser that we're putting in a special character code, we need to *escape* the code. If you're a programmer, you'll be familiar with this term, but for the rest of us, all it means is that you have to put a backslash in front of the code. This alerts the browser that what follows the slash is not to be taken as literal text, but is instead a code for something else.

With the backslash, we finally have all the correct characters and punctuation needed to insert a simple non-breaking space:

```
blockquote:after {
    content:"\00A0";
}
```

Once you do this, the page will look exactly the same; the non-breaking space is invisible, of course. Let's add the borders around it to make it show up. We also need to set its `width` and `height` to zero and make it display as a block element so we can move it around to place the tail against the side of the speech bubble:

```
blockquote:after {
    content: "\00a0";
    display: block;
    width: 0;
    height: 0;
    border-width: 10px 20px 10px 0;
    border-style: solid;
    border-color: transparent #000 transparent transparent;
}
```

If we had made all four borders the same width, we'd end up with a rather fat triangle, like the one shown in Figure 2.7. To make the triangle a little longer and thinner, we've set the top and bottom borders to only 10 pixels, and the left border is nonexistent at zero pixels. The right border—the one we use to create the appearance of a left-pointing triangle—is a nice, wide 20 pixels. All the borders except the right one are transparent; here I've set the right border's color to black temporarily just so we can see it in order to place it correctly (**Figure 2.9**).

The triangle is currently placed right after the `blockquote`'s content—not the right spot for a speech bubble's tail. You can correct this by moving it with absolute positioning. First, add `position: relative;` to the `blockquote` rule; this establishes it as the reference point for the absolute element's positioning:

```
blockquote {
    position: relative;
    margin: 0 0 0 112px;
    padding: 10px 15px 5px 15px;
    -moz-border-radius: 20px;
    -webkit-border-radius: 20px;
    border-radius: 20px;
    border-top: 1px solid #fff;
    background-color: #A6DADC;
    word-wrap: break-word;
}
```

FIGURE 2.9 The black right border creates the appearance of a left-pointing triangle.

Then, add the absolute positioning to the generated content, along with top and left values:

```
blockquote:after {
    content: "\00a0";
    display: block;
    position: absolute;
    top: 20px;
    left: -20px;
    width: 0;
    height: 0;
    border-width: 10px 20px 10px 0;
    border-style: solid;
    border-color: transparent #000 transparent transparent;
}
```

FIGURE 2.10 **Absolute positioning places the triangle where we want it.**

You can set the top value to whatever you want; just make sure it's equal to or greater than the border-radius value so it lands on the straight edge of the box, below the corner curve. The left value should be a negative value in order to pull the triangle to the left, and it should match the width of the triangle. In this case, the width of the triangle is 20 pixels, because that's the width of the right border, so we're using a left value of –20px. This places the triangle right up against the left edge of the comment box (**Figure 2.10**).

It's possible that a comment might be so short that the tail hangs off the bottom, as seen in the second comment in Figure 2.10. To fix this, add min-height: 42px; to the blockquote rule.

```
blockquote {
    position: relative;
    min-height: 42px;
    margin: 0 0 0 112px;
    padding: 10px 15px 5px 15px;
    -moz-border-radius: 20px;
    -webkit-border-radius: 20px;
    border-radius: 20px;
    border-top: 1px solid #fff;
    background-color: #A6DADC;
    word-wrap: break-word;
}
```

Now that the triangle isn't layered over the blockquote, we can change its color to match the blockquote:

```
blockquote:after {
    content: "\00a0";
    display: block;
    position: absolute;
    top: 20px;
    left: -20px;
    width: 0;
    height: 0;
    border-1width: 10px 20px 10px 0;
    border-style: solid;
    border-color: transparent #A6DADC transparent
                  transparent;
}
```

NOTE: The page with all the changes to this point is named speech-bubble_1.html in the exercise files that you downloaded for this chapter.

This creates a seamless appearance between the bubble and the tail parts of each speech bubble (**Figure 2.11**).

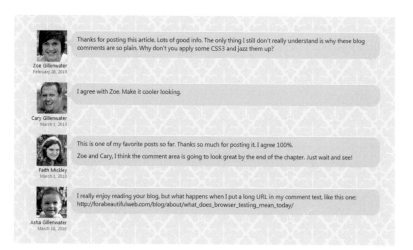

FIGURE 2.11 **Each tail is now colored and placed correctly.**

WORKAROUNDS FOR IE

Our tail shows up fine in IE 8 and later versions, but IE 7 and earlier versions don't support generated content, so they don't see the tail. I think this is fine in this case, as there's no reason users of those browsers would see the plain rectangles and think, "Hey wait a second! Why isn't there a little triangle sticking out of each comment block?"

To add tails in IE 7 and earlier, you'd need to manually add another element to the HTML of each comment, such as an empty span, and turn this element into the triangle.

Semitransparent Backgrounds with RGBA or HSLA

There's nothing more that we have to do to create the appearance of a speech bubble—we've got the rounded corners and the tail—but it would be nice to add a little more depth and visual richness with some extra graphic details.

One great way to add depth is to make backgrounds semitransparent (also called alpha transparency). By letting a little bit of the page background show through, you create more of a layered appearance, as if the semitransparent element is floating over the background. I think this look is especially well-suited to speech bubbles, because, well, they're bubbles—light and airy.

Before CSS3, you could create semitransparent backgrounds using an alpha-transparent PNG as a tiling background image. Using a background image has the disadvantage of adding another hit to your server, making pages load a little slower for your users. Performance is impacted even more if you need to support IE 6, since it needs a script to be able to understand alpha-transparent PNGs. Plus, you can't use a background image on a border, so you wouldn't be able to make the speech bubble's tail semitransparent. It would look pretty weird for the body of the bubble to be semitransparent and the tail to be totally opaque.

CSS3'S RGBA AND HSLA SYNTAX

Luckily, in CSS3 we have both RGBA and HSLA to turn to. Both are methods for specifying a color and its level of transparency at the same time. RGBA stands for red-green-blue-alpha (for alpha transparency) and HSLA stands for hue-saturation-lightness-alpha.

We could specify the shade of blue that we're using as the speech bubble's background using any of these syntaxes:

♦ Hexadecimal: #A6DADC

♦ RGB: 166, 218, 220

♦ RGBA: 166, 218, 220, 1

♦ HSL: 182, 44%, 76%

♦ HSLA: 182, 44%, 76%, 1

They all get us to the same exact color, just through different routes. It's a "you say toe-may-toe, I say toe-mah-toe" sort of thing.

In the RGBA syntax, the first three values are the amounts of red, green, and blue, either from 0–255 or 0%–100%. (You'll most often see the 0–255 values, not the percentages.) In the HSLA syntax, the first three values are the hue value, from 0 to 360; the percentage level of saturation; and the percentage level of lightness. In both RGBA and HSLA, the fourth value is the opacity level, from 0 (completely transparent) to 1 (completely opaque).

NOTE: CSS3 also has an opacity property, but it makes the entire element semitransparent, including its content, instead of just the background.

You can use most graphic editors to determine the correct red, green, and blue values needed to create your chosen color. Use the color picker to choose a color, and in the color dialog box or picker window, most graphic editors will tell you that color's hexadecimal code as well as RGB values (**Figure 2.12**). Finding HSL values can be a little trickier, as not all image-editing software uses HSL; for instance, Photoshop uses HSB (also called HSV), which is similar, but not quite the same. If you're on a Mac running Snow Leopard, check out the free app Colors by Matt Patenaude (http://mattpatenaude.com), which lets you pick colors from anywhere on your screen and can display values in HSLA as well as other syntaxes. If you're not on a Mac, I recommend you use one of the online HSL color picker or converter tools (see the "Online color tools" sidebar).

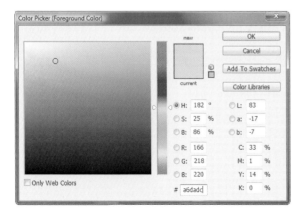

FIGURE 2.12
Photoshop's Color Picker dialog box shows the equivalent RGB values for the chosen hex color.

ONLINE COLOR TOOLS

There are many free web-based color picker and converter tools that you can find through Googling, but here are a couple that are particularly handy for working with RGB and HSL values:

◆ The color converter tool at http://serennu.com/colour/hsltorgb.php allows you to convert color values you already have into hex, RGB, and HSL syntaxes.

◆ The Doughnut Color Picker at www.workwithcolor.com/doughnut-color-picker-01.htm lets you both pick and convert colors. The picker uses HSL, but gives the hex and RGB equivalents, and lets you input colors in any of the three syntaxes.

Some browser-based color pickers make finding HSL or RGB values even easier and faster. I'm a big fan of the Rainbow extension for Firefox (https://addons.mozilla.org/en-US/firefox/addon/14328). After you install the extension, you can tell it which syntax to use to display color values (**Figure 2.13**). Then, when you use its Inspector tool to choose colors from a web page, it gives you the option to automatically copy those values to your clipboard (**Figure 2.14**), and you can then easily paste them into your CSS. Note that, as of this writing, the extension doesn't include the "A" part of either RGBA or HSLA, so you'll have to add that part in by hand. But I think you can handle all that typing.

FIGURE 2.13 In the options for the Rainbow extension, set the "Display color values in" option to "Hsl."

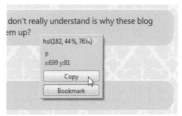

FIGURE 2.14 Using Rainbow's Inspector tool, you can click on a color to display and copy its color code.

RGBA VERSUS HSLA

The main reason I recommend the Rainbow Firefox extension over some other color picker extensions is that many others don't include HSL values, while Rainbow does, and I prefer HSLA over RGBA.

I'm in the minority here. Many more people use RGBA than HSLA, but I think that's mainly because most people haven't heard of HSLA. It's a shame, because the majority of people who use HSLA find it more intuitive.

With RGB and RGBA values, it's hard to tell at a glance what the color is going to be. If you take a minute to study a whole RGB or RGBA value, such as `rgb(166,218,220)`, you can get a fair idea of the resulting color, based on which of the three component color values (red, green, or blue) are highest. But I'm not a big fan of taking that minute to parse it out while I'm trolling through my style sheet trying to track down where some mysterious color is coming from. And even after I determine that an RGB value is producing a greenish-blue hue, for instance, it's hard to tell how muted or dark that greenish-blue is by looking at only its red, green, and blue values.

HSL AND HSLA HUE VALUES CHEAT SHEET

If you're going to use HSLA, it's helpful to memorize the hue values of a few key colors (or at least approximately where they are between 0 and 360, so you can tweak your way to the shade you want).

- 0 or 360 = red
- 30 = orange
- 60 = yellow
- 120 = green
- 180 = cyan
- 240 = blue
- 270 = purple
- 300 = magenta

To get black in HSL and HSLA, just set the lightness value to zero percent. For white, set the lightness value to 100 percent. In both cases, the hue and saturation values can be whatever you want.

To get gray in HSL and HSLA, just set the saturation value to zero percent. The lightness value will control the shade of the gray, and the hue value is irrelevant.

Another problem with RGB and RGBA is that if you want to tweak a color—make it a little darker or brighter or greener—you have to guess at how to change each of the values to get to the hue you want. In web design, it's common to use multiple shades of the same hue in different places in the page, such as a brightened version of a color on the current tab in a nav bar. But with RGB, different shades of the same hue don't necessarily have very similar color values. For instance, a just slightly darker version of the shade of blue we've been working with would have an RGB value of 155, 209, 211 instead of the original 166, 218, 220. All three numbers have to change to produce a very slight shift in darkness.

With HSL and HSLA, you don't have to add amounts of red, green, and blue to get a specific hue, but instead set that hue as one specific number. All you have to do is remember that both 0 and 360 equal the same shade of pure red. As you increase the hue value from 0, you simply move through the rainbow from red to purple and then back around to red again, as if you were going around a color wheel (**Figure 2.15**).

FIGURE 2.15
The 360 hue values in
the HSL color syntax

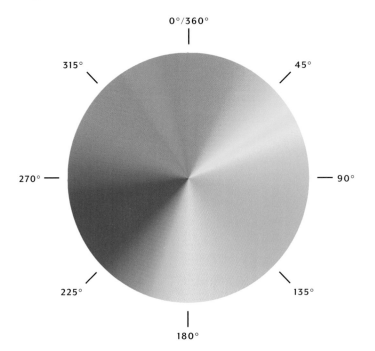

THE LOWDOWN ON RGBA AND HSLA

RGBA and HSLA are part of the Color module found at www.w3.org/TR/css3-color. Both allow you to set a color and its level of transparency at the same time.

In the RGBA syntax, the first three values are the amounts of red, green, and blue, either from 0–255 or 0%–100%. In the HSLA syntax, the first three values are the hue value from 0 to 360, the percentage level of saturation, and the percentage level of lightness. In both RGBA and HSLA, the fourth value is the opacity level from 0 (completely transparent) to 1 (completely opaque).

Other than ghostly bubble backgrounds, you might want to use RGBA or HSLA for:

◆ Drop shadows that tint the background beneath them (you'll learn how to do this later in this chapter)

◆ Gradient highlights on buttons or any other objects (again, you'll learn how to do this soon)

◆ Tinting the chosen link in a nav bar a slightly lighter or darker shade of the main color

◆ Semitransparent caption boxes laid over photos; see http://css-tricks.com/text-blocks-over-image and www.htmldrive.net/items/show/381/Snazzy-Hover-Effects-Using-CSS3.html

◆ Semitransparent dialog boxes, modal windows, or tooltips laid over content

TABLE 2.3 RGBA and HSLA browser support

IE	FIREFOX	OPERA	SAFARI	CHROME
Yes, 9+	Yes	Yes	Yes	Yes

Once you have the hue you want, you can then adjust its saturation if you want it duller or brighter, or adjust its lightness if you want it darker or lighter. It's easy to get multiple shades of the same color, or to tweak the color's hue just a little bit in one direction. Once you've worked with HSLA for a while and are more familiar with what each hue value computes out to, it's easier to tell at a glance what color you're going to get when you're glancing through the HSLA values in your style sheets.

The bottom line is this: RGBA and HSLA both have the same browser support and produce the same colors. I'm using HSLA throughout this book because it's more intuitive to me, but if you find RGBA easier, it's perfectly fine to use it instead.

CREATING SEMITRANSPARENT SPEECH BUBBLES

Now that we've gotten all that syntax out of the way, we can switch the speech bubbles' background color from hexadecimal to HSLA notation and make them semitransparent.

The speech bubbles' background color is currently set to #A6DADC. We can figure out the HSLA equivalent using the Rainbow extension. Just open your speech-bubble page in Firefox, and use the Rainbow Inspector to click on the speech bubble background color. It will show you that the HSL value is hsl(182, 44%, 76%). Copy this value, go back to your code editor, and paste it over the current hexadecimal background color:

NOTE: Having spaces after the commas between the three HSL values is completely optional—it works the same way with or without spaces. (I took them out.)

```
blockquote {
    position: relative;
    min-height: 40px;
    margin: 0 0 0 112px;
    padding: 10px 15px 5px 15px;
    -moz-border-radius: 20px;
    -webkit-border-radius: 20px;
    border-radius: 20px;
    border-top: 1px solid #fff;
    background-color: hsl(182,44%,76%);
    word-wrap: break-word;
}
```

If you save and refresh the page after this change, it will look exactly the same. You haven't changed the color yet—just changed the syntax for specifying it.

Now we'll modify this new syntax to make the speech bubbles semitransparent. Change background-color: hsl(182,44%,76%); to background-color: hsla(182, 44%,76%,.5); . Make sure to add the "a" of "hsla"!

NOTE: I've written the alpha value as ".5," but "0.5" is also perfectly fine.

You also want to change the tail to match. Copy and paste the HSLA value over the hexadecimal value in the border-color declaration:

```
blockquote:after {
    content: "\00a0";
    display: block;
    position: absolute;
    top: 20px;
    left: -20px;
    width: 0;
    height: 0;
    border-width: 10px 20px 10px 0;
```

```
    border-style: solid;
    border-color: transparent hsla(182,44%,76%,.5)
                  transparent transparent;
}
```

Save and refresh the page in your browser. You can now see the page background pattern showing through the speech bubbles slightly, as well as each commenter's avatar showing through the little bit of the tail that overlaps each picture (**Figure 2.16**).

FIGURE 2.16 Each speech bubble's background is the same shade of blue, but now semitransparent.

WORKAROUNDS FOR IE

You have a few options for working around the lack of HSLA/RGBA support in IE 8 and earlier.

◆ Provide a replacement solid background color (in hexadecimal, RGB, or HSL syntax). If you declare the solid background color before the HSLA/RGBA version, using the background shorthand property on either both the colors or just the HSLA/RGBA one, IE 8 and earlier will use it and correctly ignore the HSLA/RGBA one. But if you use the background-color property instead of background to declare the HSLA/RGBA color, IE 7 and 6 won't use the solid color; they try to apply the HSLA/RGBA color and can't, so they display no color at all. In some pages, where the text is still readable even without a background color behind it, this would be acceptable. In those cases where it's not, and where you can't use the background shorthand property, you would need to feed IE 7 and earlier the solid background color in a rule that only IE can read. See Chapter 1 for your IE-feeding options.

◆ Tile a tiny semitransparent PNG image as the background image. This has the advantage over the first option of actually making the background semitransparent, instead of opaque. It works in IE 8 and 7, but not IE 6 and earlier, since those versions don't support alpha-transparent PNGs. To work around this, you could use IE's AlphaImageLoader filter (or one of the many IE transparency scripts

TIP: You can use server-side programming to generate the PNGs for you. See http://leaverou.me/2009/02/bulletproof-cross-browser-rgba-backgrounds for a PHP script that generates them based on the RGBA values in your CSS.

NOTE: The PIE script mentioned earlier can also be used to make RGBA work in IE, but only in limited contexts. See http://css3pie. com/documentation/ supported-css3-features for more information.

that makes use of the filter), feed IE 6 a solid background color, or feed IE 6 a GIF or PNG8 image. But all of this is a lot of extra work and could have a big impact on the performance of your pages—the AlphaImageLoader filter is horribly slow and an image is another HTTP request. (Plus, in our case, we couldn't use it on the speech bubbles' tails, since they are just borders and don't have background images.) I don't recommend using a PNG background image unless you don't need to worry about IE 6 and thus won't be providing any workarounds for its lack of alpha-transparent PNG support.

♦ Use IE's Gradient filter, which works since version 5.5, and allows semitransparent colors (using its own proprietary syntax, of course). Just set both the starting and ending colors to the same color so you don't create the appearance of a gradient.

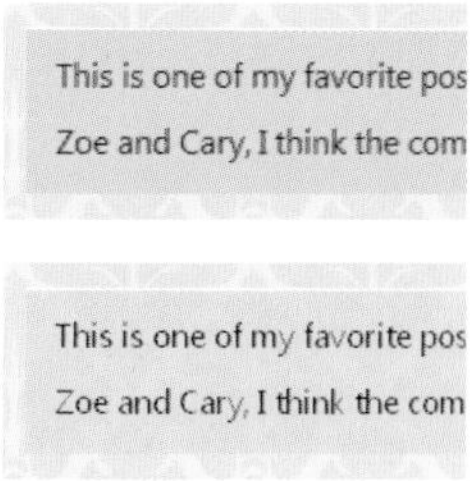

I recommend either the first or third option. The third more closely resembles the appearance we're going for, since the background will be semitransparent instead of solid. However, it's worth noting that the Gradient filter can do strange things to the anti-aliasing of the element's text and make it look a little uneven (peek ahead at **Figure 2.17**). You'll have to decide if the less pretty text is worth the more pretty background. Also, adding the filter will make the generated content tail disappear in IE 8 (it never appeared in 7 and 6 to begin with). I can't give you any explanation for this—it's just one of those weird IE bugs.

FIGURE 2.17
Before (top) and after (bottom) the Gradient filter is applied in IE 8. With the filter, the background color is semitransparent, but the anti-aliasing of the text is now a little uneven-looking.

In this case, I say let's go for the semitransparent background using the filter. Since we don't have rounded corners in IE to create the speech-bubble appearance, I don't mind losing the speech bubble's tail.

We could add the filter right inside the blockquote rule—non-IE browsers will just ignore it—but as discussed in Chapter 1, it's always nice to keep hacks and workaround separate from the standard rules. To keep the filters separate, we should either create a separate IE sheet, or use the conditional comments html tag trick described in Chapter 1. Let's use the html tag trick.

TIP: If you don't want to type all this by hand (I don't blame you), open speech-bubble_final. html from this chapter's exercise files, and copy and paste it from there.

Go to the opening html tag of the page, and change it to the following HTML:

```
<!--[if lt IE 7]><html lang="en" class="ie6"><![endif]-->
<!--[if IE 7]><html lang="en" class="ie7"><![endif]-->
<!--[if IE 8]><html lang="en" class="ie8"><![endif]-->
<!--[if IE 9]><html lang="en" class="ie9"><![endif]-->
<!--[if gt IE 9]><html lang="en"><![endif]-->
<!--[if !IE]>--><html lang="en"><!--<![endif]-->
```

Now we can create one rule for IE 5.5, 6 and 7, and another rule for IE 8, since its filter syntax is a little different than that used in earlier versions of IE. Add the IE 7 and earlier rule first:

```
.ie6 blockquote, .ie7 blockquote {
    background: none;
    filter: progid:DXImageTransform.Microsoft.gradient
        (startColorstr=#99A6DADC, endColorstr=#99A6DADC);
    zoom: 1;
}
```

The Gradient filter simply declares a starting and ending color, both the same. The color values look strange, though, don't they? They're not your standard six-digit hexadecimal codes. The first two digits are the alpha transparency value. You can use any hexadecimal value between 00 and FF, with 00 being transparent and FF being opaque. The last six digits are the standard hexadecimal code for a color. So, the color #99A6DADC sets the alpha transparency to 99, the hexadecimal equivalent of the .6 level of transparency we're using in HSLA, and the color to A6DADC, the same blue we've been using all along.

In addition to applying the filter, this IE 7 and earlier rule removes the background color, which would override the filter. Also, IE 6 and earlier need to have hasLayout triggered on the blockquotes to make the filter work, which zoom: 1; accomplishes.

CONVERTING HSLA AND RGBA TO IE'S GRADIENT FILTER

To use the exact same level of transparency in the IE filter as the HSLA notation, you need to multiply the level of HSLA transparency value, .6 in this case, with 255, and then convert this into hex. Robert Nyman explains how to do this at http://robertnyman.com/2010/01/11/css-background-transparency-without-affecting-child-elements-through-rgba-and-filters.

A much easier way to do this is to use Michael Bester's "RGBa & HSLa CSS Generator for Internet Explorer" at http://kimili.com/journal/rgba-hsla-css-generator-for-internet-explorer. Put in an RGBA or HSLA value and it will automatically convert it to the Gradient filter equivalent.

NOTE: The line breaks in the filter value are there just to make it easier to read. You can add or remove line breaks within it without affecting how the code functions.

NOTE: Understanding hasLayout is important when working with IE. If you need a refresher on this strange "property," see Ingo Chao's article "On having layout" at www.satzansatz.de/cssd/onhavinglayout.html.

IE 8 doesn't need the background color removed, as it correctly ignores the HSLA background color on the main blockquote rule. It also doesn't need hasLayout triggered. But, it does have a slightly different syntax for filter properties. Add the following rule for IE 8:

```
.ie8 blockquote {
    -ms-filter: "progid:DXImageTransform.Microsoft.gradient
    (startColorstr=#99A6DADC, endColorstr=#99A6DADC)";
}
```

The differences in the filter syntax are that it's called -ms-filter instead of filter, and the value of the -ms-filter property is put in quotation marks. This syntax is more in line with the CSS specifications and how other browsers designate their proprietary properties.

Image-free Gradients

We can enhance the speech bubbles' backgrounds even further by giving each a subtle gradient to make them appear more rounded and three-dimensional. CSS3 allows you to create gradients without images, speeding up your development time and decreasing page-loading times, just as our image-free rounded corners can do. CSS-generated gradients also have the advantage of being able to scale with their containers in ways that image gradients can't, making them more versatile.

Unfortunately, CSS3 gradients are still very much in development at the time of this writing; their syntax is laid out only in a W3C editor's draft, not a more finalized working draft or candidate recommendation. Thus, be aware that the syntax for gradients is more likely to change than most of the CSS I'll describe in this book. Still, I think it's fine to add CSS that is a little experimental if you're using it in a very limited manner; non-supporting browsers won't be harmed by its lack, and supporting browsers won't be harmed if the syntax later changes. The (unlikely) worst-case scenario is that the syntax will totally change, making the gradients fail to appear in all browsers. I think I can live with this.

You can create both linear (straight) gradients and radial (circular or elliptical) gradients; we're just going to focus on linear gradients here. There is no gradient property; you specify a gradient using the linear-gradient or radial-gradient function as the *value* for any property that allows an image value, such as background-image and list-style image (though Firefox currently supports it only on background-image). When you specify a linear gradient, you tell the browser its starting point, angle, and starting and ending colors. You can also add extra colors in between the starting and ending colors and specify the exact position of each color along the line of the gradient.

This sounds simple enough, but unfortunately, Firefox and Webkit (the only browsers that currently support gradients) differ on the syntax required to feed the browser this information; Firefox matches the official W3C syntax, and Webkit uses a very different (and more complicated) syntax that they developed first. Not only that, but even within each single syntax there are many variations on how you can specify the same gradient. It can get pretty confusing. To start off simply, let's first apply a simple linear gradient to the speech bubbles to see a real example, before diving into the details of the full syntax.

THE FIREFOX AND W3C SYNTAX

Firefox's syntax matches the official syntax being developed by the W3C and is generally easier to understand and use, so we'll start with the gradient for Firefox.

First, add a linear gradient for Firefox in the background-image property of the blockquote rule, using the -moz-linear-gradient function:

```
blockquote {
    position: relative;
    min-height: 40px;
    margin: 0 0 0 112px;
    padding: 10px 15px 5px 15px;
    -moz-border-radius: 20px;
    -webkit-border-radius: 20px;
    border-radius: 20px;
    border-top: 1px solid #fff;
    background-color: hsla(182,44%,76%,.5);
    background-image: -moz-linear-gradient(
            hsla(0,0%,100%,.6),
            hsla(0,0%,100%,0) 30px
            );
    word-wrap: break-word;
}
```

NOTE: The line breaks in this gradient function are there just to make it easier to read. Just like with any piece of CSS, you can add or remove line breaks within it without affecting code functionality.

This specifies a starting color (hsla(0,0%,100%,.6)), ending color (hsla(0,0%,100%,0)), and the position of the ending color (30px). Because we haven't specified any starting point for the gradient or its angle, Firefox will simply use the default values, which makes the gradient start at the top of the box and run straight down. (If we did want to specify a starting point and/or angle, we'd do it at the start of the function. See "The lowdown on linear gradients" for the exact syntax.)

The starting color is white at 60 percent opacity, and the ending color is white at zero percent opacity (completely transparent). Laying semitransparent white over the background color creates a tint of whatever that background color is. In this case, it makes the gradient appear to be very light blue at the top and then fade away to nothing (**Figure 2.18**). We could have used an actual shade of light blue, but using semitransparent white in HSLA or RGBA is much more flexible. If we were to later change the color of the speech bubbles' backgrounds to orange, for instance, we'd have to also change the light blue gradient to light orange. But since it's white, it will always be a tint of whatever the background color is. Sticking with semitransparent white and black is the smartest way to create tints and shades of colors.

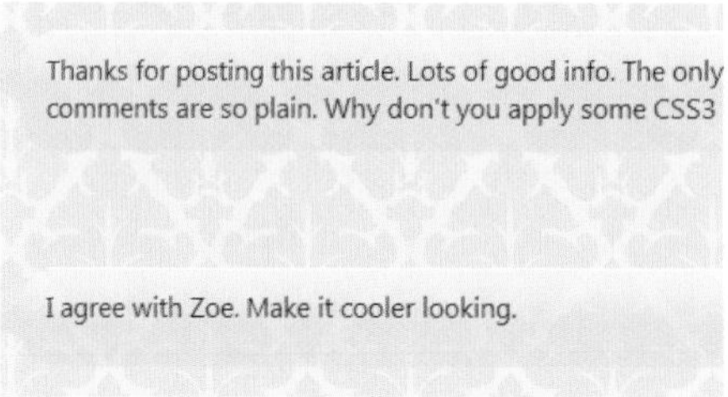

FIGURE 2.18 A gradient over the background makes the speech bubbles look more three-dimensional.

Right after the ending color value, there's a space and then a value of `30px`. This tells Firefox that you want it to place the ending color 30 pixels down the gradient. The gradient will run from the top of the box down 30 pixels, and then the ending color of the gradient will fill the rest of the vertical space. Since the ending color is completely transparent, it creates the appearance that the gradient covers only the top 30 pixels of the speech bubble.

That's all you need to create the gradient in Firefox. Normally, I would tell you to copy and paste the `background-image` declaration and remove the `-moz-` bit from the second declaration to add the non-browser-specific version at the end. But in this case, the official syntax is still so early in its development that I think it's best to leave it off and wait for it to become more finalized. We'll stick with just the Firefox syntax, and add the Webkit syntax now.

THE WEBKIT SYNTAX

For Webkit-based browsers, add another background-image declaration to the blockquote rule, this time containing the -webkit-gradient function:

```
blockquote {
    position: relative;
    min-height: 40px;
    margin: 0 0 0 112px;
    padding: 10px 15px 5px 15px;
    -moz-border-radius: 20px;
    -webkit-border-radius: 20px;
    border-radius: 20px;
    border-top: 1px solid #fff;
    background-color: hsla(169,41%,76%,.5);
    background-image: -moz-linear-gradient(hsla(0,0%,
    ¬100%,.6), hsla(0,0%,100%,0) 30px);
    background-image: -webkit-gradient(linear,
                      0 0, 0 30,
                      from(hsla(0,0%,100%,.6)),
                      to(hsla(0,0%,100%,0))
                      );
    word-wrap: break-word;
}
```

As you can see, the Webkit syntax is very different—and more complicated.

RADIAL GRADIENTS

We're not covering radial gradients here, but you can learn more about them in these articles:

- ◆ "CSS gradient syntax: comparison of Mozilla and WebKit (Part 2)," by Peter Gasston (www.broken-links.com/2009/11/30/css-gradient-syntax-comparison-of-mozilla-and-webkit-part-2)

- ◆ "css gradients in Firefox 3.6," by Alix Franquet (http://hacks.mozilla.org/2009/11/css-gradients-firefox-36)

THE LOWDOWN ON LINEAR GRADIENTS

The gradient functions are part of a draft of the Image Values module; this draft is found at http://dev.w3.org/csswg/css3-images/#gradients-, but ultimately the finalized module can be found at www.w3.org/TR/css3-images.

You specify a gradient using the `linear-gradient` or `radial-gradient` function as the value for any property that allows an image value. **Figure 2.19** shows a diagram of a `linear-gradient` function with every possible piece of the gradient syntax included.

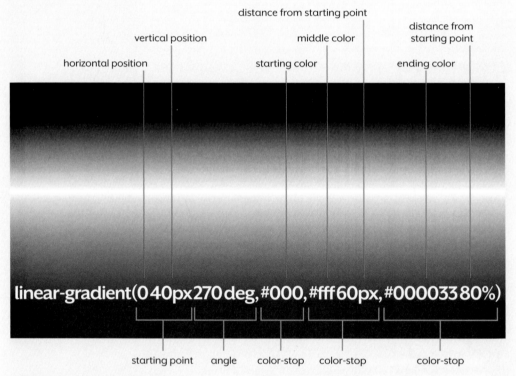

FIGURE 2.19 **All the possible pieces of a linear gradient function, shown over the gradient it would produce.**

You don't need to include all of the pieces shown in Figure 2.19. The important points to remember are:

◆ All you need for a gradient to work are the two colors (in any syntax). The rest of the pieces shown in Figure 2.19 are optional and just uses the default values if you leave them out.

◆ If you don't specify any positions for the colors or the gradient's angle, the gradient will run from top to bottom.

◆ You can specify the starting point for the gradient at the beginning of the function, using either keywords (like `center`) or numbers (like `20px` or `60%` or `1em`), which can be negative. If you use numbers, the first value is how far *across* the box the gradient starts (the x-axis or horizontal starting point position) and the second value is how far *down* the box the gradient starts (the y-axis or vertical starting point position).

◆ After the starting point (if present), you can specify the angle at which the gradient will run. The angle is measured between a horizontal line and the gradient line, going counterclockwise. For instance, `0deg` produces a left-to-right gradient, `90deg` goes bottom to top, `180deg` goes right to left, and `270deg` goes top to bottom. You can also use negative values.

◆ Each color-stop includes a color (in any syntax) and, optionally, a point where that color should be placed along the gradient's line. The value is measured from the starting point of the gradient, which may not necessarily be the edge of the box (as is the case in Figure 2.19, where the gradient starts 40 pixels down from the top edge of the box).

Since gradients placed in the `background-image` property are essentially browser-generated images, you can use other CSS background properties to further control them, just like you would any other background image. For instance, you can use the new CSS3 `background-size` property to control the gradient's size and `background-repeat` to control its tiling.

Other than adding a highlight, you may want to use CSS3 gradients for:

◆ Making something's surface appear to be rounded, like a button; see www.webdesigner-wall.com/tutorials/css3-gradient-buttons and http://blog.brandoncash.net/post/525423850/sexy-css-buttons

◆ Make something appear to be shiny, like metal, glass, or a CD

◆ Creating the appearance of a reflection; see www.broken-links.com/2010/03/22/create-a-studio-style-backdrop-with-css3

◆ Creating a vignette effect, where the edges of an image or box are gradually darkened, like in an old photograph; see http://sickdesigner.com/index.php/2010/html-css/css3-vignette-a-wicked-cool-technique

◆ Fading in or out a background image by layering it with a gradient; see http://atomicrobotdesign.com/blog/htmlcss/make-the-thinkgeek-background-effect-using-css3

◆ Equal-height columns; see http://aext.net/2010/08/css3-sidebar-full-height-background-color

TABLE 2.4 **Gradients browser support**

IE	FIREFOX	OPERA	SAFARI	CHROME
No	Yes, 3.6+, with -moz-	No	Yes, with -webkit-	Yes, with -webkit-

First, you specify the type of gradient—linear or radial—within the `-webkit-gradient` function itself, instead of having separate `linear-gradient` and `radial-gradient` functions.

Next, you specify the horizontal and vertical positions of the starting point (here, `0 0`), followed by the horizontal and vertical positions of the ending point (here, `0 30`). You can do this using keywords (such as `top` and `left`), percentages, or pixels, but strangely, Webkit requires you to leave off the "px" if you want to use pixels. So, in this case, we're telling Webkit that we want the gradient to start at a point zero pixels across and zero pixels down the box (the top left corner) and end at zero pixels across and 30 pixels down the box. This makes the gradient run from the top to 30 pixels down the box, and then fill the rest of the box with the ending color, just like in Firefox.

After the starting and ending points, we have the starting color and the ending color. Just like with Firefox, you can use whatever color syntax you wish, but note that you must include `from` and `to` before each color.

The result of this `-webkit-gradient` CSS should look the same as Figure 2.18.

The CSS syntax differences between Firefox and Webkit can be hard to remember. Luckily, you don't have to memorize them if you don't want to. There are some great gradient-generator tools online that allow you to use a visual editor to create the gradient, and then they write the corresponding CSS you need to use. Just copy and paste! Find these gradient generators at http://gradients.glrzad.com, http://westciv.com/tools/gradients, http://westciv.com/tools/radialgradients, and www.display-inline.fr/projects/css-gradient.

WORKAROUNDS FOR NON-SUPPORTING BROWSERS

The CSS we've used so far works only in Safari, Chrome, and Firefox 3.6 and later, making gradients one of the less-supported features of CSS3. However, it's one of the easiest features to provide work-arounds for non-supporting browsers. (If you even choose to provide a workaround, that is—letting non-supporting browsers see the solid background color is an acceptable fallback in most cases.)

Picture it. The most obvious workaround for non-supporting brows-ers is to just go back to the good old-fashioned way of creating gradients: create an actual image gradient as an alpha-transparent PNG, set it as the background image on the blockquote, and tile it horizontally. Just make sure to declare this image *before* the two background-image declarations that contain the -moz-linear-gradient and -webkit-gradient functions. This allows browsers that *do* support gradients to override the first background-image property that uses an image with the later background-image property that creates a CSS3 gradient.

Of course, creating and using an image negates the efficiency benefits of using CSS3 to generate gradients for you. Firefox 3.6 won't load the image that it doesn't need, but Safari and Chrome *will*, even though they use the CSS3 gradient and never show the image. So, you keep the performance advantage of CSS3 gradients in Firefox 3.6, but lose it in Safari. Granted, you still get the other advantages of CSS3 gradients over image gradients, but the performance benefit is one of the most important.

MORE DETAILS ON THE WEBKIT LINEAR GRADIENT SYNTAX

In a Webkit linear gradient, if you want to include any extra colors between the starting and ending colors, you'd use syntax like color-stop(50%, #333). In this example, 50% specifies how far along the gradient you want the color to appear; it can also be written as a number between 0 and 1. #333 is the color value, written in any syntax you like. The color-stop can be written between the starting and ending colors or after them, with each color-stop separated by commas.

For even more details on the Webkit syntax, see these articles:

◆ "Safari CSS Visual Effects Guide: Gradients" (http://developer. apple.com/safari/library/documentation/InternetWeb/Conceptual/ SafariVisualEffectsProgGuide/Gradients/Gradients.html)

◆ "CSS gradient syntax: comparison of Mozilla and WebKit," by Peter Gasston (www.broken-links.com/2009/11/26/ css-gradient-syntax-comparison-of-mozilla-and-webkit)

◆ "CSS gradient syntax: comparison of Mozilla and WebKit (Part 2)," by Peter Gasston (www.broken-links.com/2009/11/30/ css-gradient-syntax-comparison-of-mozilla-and-webkit-part-2)

TIP: Another way to fake a gradient is to use an inset box-shadow, which has more browser support than CSS3 gradients (but not as much as plain old background images, of course). I'll go over the box-shadow property further down in this chapter.

Because of this performance hit in Webkit-based browsers, I recommend you either forgo the background image fallback, letting non-supporting browsers just miss out on the gradient, or hide the background image fallback from gradient-supporting browsers by using Modernizr (explained in Chapter 1). Of course, if you're going to go to all the trouble of creating and applying a gradient image, you may decide it's best to just use the image for all browsers and not use CSS3 gradients at all. There's no right answer here, but my recommendation is to either use CSS3 gradients exclusively, or don't use them at all and stick with images.

Use a script. For IE 6 through 8, you can use PIE (http://css3pie.com/documentation/supported-css3-features). For other browsers, check out Weston Ruter's css-gradients-via-canvas script (http://weston.ruter.net/projects/css-gradients-via-canvas). It works in browsers that support the HTML5 canvas element, so it makes gradients possible in Firefox 2 and 3 as well as Opera 9.64 and later. It doesn't work in IE, but you could use it in combination with IE's Gradient filter. Which leads us nicely to the next workaround...

Change color values for a different effect. We're already using IE's Gradient filter to create single-color semitransparent backgrounds on the blockquotes. We can modify the starting color values to be a lighter shade of blue to simulate the CSS3 gradient that we're using.

In both IE rules, change the starting color in the Gradient filter from #99A6DADC to #99E3F4EE:

```
.ie6 blockquote, .ie7 blockquote {
    background: none;
    filter: progid:DXImageTransform.Microsoft.gradient
        (startColorstr=#99E3F4EE, endColorstr=#99A6DADC);
    zoom: 1;
}
.ie8 blockquote {
    -ms-filter: "progid:DXImageTransform.Microsoft.gradient
        (startColorstr=#99E3F4EE, endColorstr=#99A6DADC)";
}
```

By default, IE gradients run from top to bottom, so the resulting gradients in IE look reasonably similar to the ones in Firefox and Webkit-based browsers (**Figure 2.20**). We can't control the placement of the color stops in IE like we can with CSS3 gradients, but the filter works well for simple, two-color, linear gradients. It works only in IE 8 and earlier, though; IE 9 doesn't support Microsoft filters. Thus, no gradient shows in IE 9, but at least IE 9 shows the semitransparent background color.

TIP: Find out more about IE's Gradient filter at http://msdn.microsoft.com/en-us/library/ms532997(VS.85).aspx.

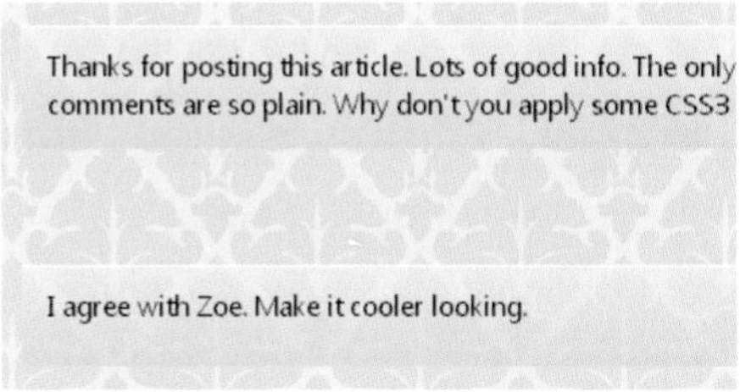

Thanks for posting this article. Lots of good info. The only comments are so plain. Why don't you apply some CSS3

I agree with Zoe. Make it cooler looking.

FIGURE 2.20 IE's Gradient filter can simulate simple CSS3 gradients (shown here in IE 8).

Note that if you have a fallback background image declared for other browsers, IE will let it override the Gradient filter. The IE 7 and earlier rule already removes any background that might be present, but the IE 8 rule doesn't. Remember to add background: none; to the IE 8 rule if you add a background image to the main blockquote rule (because you're adding a gradient image fallback, for instance).

NOTE: The page with all the changes to this point is named speech-bubble_2.html in the exercise files that you downloaded for this chapter.

Image-free Drop Shadows

In our continuing quest for three-dimensionality, we can add a drop shadow behind each speech bubble. Once again, we'll do it without images.

Drop shadows on boxes are created in CSS3 using the box-shadow property. In the property, you set the shadow's horizontal and vertical offsets from the box, its color, and you can optionally set blur radius as well as spread radius.

Add the following three lines of CSS to the blockquote rule:

```
-moz-box-shadow: 1px 1px 2px hsla(0,0%,0%,.3);
-webkit-box-shadow: 1px 1px 2px hsla(0,0%,0%,.3);
box-shadow: 1px 1px 2px hsla(0,0%,0%,.3);
```

Just as with border-radius, all three lines accomplish the same thing, but are read by different browsers; the non-prefixed box-shadow property will work only in IE 9 and Opera at the time of this writing.

The first value in each property, 1px, is the horizontal offset from the box, and it tells the browser to move the shadow one pixel to the right of the box's edge. The second value, 1px, is the vertical offset, moving the shadow one pixel down. You can use negative values to move the shadow to the left and up instead.

The third value, 2px, is the blur radius, which specifies over how many pixels the shadow should stretch. A larger value makes the shadow blurrier and softer; a value of zero would make it completely sharp-edged.

NOTE: The number values in the box-shadow property have to be specified in the exact order shown, but you don't have to put the color value at the end. You can put the color value first if you want.

The fourth value is the color—in this case, black at 30 percent opacity. You can use any syntax for declaring the color in box-shadow, but HSLA or RGBA—the only syntaxes that can make a color semitransparent—are your best bets. Semitransparency is very handy for drop shadows, since you want to be able to see the background of whatever is behind the shadow peeking through a bit. If you made the shadow solid light gray, for instance, and then changed the page's background to dark navy blue, you'd end up with a light gray shadow on top of a navy blue background. What you really want is an even darker navy blue shadow, as that's how a shadow on something navy blue would look in real life. Using HSLA or RGBA for your drop shadows, and keeping the colors either black (for a shadow) or white (for a glow effect) allows you to switch the background color or image under the drop shadow and not have to make a corresponding change to the color of the shadow itself. It will appear to adjust its color to whatever is beneath it.

With box-shadow added to the blockquote rule, save the page, and check it out in an up-to-date browser to see the subtle greenish-gray shadow to the right and bottom of each speech bubble (**Figure 2.21**). You'll notice that the shadow pays attention to the border-radius and is also rounded to match the corners.

FIGURE 2.21
The box-shadow **property adds a shadow beneath each speech bubble.**

Our drop shadow does add that extra little hint of three-dimension-ality, but we can increase that 3D appearance by making the speech bubbles appear to move forward a bit when each is hovered over. The farther away the speech bubble is from the background, the larger its shadow should appear. You increase the offset of the shadow on hover by adding this rule:

```
blockquote:hover {
    top: -2px;
    left: -2px;
    -moz-box-shadow: 3px 3px 2px hsla(0,0%,0%,.3);
    -webkit-box-shadow: 3px 3px 2px hsla(0,0%,0%,.3);
    box-shadow: 3px 3px 2px hsla(0,0%,0%,.3);
}
```

The negative top and left values are what actually shift the speech bubble and create the appearance of movement, but increasing the shadow as well—from 1 pixel offset to 3 pixels offset—makes the movement look more realistic (**Figure 2.22**). Increasing the shadow also makes it appear more like the speech bubble is moving away from the background and closer to the user, instead of just farther up the page.

TIP: For help creating more complicated shadows, use the box-shadow generator at http://westciv.com/tools/boxshadows. Unfortunately, however, it doesn't include spread radius or inset.

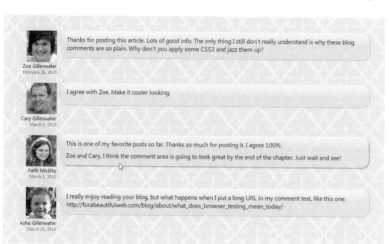

FIGURE 2.22 The larger shadow on hovered speech bubbles makes them appear to jump out at you a bit.

THE LOWDOWN ON THE box-shadow PROPERTY

The box-shadow property is part of a draft of the Backgrounds and Borders module; this draft is found at http://dev.w3.org/csswg/css3-background/#the-box-shadow, but ultimately the finalized module can be found at www.w3.org/TR/css3-background.

In the property, you set the shadow's horizontal and vertical offsets from the box, and you set the shadow's color. You'll usually also want to set a blur radius (it's zero otherwise) and can optionally set a spread radius to expand or contract the overall width of the shadow, using positive or negative values, respectively. You can make a shadow appear inside a box instead of outside or behind it using the inset keyword, added at the start or end of the box-shadow value. (Spread radius and inset are not supported in Safari 4 and earlier, Safari on iOS 3 and earlier, or IE 9.)

You can apply multiple shadows to the same box by writing each in the same box-shadow property, separated by commas. They'll be stacked on top of each other, with the first shadow declared on top.

Other than creating basic shadows behind boxes, you might want to use box-shadow for:

◆ Glows (by not offsetting the shadow at all and also optionally using a positive spread radius value)

◆ 3D-looking buttons

◆ Simulating multiple borders around a box (using multiple box-shadows, each set to 0 blur radius to give them hard edges); see http://weston.ruter.net/2009/06/15/multiple-borders-via-css-box-shadow

◆ Simulating gradients (using inset box-shadow); see http://girliemac.com/blog/2010/02/04/css3-box-shadow-with-inset-values-the-aqua-button-rerevisited, http://graphicpush.com/experiments-with-css3-border-radius-and-box-shadow, and http://nimbupani.com/vignettes-with-css3-box-shadows.html

TABLE 2.5 box-shadow **browser support**

IE	FIREFOX	OPERA	SAFARI	CHROME
Partial, 9+	Yes with -moz-, 3.5+	Yes, 10.5+	Yes with -webkit-	Yes with -webkit-

WORKAROUNDS FOR IE

The box-shadow property is not supported by IE 8 and earlier, but as with gradients, you can use IE's filters to fake it. The DropShadow and Shadow filters are specifically designed to create drop shadows, and Glow works if you want an even glow around all sides of the box. Unfortunately, these filters don't offer as many customization options for the drop shadow as you have with CSS3 box-shadow, as Chris Casciano demonstrates and explains in his article "CSS3 Box Shadow in Internet Explorer [Blur-Shadow]" at http://placenamehere.com/article/384/CSS3BoxShadowinInternetExplorerBlurShadow. I don't think any of these filters will create the particular effect we want in this case.

Also in this article, Chris shows a clever technique using IE's Blur filter instead of DropShadow, Shadow, or Glow to create a more realistic-looking drop shadow, but the technique requires making a copy of the box in the HTML, and then blurring this copy. Another article at http://dev.opera.com/articles/view/cross-browser-box-shadows uses the same technique, and also shows how to use Blur to create the appearance of an inset shadow. The extra HTML elements required in these tutorials are an acceptable compromise when you really must have a drop shadow in IE, but in the case of our speech bubbles, I don't think the extra work and extra file size that would result from all those extra divs is worth the small visual gain. So we're not going to walk through the steps to implement the Blur filter solution here; we'll be satisfied with no drop shadows in IE.

> **NOTE:** The PIE and IE-CSS3 scripts mentioned earlier in the chapter can also create drop shadows in IE. But with the IE-CSS3 script, the drop shadows have to be black.

Image-free Text Shadows

Why should the boxes get to have all the fun—shouldn't text be able to have drop shadows too? Happily for us, CSS3 has a property named text-shadow that does just that.

The text-shadow property can give you a nice accessibility and usability benefit. With the graphic effects we've already looked at in this chapter, the CSS3 equivalent just replaces a decorative image, such as replacing a GIF of a curved corner with a CSS-generated curved corner—kind of trading an image for a faux-image. The text-shadow property, on the other hand, allows you to replace an image of text with real text. For instance, you may have a headline that you want to have a shadow behind it. Before text-shadow, you might create an image of that headline and its shadow and display that image in your page. The user has no control over text in an image to make it more readable for him or herself by scaling it, changing its color, changing the font, and any number of other things you can do to real text. Using `text-shadow` on real text gives control back to the user.

Using real text with `text-shadow` applied can also improve readability by creating more contrast between the text and its background. Have you ever watched a movie with closed captioning? The captions probably had a small shadow or outline around them to make the text stand out more on a variety of background colors. Slight drop shadows behind text in web pages can give the same readability boost.

Other advantages of real text: it's searchable, it can be selected to copy and paste, and it's more quickly and easily editable by you or your client than an image or Flash movie would be.

Of course, like many web techniques, `text-shadow` can backfire and decrease usability if not used well. I'm certainly not saying you should go out and add drop shadows to all your text; there are many cases where it would impede readability. You also always need to make sure that the text is still readable if the shadow isn't there. But `text-shadow` is another tool in your arsenal that you can choose to use when appropriate.

So, `text-shadow` sounds great—how do you apply it?

MAKING TEXT STAND OUT USING SHADOWS

Let's add a `text-shadow` on hover to highlight the chosen comment just a bit. Add the following line to the `blockquote:hover` rule:

```
text-shadow: 1px 1px 1px hsla(0,0%,100%,.7);
```

TIP: Just like with box-shadow, text-shadow usually looks best when the color is semitransparent using HSLA or RGBA.

The syntax is almost exactly the same as the syntax for `box-shadow`. (The only difference is that you can't set spread radius or `inset` on `text-shadow`.) We have a horizontal offset, vertical offset, optional blur radius, and color. In this case, there's no need to add any browser-specific prefixes; Firefox, Safari, Chrome, and Opera all support the standard `text-shadow` property. **Figure 2.23** shows the subtle shadow that appears behind the text of a `blockquote` that's being hovered over.

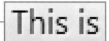

FIGURE 2.23 A white shadow appears to the right and bottom of the text in the speech bubble that the user has her mouse over.

Another nice place to add a shadow behind text is the commenter's name and date of comment. These two pieces of text are pretty small and are sitting on top of a patterned background. A very slight, sharp-edged text shadow would give it a subtle outline to make it stand out more and be a little easier to read.

Add the following line to the existing `.comment-meta` rule:

```
text-shadow: 1px 1px 0 hsla(0,0%,100%,.7);
```

The effect this produces is very subtle, but it needs to be. A thick outline around such small text would look strange and probably make it *harder* to read. But the slight text shadow we're using adds just a little bit of contrast to make the text just a little bit more readable (**Figure 2.24**).

NOTE: The page with all the changes to this point is named speech-bubble_3.html in the exercise files that you downloaded for this chapter.

TIP: For help creating more complicated shadows, use the `text-shadow` generator at http://westciv.com/tools/shadows.

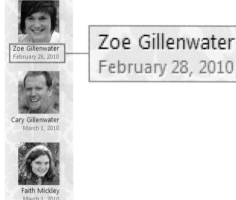

FIGURE 2.24 The sharp-edged shadow on the commenter's name and date makes the text stand out a bit more compared to the non-shadowed text.

THE LOWDOWN ON THE `text-shadow` PROPERTY

The `text-shadow` property is part of the Text module found at www.w3.org/TR/css3-text. It was part of CSS 2, removed from 2.1, and is back in 3.

In the property, you set the shadow's color and its horizontal and vertical offsets from the text. You can also set a blur radius; the default (if you leave it out) is zero.

You can apply multiple shadows to the same text by writing each in the same `text-shadow` property, separated by commas. They'll be stacked on top of each other, with the first declared shadow on the top.

Other than creating basic shadows behind text, you might want to use `text-shadow` for:

- Glows; see http://desandro.com/articles/the-new-lens-flare

- Letterpress, engraved, cut-out or embossed text (using a light shadow on one side of the text and a dark shadow on the other side); see http://sixrevisions.com/css/how-to-create-inset-typography-with-css3

- Fiery text (using multiple yellow, orange, and red shadows); see www.css3.info/preview/text-shadow

- Blurred text (using a shadow the same color as the text, or simply transparent color for the text); see http://simurai.com/post/684792689/text-blur

- Creating the appearance that text is stacked into a 3D column (using multiple shadows); see http://css-tricks.com/3d-text-tower

- Creating the appearance that links are pushed inwards like a button when clicked, by decreasing text-shadow; see www.impressivewebs.com/text-shadow-links

Also check out http://maettig.com/code/css/text-shadow.html for many examples of `text-shadow` effects; some are more practical than others, but all are good for jogging your creativity.

TABLE 2.6 `text-shadow` **browser support**

IE	FIREFOX	OPERA	SAFARI	CHROME
No	Yes	Yes	Yes	Yes

WORKAROUNDS FOR IE

The DropShadow, Shadow, or Glow filters for IE that I mentioned earlier can actually create shadows behind text too, not just boxes. To get a text shadow instead of a box shadow, you write the filter in the exact same way, but make sure there is no background color or background image on the element. If it has a background, IE will apply the shadow to the box; if it doesn't have a background, it will apply the shadow to the content.

Unfortunately, when any of these filters are applied to text, they make that text very jagged. It's similar to the unevenness of the text that showed up when we applied the gradient filter in IE (see Figures 2.17 and 2.20), but more extreme. In the case of our speech bubbles, I think it really impairs the readability, and the whole point of adding `text-shadow` here was to enhance readability. So, we won't be adding IE filters to any text here. If you do want to add filters yourself, see http://msdn.microsoft.com/en-us/library/ms673539(VS.85).aspx for the syntax. There are also a couple jQuery plugins that uses IE filters, available at http://kilianvalkhof.com/2008/javascript/text-shadow-in-ie-with-jquery and www.hintzmann.dk/testcenter/js/jquery/textshadow.

NOTE: If you're using the Mootools JavaScript framework, you may want to check out the MooTools text drop-shadow script, which works in IE and non-IE browsers, at http://pr0digy.com/mootools/text-dropshadows.

Transforming the Avatars

We've completed all the styling for the speech bubbles themselves. What about the avatars, the little images next to each speech bubble? We could reuse some of the CSS3 effects such as `box-shadow` on them, but let's do something new and use CSS3 transforms.

NOTE: Firefox currently doesn't allow `-moz-border-radius` on `img` elements, so—sadly—you can't round the avatars' corners in that browser.

What are Transforms?

Transforms are a collection of effects, each called a *transform function*, that manipulate the box in ways like rotating, scaling, and skewing. These effects would previously have had to be accomplished with images, Flash, or JavaScript. Transforming objects with pure CSS avoids the need for these extra files, once again increasing the efficiency of both your development and the pages themselves.

THE LOWDOWN ON THE transform PROPERTY

The transform property is part of both the 3D Transforms module found at www.w3.org/TR/css3-3d-transforms, and the 2D Transforms module, at www.w3.org/TR/css3-2d-transforms. All of the 2D transform functions are also included in the 3D spec, so you may just want to refer to the 3D spec.

There are too many transform functions to list here, but here's sample syntax for the most important and supported ones:

◆ translate moves the object to a new location, specified as an X and Y coordinate. Positive values move it right and down, respectively, and negative values move it left and up. Example: translate(20px, -10px)

◆ scale scales the dimensions of the object X number of times. Negative values flip the object. To scale something smaller, use a number between 0 and 1. If you use two values, separated by commas, the first is the horizontal scaling factor and the second is the vertical scaling factor. Example: scale(2.5) or scale (1, .5)

◆ rotate turns an object a specified number of degrees (deg). Positive values turn it clockwise; negative values turn it counter-clockwise. Example: rotate(45deg)

◆ skew skews or warps an object, again in degrees. The first value controls the horizontal slope and the second the vertical; if you use only one value, the skew on the Y axis is set to zero. Example: skew(10deg, 20deg)

You can include multiple transform functions in one transform property, separated with spaces. The transforms are applied in the order listed.

You can use the transform-origin property to specify the point of origin from which the transform takes place, using keywords, numbers, or percentages. The default is the center.

When you transform an object, the other objects around it don't move to make way for the transformation (similar to relative positioning). The object is placed first in the flow, and then transformed.

Other than rotating avatars, you might want to use transforms for:

◆ Increased link, button, or table row size on hover

◆ Display of an image gallery where thumbnails scale up when hovered

◆ Angled photos (to create the appearance of that they've been tacked-up or are scattered across a table, for instance)

◆ Angled sticky-note-style boxes

◆ Randomly angled tags in a tag cloud; see http://code.almeros.com/how-to-create-a-css3-enabled-tag-cloud

◆ Skewed boxes or images (to imply perspective)

◆ Small diagonal banner in the top corner of a page

◆ Sideways text (popular in date stamps on blog posts, for instance); see http://snook.ca/archives/html_and_css/css-text-rotation

◆ Printable folding card; see http://natbat.net/2009/May/21/pocketbooks

◆ Slideshow where images slide in and out of viewing window (using `translate`); see http://css3.bradshawenterprises.com/#slide2

◆ Links or tabs that slide up into full view when hovered (using `translate`); see http://creativefan.com/css3-tutorial-create-card-pockets-how-to

◆ 3D cube (using 2D `skew`); see http://depotwebdesigner.com/tutorials/how-to-create-3d-cube-with-css3.html

TABLE 2.7 2D transforms browser support

IE	FIREFOX	OPERA	SAFARI	CHROME
No	Yes with -moz-, 3.5+	Yes with -o-, 10.5+	Yes with -webkit-	Yes with -webkit-

TABLE 2.8 3D transforms browser support

IE	FIREFOX	OPERA	SAFARI	CHROME
No	No	No	Yes with -webkit-, 5+	No

Just like `text-shadow`, transforms can sometimes have a usability and accessibility benefit by allowing you to replace an image of text with real text. For instance, you may have a feature box or ad containing text that you want to be at a slight angle. Before transforms, you might have created an image of that angled box—text and all—and used that image in your page. Image text is less accessible, not searchable, and takes more work to create and edit.

Obviously, you don't want to start skewing and rotating all the text on your page. That certainly wouldn't improve readability! But in small doses, and in cases where you were going to use an image or Flash movie instead, transforms can improve accessibility by allowing you to accomplish the same effect with real text.

Rotating the Avatars

Let's look at the syntax for transforms by rotating the avatars. Add this new rule to the styles:

```
.comment-meta img {
    -moz-transform: rotate(-5deg);
    -o-transform: rotate(-5deg);
    -webkit-transform: rotate(-5deg);
    transform: rotate(-5deg);
}
```

> **NOTE:** You can have the syntax for all the different transforms written for you using the handy transforms CSS generator at http://westciv.com/tools/transforms.

The prefix-free `transform` property is not yet supported by any browser; we've included it for future compatibility.

> **NOTE:** At the time of this writing, Chrome does a really bad job anti-aliasing the edges of the avatars when they're rotated, making them very jagged. There's no workaround. You can either remove the -webkit- declaration, which would also remove the rotation in Safari, or just live with the jaggedness.

The `transform` property (and, for now, all three browser-specific equivalents) tells the browser that you want to apply a transform. You then specify that the particular transform function you want is `rotate`, and that the number of degrees of rotation, using the `deg` unit, is negative five. You can use either positive or negative values. Other transform functions take different types of measurements—a value of `-5deg` doesn't make much sense for `scale`, does it?—but the pattern is always the same:

```
transform: function(measurements);
```

You can also use the `transform-origin` property to specify the point of origin from which the transform takes place, such as the center or top right corner of the object. The default is the dead center, which is fine in our case, so there's no need to add the `transform-origin` property here.

Save the page and refresh your browser. You'll see that the avatars are now at an angle (**Figure 2.25**).

WORKAROUNDS FOR IE

IE's Matrix filter can emulate several of the CSS3 transforms. Unfortunately, you have to do some complicated calculations using matrix mathematics to find the correct values to use in the filter. I'm guessing you're not reading a web design book because you're wild about math, so I'll spare you that (I wouldn't be able to explain it anyway) and point you to an online CSS generator called IE's CSS3 Transforms Translator at www.useragentman.com/IETransformsTranslator, developed by Zoltan Hawryluk and yours truly.

To use the Transforms Translator, type `rotate(-5deg)` into the Step 1 input box and any width and height values you want (we're not going to be using them, but they're required to use the tool). Then click the Translate to IE Matrix button. The Step 2 box will appear below with two code blocks in it, one for CSS3-supporting browsers, and one for IE (**Figure 2.26**).

FIGURE 2.25
The rotate transform function angles the avatar images.

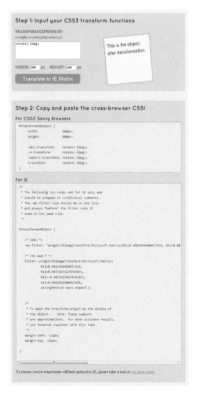

FIGURE 2.26 The Transforms Translator web site generates IE Matrix filter values that are equivalent to the CSS3 2D transforms you feed it.

Copy the code from the IE box and paste it into the styles in the head of the page. Remove any comments from within the CSS:

```
#transformedObject {
    -ms-filter: "progid:DXImageTransform.Microsoft.
    ¬Matrix(M11=0.9961946980917454, M12=0.08715574274765871,
    ¬M21=-0.08715574274765871, M22=0.9961946980917454,
    ¬SizingMethod='auto expand')";
    filter: progid:DXImageTransform.Microsoft.Matrix(
            M11=0.9961946980917454,
            M12=0.08715574274765871,
            M21=-0.08715574274765871,
            M22=0.9961946980917454,
            SizingMethod='auto expand');
    margin-left: -11px;
    margin-top: -11px;
}
```

This rule includes the `filter` property for IE 6 and 7, and the `-ms-filter` property for IE 8. Note that although the `-ms-filter` property shown above has line breaks in it, in order to fit within the page of this book, these are not there in the value generated by the Transforms Translator. Make sure you keep the `-ms-filter` property all on one line—it won't work otherwise. The `filter` property works with or without line breaks in it. The `margin` values are there because IE doesn't use the same origin point for the transform as other browsers, which would make the avatars slightly overlap the commenters' names. Using margins or relative positioning nudges the elements into place to match up with the other browsers.

Now we need to change the selector to match the name of the element we want to transform, in this case `.comment-meta img`. We also need to divide the single rule into two rules: one for IE 6 and 7, and one for IE 8. Make sure you include the margin values in both rules.

```
.ie6 .comment-meta img, .ie7 .comment-meta img {
    filter: progid:DXImageTransform.Microsoft.Matrix(
            M11=0.9961946980917454,
            M12=0.08715574274765871,
            M21=-0.08715574274765871,
            M22=0.9961946980917454,
            SizingMethod='auto expand');
    margin-left: -11px;
    margin-top: -11px;
}
.ie8 .comment-meta img {
```

```
    -ms-filter: "progid:DXImageTransform.Microsoft.Matrix(
    M11=0.9961946980917454, M12=0.08715574274765871,
    ¬M21=-0.08715574274765871, M22=0.9961946980917454,
    ¬SizingMethod='auto expand')";
    margin-left: -11px;
    margin-top: -11px;
}
```

If you save the page and preview it in IE now, you'll discover that
it works perfectly in IE 7, but in IE 6 the tops of the images are cut
off, and in IE 8 the images overlap the commenters' names slightly
(**Figure 2.27**).

The IE 6 problem is due to the negative margins on the images—IE 6
doesn't display the part of an element that is outside its box if negative margins have moved it outside. To fix it, just add `position: rel-
ative` to the IE 6 and 7 rule:

```
.ie6 .comment-meta img, .ie7 .comment-meta img {
    filter: progid:DXImageTransform.Microsoft.Matrix(
            M11=0.9961946980917454,
            M12=0.08715574274765871,
            M21=-0.08715574274765871,
            M22=0.9961946980917454,
            SizingMethod='auto expand');
    margin-left: -11px;
    margin-top: -11px;
    position: relative;
}
```

The IE 8 overlapping problem is due to the fact that the negative margins don't interact well with the other styles we already have in place.
Let's use relative positioning to reposition the images instead of negative margins:

```
.ie6 .comment-meta img, .ie7 .comment-meta img {
    filter: progid:DXImageTransform.Microsoft.Matrix(
            M11=0.9961946980917454,
            M12=0.08715574274765871,
            M21=-0.08715574274765871,
            M22=0.9961946980917454,
            SizingMethod='auto expand');
    position: relative;
    top: -5px;
    left: -5px;
}
```

Zoe Gillenwater
February 28, 2010

Cary Gillenwater
March 1, 2010

Faith Mickley
March 1, 2010

Asha Gillenwater
March 10, 2010

FIGURE 2.27
**The rotation (in IE 8)
looks good, but the
avatars overlap the
commenters' names.**

NOTE: Remember,
the line breaks shown
in the -ms-filter
property are just there
for book formatting
purposes. Make sure
your -ms-filter prop-
erty is all on one line.

```
.ie8 .comment-meta img {
  -ms-filter: "progid:DXImageTransform.Microsoft.
  ¬Matrix(M11=0.9961946980917454, M12=0.08715574274765871,
  ¬M21=-0.08715574274765871, M22=0.9961946980917454,
  ¬SizingMethod='auto expand')";
  position: relative;
  top: -5px;
  left: -5px;
}
```

With these changes, the avatars are now rotated in IE 6 through 8 the
same amount as in the transforms-supporting browsers, and they don't
overlap the commenters' names below or the comment text to the right.

Instead of using the Matrix filter directly, you can use a premade
script that uses it behind the scenes. A script has the advantage that
you can then script changes in the transforms, to create animations or other effects, more easily. The cssSandpaper script (www.
useragentman.com/blog/csssandpaper-a-css3-javascript-library),
also by Zoltan Hawryluk, makes several transform functions as well as
box-shadow, gradients, RGBA, and HSLA work in IE. The Transformie
script by Paul Bakaus (http://paulbakaus.com/?p=11) is a simpler script
that uses jQuery.

The Finished Page

We've completed all the styling for the comments area, so check out
your work in an up-to-date browser; you should see something like
Figure 2.28. Compare it to Figure 2.1 showing the base page. It's not
a radical difference, but the completed page is visually richer and
more unique.

IE is missing some of the effects, but looks fairly close to Figure 2.28
overall (**Figure 2.29**). The small differences that do exist are OK; the
effects we've added are purely decorative, and IE users will have no
reason to think that they're missing anything. Even if you choose not
to add any of the IE workarounds such as filters that we've used in this
chapter, your page will still look like Figure 2.1 in IE 8 and earlier and
be perfectly usable and attractive.

NOTE: The completed
page showing all of
these effects is named
speech-bubble_final.
html in the exercise
files for this chapter.

FIGURE 2.28
The page with all
CSS3 applied, shown
here in Firefox 3.6.

FIGURE 2.29 IE 8 (top left), IE 6 (top right), and the preview version of IE 9 (left) don't display all of the CSS3 effects we've added, but the page is still attractive and usable.

Notebook Paper

Chapter 2 was all about creating graphic effects without any graphics. In this chapter, we'll use plenty of images, but new CSS3 properties allow us to use them with more streamlined markup and to make them behave in ways not possible with CSS 2.1. You'll also learn how to use unique, non-web-safe fonts in your pages without resorting to Flash, images, or scripting—even in Internet Explorer. Altogether, we'll be able to use these image and font techniques to make a web page look like a realistic piece of notebook paper.

WHAT YOU'LL LEARN

We'll create the appearance of a piece of notebook paper using these CSS3 properties and concepts:

- The `background-size` property to scale a background image with the text

- Multiple background images on one element

- The `border-image` property to create graphic borders

- The `background-clip` property to move a background image out from under a border

- The `@font-face` rule to embed unique fonts in the page

The Base Page

Creating the appearance of real objects, like sticky notes and file folders, has always been popular in web design. If you wanted an article to look like it was written on a piece of real paper, the first step might be to apply a simple lined paper background image to it. **Figure 3.1** shows this starting point.

FIGURE 3.1 The article with a single background image, before any CSS3 is applied.

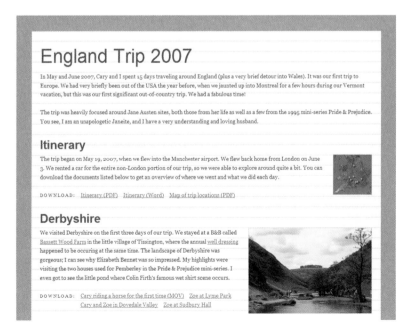

Beyond the Basic Background

To make the web page shown in Figure 3.1 look more like a realistic piece of paper, you would want to add some extra graphic details beyond the lined background, like a torn edge or a coffee stain. Without CSS3, it's certainly possible to add these graphic details. But new properties in CSS3 make it easier and keep your markup cleaner. Let's add some of these new properties now to enhance the background.

Scaling the Background Image

One thing that would make the background look more realistic is if the text were aligned to the notebook paper lines, instead of overlapping them indiscriminately. To fix this without CSS3, you would need to set a base `font-size` and `line-height` in pixels, and then adjust the spacing between the lines in your background image to match. This would work for most users. But if anyone resized the text, or had non-standard user settings to override the pixel font sizes, the text would become mis-aligned. The text could scale, but the background image couldn't.

But that was then—before the CSS3 `background-size` property was introduced. With `background-size`, you can control the horizontal and vertical scaling of a background image as well as how it stretches to cover the background area and gets clipped.

HOW background-size WORKS

Before we apply `background-size` to our page, let's look at a couple of simple examples to get a better grip on how the property works.

Figure 3.2 shows an image 200 pixels wide by 120 pixels tall. **Figure 3.3** shows how the image looks when set as a normal repeating background of a `div` that's 500 pixels wide by 200 pixels tall; since the `div`'s dimensions aren't an even multiple of the image's dimensions, some of the image gets cut off on the right and bottom.

FIGURE 3.2 An image that's 200 pixels wide by 120 pixels tall

FIGURE 3.3 When the image is repeated across the background of the div, some of it gets cut off on the right and bottom.

We can use the background-size property to scale the image down from 200 pixels to 100 pixels wide:

```
div {
    width: 500px;
    height: 200px;
    border: 1px solid #999;
    background-image: url(images/stars.gif);
    background-size: 100px auto;
}
```

The first value in the background-size property, 100px, sets the width of the background image. The second value, auto, sets the height. A value of auto makes the height whatever it needs to be to preserve the aspect ratio of the image. If you leave the second value off, the browser assumes it to be auto, so a value of background-size: 100px; would have worked identically here. Compare **Figure 3.4** to Figure 3.3 to see how the background image has been shrunk but kept its aspect ratio.

FIGURE 3.4
The browser has scaled the image to 100 pixels wide, so it now fits in the div exactly five times and doesn't get cut off on the right.

If you use percentages in the background-size property, they're relative to the box the background is on, not to the background image itself. If you wanted exactly two copies of the image to show in the div, with neither cut off at all, you could use this CSS:

```
div {
    width: 500px;
    height: 200px;
    border: 1px solid #999;
    background-image: url(images/stars.gif);
    background-size: 50% 100%;
}
```

The image is stretched to fill half the width of the div and all of its height, and then repeated (**Figure 3.5**). In this case, the browser has to both distort the shape of the image and scale it up, making the edges in the image look a little blurry or pixelated. As with any browser-based scaling, background sizing is not going to look good with all images, but can work quite well with grungy, abstract, or very simple images that don't have super-clean edges—such as our lined-paper background.

FIGURE 3.5
The browser has scaled the image to fit twice across the width and once across the height, distorting it but keeping it from cutting off.

MORE NEW WAYS TO TILE BACKGROUNDS

Besides setting background-size to a value that fits perfectly within the width of a box, another way to keep background image tiles from getting cut off on one or more sides is to use the values of round and space in the background-repeat property. These values are new to CSS3, and can be used in conjunction with background-size or without it.

A value of round repeats the background image but rescales it so it will fit an even number of times without getting cut off. A value of space repeats the background image as often as it will fit without getting cut off, and then spaces the tiles out to fill any leftover room.

Unfortunately, at the time of this writing, the only browsers that support these values are IE 9 and Opera, but Opera does so incompletely and incorrectly. Until these background-repeat values have better support, background-size is your best bet for ensuring background images don't get cut off, though it's not as flexible as round and space are.

MAKING THE PAPER LINES SCALE WITH THE TEXT

In order to make our paper background image scale with the text, we need to set its dimensions not in percentages or pixels, but in ems. Ems are a relative unit of measurement based on the current font height.

To get started, download the exercise files for this chapter at www.stunningcss3.com, and open paper_start.html in your code editor of choice. Its CSS is contained in a `style` element in the head of the page.

Find the `#paper` rule in the CSS, and add the `background-size` property, plus the Mozilla and Webkit equivalents:

```
#paper {
    float: left;
    margin: 40px;
    padding: 3.2em 1.6em 1.6em 1.6em;
    background: url(images/paperlines.gif) #FBFBF9;
    -moz-background-size: auto 1.6em;
    -webkit-background-size: auto 1.6em;
    background-size: auto 1.6em;
}
```

Opera, Chrome, Safari 5, Firefox 4, and IE 9 use the standard `background-size` property; Firefox 3.6 and Safari 4 and earlier use the `-moz-` and `-webkit-` versions of the property, respectively. In each property, we're telling the browser that we want the height of the image to be 1.6 ems and that we want the width to just size itself proportionally. The image depicts one line on the paper, so that means that the space between every line will now be 1.6 ems tall. Why 1.6 ems? The height of each line of text is 1.6, specified by the `line-height` already in place on the `body` element:

```
body {
    margin: 0;
    padding: 40px;
    background: #CCC url(images/background.gif);
    color: #333;
    font-size: 87.5%;
    font-family: Georgia, "Times New Roman", Times, serif;
    line-height: 1.6;
}
```

Figure 3.6 shows that the background image's size has indeed changed, but the text is still not lining up with the lines in the image. This is because we haven't set all the text sizes and margins to line up with a regular spacing of 1.6 ems. The paragraph and list text have the correct spacing for the background image, since their `line-height` is already 1.6 and their bottom margins are 1.6 ems, as you'll see in the CSS. But the headings need to have their margins tweaked to fall in line.

FIGURE 3.6 The background image lines are closer together after applying background-size.

```
h1 {
    margin: -.3em 0 .14em 0;
    color: #414141;
    font-family: Helvetica, "Helvetica Neue", Arial,
    ¬ sans-serif;
    font-size: 3.5em;
    font-weight: normal;
}
h2 {
    clear: left;
    color: #414141;
    margin: 0 0 -.14em 0;
    font-family: Helvetica, "Helvetica Neue", Arial,
    ¬ sans-serif;
    font-size: 2.17em;
    font-weight: bold;
}
```

These margin values are based on trial and error. Unlike with absolute pixel-based measurements, you're not going to be able to find values that work perfectly for all browsers; each browser has different ways of rounding and translating relative measurements like ems into the pixels displayed on the screen. In this case, these margin values work well for Firefox, Safari, and Chrome. Everything is spaced out at regular intervals of 1.6 ems, keeping the text aligned to the lines in the background image (**Figure 3.7**).

FIGURE 3.7 The text is now aligned to the lines in the background image, shown here in Firefox 3.6.

FIGURE 3.7 The text is now aligned to the lines in the background image, shown here in Firefox 3.6.

But in Opera, the text isn't aligned, as Opera sizes the background image just slightly smaller than the other browsers. If we were to adjust the font sizes and margins to make everything line up in Opera, it would mess up the alignment in the other browsers. You'll have to decide which browsers are more important to you, based on your own site's visitor statistics, and cater your measurements to those.

Once the text is aligned with the background image, if the user has a different default text size from the norm, or scales the text size up or down, the background image scales with it, keeping the lines always aligned with the text (**Figure 3.8**). Also, if you were to later change the base font size on the body element, everything would scale to match, without your having to remake the background image.

FIGURE 3.8 Even if the user has a larger text size, the text stays aligned with the background image lines.

WORKAROUNDS FOR IE

The background-size property doesn't work in IE 8 and earlier, and there are no workarounds to directly emulate it. In this case, it's a minor visual effect, so I think we can chalk it up as progressive enhancement and not worry about its lack in IE.

You can, however, provide alternate styles using Modernizr, which does detect for support of the background-size property. For instance, you could provide a different background image altogether, or you could provide an alternate version of the lined paper background image that has been designed to fit with a particular pixel font size; you would set this pixel font size only for browsers that don't support background-size. I don't recommend doing this here, as pixel-based font sizes are bad for accessibility. However, Modernizr is a good option in general for providing alternate styles when you're trying to scale a background image using background-size.

THE LOWDOWN ON THE background-size PROPERTY

The background-size property is part of the Backgrounds and Borders module, found at www.
w3.org/TR/css3-background. Its value can be a width and height in any unit, or it can be auto.

Alternately, background-size can be set to either contain or cover. Both make the browser scale
the image proportionally. A value of contain scales it to the largest size where both its width and
height will fit inside the background area, so it doesn't get cut off at all, but often leaves some area
with no background on it. A value of cover scales it to the smallest size where one tile of it will completely cover the background area, but allows it to get cut off where necessary to make sure the
whole area has a background image covering it.

Other than scaling lines to match text spacing, you might want to use background-size for:

♦ Making the non-repeating background of the header of a page scale in a liquid or elastic layout
  to always fill the whole header width

♦ Making a repeating background image tile a full number of times instead of the tiles getting cut
  off on the edges of the box

♦ Making a large background image always fill the entire page; see www.alistapart.com/articles/
  supersize-that-background-please

♦ Scaling a faux-columns background image in a liquid layout; see www.css3.info/liquid-faux-
  columns-with-background-size

♦ Scaling a link or list item's background image icon with its text

♦ Scaling background images for the iPhone 4's high-resolution display down by half, so that
  when it doubles the pixels, as it always does, the images won't look blurry; see http://dryan.com/
  articles/posts/2010/6/25/hi-res-mobile-css-iphone-4

♦ Changing the size of background images based on the size of the user's window, using media
  queries, which you'll learn about in Chapter 6

TABLE 3.1 background-size **browser support**

IE	FIREFOX	OPERA	SAFARI	CHROME
Yes, 9+	Yes, 4+; 3.6 with -moz-	Yes	Yes, 5+; 3+ with -webkit-	Yes

Multiple Background Images on One Element

One of the changes to CSS that has brought web designers the most joy is the ability to apply multiple background images to a single element. In our example, we'll be able to use this function to make the paper look a little more realistic—we'll beat it up a bit by adding some stain images, as well as adding a thumbtack at the top.

Before CSS3, only one background image per box was allowed, so you'd have to add an extra div for each extra image and apply one image to each div. If you could count on other particular blocks already being inside your divs, such as a h3 element always being the first nested element, you could apply background images to these other blocks instead of adding extra divs. However, doing so could be risky, as you would be relying on certain types of content always being present and in particular places; if those pieces of content weren't there, of course their background images wouldn't show up.

This nesting divs method wasn't difficult, but it was messy. It junked up your markup and increased the pages' file size. To add more images later, you'd need to not only change the CSS, but the HTML as well.

With CSS3, you can leave the HTML alone and instead simply list each background image in the background-image or background property, separated by commas. Each image can be positioned, repeated, sized, and otherwise controlled independently.

Figure 3.9 shows the extra images we want to apply to our article div. To apply them, add a new background declaration under the existing one in the #paper rule:

```
#paper {
    float: left;
    margin: 40px;
    padding: 3.2em 1.6em 1.6em 1.6em;
    background: url(images/paperlines.gif) #FBFBF9;
                background: url(images/thumbtack.png),
                url(images/stains1.png),
                url(images/stains2.png),
                url(images/stains3.png),
                url(images/stains4.png),
                url(images/paperlines.gif) #FBFBF9;
    -moz-background-size: auto 1.6em;
    -webkit-background-size: auto 1.6em;
    background-size: auto 1.6em;
}
```

NOTE: The line breaks and indentions in the background property are just there to make the CSS easier to read. You can write everything on one line, or not—it works the same regardless.

NOTE: The water stain images shown in Figure 3.9 were created with the Photoshop brushes by Obsidian Dawn from www.obsidiandawn. com/water-stains-photoshop-gimp-brushes.

The first background declaration will continue to be used by IE and other browsers that don't support multiple background images. Because they don't understand the syntax of the second background declaration, they'll ignore it. Browsers that do support multiple background images will override the first declaration with the second.

The background images are layered on top of each other, with the first declared image put on top of the stack. That's why the thumbtack image is listed first and the lines image is listed last.

We're not quite done yet, though. We haven't told the browser how we want to repeat, position, and size each image. To do this, treat each snippet between the commas as if it were its own standalone background shorthand property, and write each of the background-related properties in it accordingly. **Figure 3.10** shows all the pieces that can go in the background shorthand property. The order matters for some and not for others, so I recommend sticking with the order shown in 3.10 just so you don't get confused or accidentally make a mistake. (I know *I* would otherwise!)

FIGURE 3.10
The background **short-hand property can contain multiple layers; the top layer of this diagram includes all the possible pieces of the property (minus color, which can go only into the final layer).**

```
            image      position      size      repeat  attachment   origin       clip
              |           |           |          |         |          |           |
background: url(top.gif) 50% 0 / 10px 100px no-repeat fixed padding-box padding-box,   TOP LAYER
            url(middle.gif) 50% 0 no-repeat content-box,   SECOND LAYER
            url(bottom.gif) 0 0 / auto 20px repeat #FFF;   FINAL LAYER
                                                  |
                                                color
```

Using the order shown in the diagram in Figure 3.10, add the positioning and repeat values after each image in the background property:

```
background: url(images/thumbtack.png) 50% 5px no-repeat,
            url(images/stains1.png) 90% -20px no-repeat,
            url(images/stains2.png) 30% 8% no-repeat,
            url(images/stains3.png) 20% 50% no-repeat,
            url(images/stains4.png) 40% 60% no-repeat,
            url(images/paperlines.gif) #FBFBF9;
```

Next, modify the background-size properties to tell the browser that each image should be sized using its native dimensions, except for the last (the lines image):

```
-moz-background-size: auto, auto, auto, auto, auto,
                      auto 1.6em;
webkit-background-size: auto, auto, auto, auto, auto,
                        auto 1.6em;
background-size: auto, auto, auto, auto, auto, auto 1.6em;
```

Each comma-separated value matches up with the comma-separated value at the same spot in the background property's value list.

Although you can technically include background-size information in the background shorthand property, it won't work right now. Older versions of Firefox and Safari need background-size declared using the vendor-prefixed properties, and although Opera, Chrome, Safari 5, Firefox 4, and IE 9 might accept background-size in the background property, adding it would break those older versions of Firefox and Safari. So, to keep it working everywhere, and to keep yourself from confusing the values for background-position and background-size (very easy to do!), keep background-size written separately from background.

NOTE: The page with all the changes to this point is named paper_1.html in the exercise files that you downloaded for this chapter.

Save your page and view it in an up-to-date browser. You should still see the text aligned with the notebook paper lines, but also see four stains scattered across the paper and a thumbtack at the top (**Figure 3.11**).

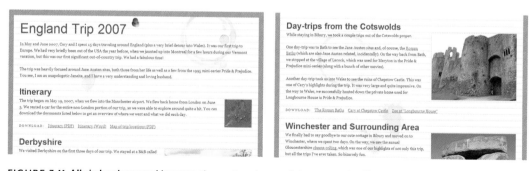

FIGURE 3.11 All six background images show at various points across the div.

The nice thing about setting each of these images independently, instead of combining them into one big image that you set on a single nested div, is that the images can move around based on the size of the div. No matter what size or dimensions the div has, there will be stain images distributed nicely across it, instead of clustered in one spot.

THE LOWDOWN ON MULTIPLE BACKGROUND IMAGES

Multiple background images are a new feature of the background and background-image properties, not a new property itself. These properties are part of the Backgrounds and Borders module, found at www.w3.org/TR/css3-background.

List each background image in the background-image or background property, separated by commas. The background images are layered on top of each other, with the first declared image put on top of the stack.

Each image can be positioned, repeated, sized, and otherwise controlled independently. To do so, include this background styling information with each image URL in the background property, or add a comma-separated list of values to each independent background property, such as background-repeat: no-repeat, no-repeat, repeat-x, repeat. Each value in the list matches up with a value in the list of background images.

Other than layering stain images over a paper background pattern, you might want to use multiple background images for:

- Flexible boxes with fancy or irregular corners or edges that other CSS3 properties like border-radius can't handle, such as ornate buttons that would still need images; see http://css-tricks.com/css3-multiple-backgrounds-obsoletes-sliding-doors

- Opening and closing quotation mark images on a blockquote; see http://css.dzone.com/news/multiple-backgrounds-oh-what-beautiful-thing

- The parallax effect, where resizing a window or hovering over a div makes the images appear to move at different speeds in relation to each other; see www.paulrhayes.com/2009-04/auto-scrolling-parallax-effect-without-javascript

- Making what appears to be a single image stretch across the whole width of a box or page, while it's really made up of multiple pieces, such as a landscape image with a sun that you always want to appear in the top right corner and a tree that you always want to appear in the bottom left corner

- Distributing images across the full width or height of a box, using percentage positions to keep them spaced out from each other, such as multiple cloud images over a blue background color

- Creating the appearance of an object from real life, using a top image slice, repeating middle slice, and bottom slice, all on the same box

- Applying a CSS3-generated gradient (remember, it goes in the background-image property, not background-color) along with a background image, to fade out a texture, blend the edges of an image into a solid color, or reveal portions of an image as the user scrolls down the page; see http://atomicrobotdesign.com/blog/htmlcss/make-the-thinkgeek-background-effect-using-css3

TABLE 3.2 Multiple background images browser support

IE	FIREFOX	OPERA	SAFARI	CHROME
Yes, 9+	Yes, 3.6+	Yes, 10.5+	Yes	Yes

WORKAROUNDS FOR NON-SUPPORTING BROWSERS

IE 8 and earlier plus older versions of Firefox and Opera don't support multiple background images. In a case like this, where the additional images are just extra decoration, you don't have to worry about providing workarounds. They'll still see the lined-paper background, which is a complete image in itself, with no clue that anything's lacking.

However, there may be times when missing out on the extra images would create an overall effect that looks incomplete or broken. For instance, if you're using multiple background images to create a complex button, with a left, middle, and right slice, the button will look broken if only one slice can be seen. Be careful about using multiple background images in cases like these, as you only have a few options for workarounds:

◆ **Use a single fallback image.** The simplest workaround for non-supporting browsers is to provide it with a single background image, either in a separate background-image declaration listed before the one using multiple images (the method we've used here) or by using Modernizr. Make sure this single image can stand on its own. This is easy to implement and doesn't harm supporting browsers, but it won't provide a sufficient appearance in cases where the page truly looks broken without the extra images.

◆ **Nest divs to hold extra images.** A more robust but work-intensive workaround than the single fallback image is to go back to the old method of nesting divs and applying separate images to separate boxes. If you do this, you'll need to use Modernizr or IE conditional comments to feed different rules to browsers with different support. Otherwise, you'd get double the backgrounds in browsers that support multiple background images. Of course, if you're going to be adding the extra divs and background rules anyway, you might as well stop using multiple background images at all and just use this old technique for all browsers, regardless of support. So I'm not sure that this workaround makes a lot of sense.

◆ **Generate the extra elements to hold extra images.** A cleaner way of implementing the "Nest divs" workaround is to use the :before and :after pseudo-elements to generate extra elements, to which you can then apply extra background images. The article "Multiple Backgrounds and Borders with CSS 2.1" by Nicolas Gallagher (http://nicolasgallagher.com/multiple-backgrounds-and-borders-with-css2) explains how to do this. This would work well for IE 8 and Firefox 3.5, for instance, but IE 6 and 7 don't support these pseudo-elements, making this technique fail to work in those browsers—unless you also added a script to force older versions of IE to support these selectors. And you'd need to make sure browsers that do support multiple background images don't see the images on the pseudo-elements. At this point, the workaround would be getting pretty complicated! Again, you'll have to decide if what may amount to simply extra decoration is worth it for you and your users.

◆ **Use canvas.** If you're comfortable with scripting, you can use the HTML5 canvas element to draw multiple images on a single element. IE 8 and earlier don't support canvas, but Google's "explorer-canvas" script (http://code.google.com/p/explorercanvas) can make it work. Explaining how to use canvas is beyond the scope of this book, but Hans Pinckaers' mb.js script (http://github.com/HansPinckaers/mb.js) has already done the work for you, making multiple backgrounds work in IE and older non-IE browsers.

Adding a Graphic Border

Another graphic detail that would be nice to add is a border on the left side of the paper to make it look like it was torn from a spiral notebook (**Figure 3.12**). There are a couple ways we can do this with CSS3.

USING BACKGROUND IMAGES

One way to add the torn paper edge is by adding it as another background image, set to repeat down only. But the edge image has transparent areas in it (the holes in the paper), so the lines background image below it will show through. If our page had a solid background color instead of a pattern, we could fill the transparent areas of the edge image with that solid color, obscuring the lines background image and blending into the page background color seamlessly. But that won't work in our page.

Without a solid background color on the page, your only option is to wrap another div around the paper div, and set the edge image as

FIGURE 3.12 Torn spiral notebook-paper edge

the background on this wrapper div. You could then give the wrapper enough left padding to keep the inner div from overlapping the edge image and obscuring it. This wouldn't be ideal, since it would add extra markup, but it would work in all browsers and with all page backgrounds.

One small disadvantage of setting the edge image as a background is that we can't control how it gets clipped at the bottom of the div. It's possible that the div would end in the middle of one of the holes in the edge, which isn't what a full sheet of real spiral notebook paper looks like (**Figure 3.13**). I will admit this is hardly a tragedy—it's a very minor, nitpicky problem. But if we can fix the problem easily with CSS, why not fix it?

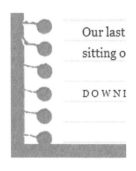

FIGURE 3.13
With the edge image as a repeating background image, it can get cut off in the middle of one of the holes.

The CSS3 solution is to set background-repeat on the edge image to round—a new value for the property introduced in CSS3. This makes the browser repeat the image as many times as it will fit, and if it doesn't fit a whole number of times, the browser rescales the image so that it will fit without clipping off at the end.

Unfortunately, only IE 9 and Opera support the round value at the time of this writing, and Opera does so imperfectly. So, background-repeat: round is not a usable solution right now. Luckily, we can forgo using a background image entirely and use the new border-image property instead.

USING border-image

CSS3 allows you to assign an image to a border, in addition to (or instead of) a color and line style. The browser will take a single image, slice it into pieces, and stretch or tile each of those pieces across each border.

For instance, let's say that **Figure 3.14** is the image we want to use for the borders on a div. We want to use the top 30 pixels of the image for the top border, the right 25 pixels for the right border, the bottom 27 pixels for the bottom border, and the left 34 pixels for the left border (**Figure 3.15**). We need to use these values as both our border widths and our border image slice locations.

NOTE: You can actually use different values for the border widths and the corresponding image slice locations. The browser will scale each image slice to fit the border width it's applied to.

```
.clouds {
    width: 400px;
    height: 150px;
    border-width: 30px 25px 27px 34px;
    border-image: url(clouds.png) 30 25 27 34 stretch;
}
```

FIGURE 3.14 **This image has irregular borders that can be stretched and tiled using** border-image.

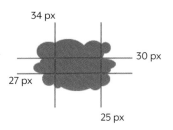

FIGURE 3.15 **The lines indicate where we want to virtually slice the image into pieces that can be tiled or stretched across the borders.**

NOTE: Strangely, you must leave the "px" unit off the slice values in the border-image property. Or, you can use percentages for slice values, relative to the image itself; in this case, you must include the % sign after the number.

The first part of the border-image value is the path to the image, which works just like any other path in CSS.

Next comes one or more numbers to specify where the browser should slice the image. In this case, we're using four numbers, since we want four different amounts sliced off from each edge. The first number, 30, is the inward offset from the top edge of the image, in pixels. The second number, 25, is the inward offset from the right edge, the third is the offset from the bottom, and the fourth is the offset from the left. The browser will slice the image at each of these lines, creating nine images that it applies to each border, each corner, and the middle of the box.

THE CENTER SLICE

The center slice of the border image is used to cover the entire middle area of the box, inside the border area. This doesn't seem very intuitive, but it does give you more styling options. If you don't want the middle of the border image to obscure the background image or color beneath it, use your graphics program to make the middle portion of the image you're using transparent, and save the image as a transparent GIF or PNG.

The spec says that this center slice should be discarded by default, unless you add the word fill to your border-image value. However, right now no browser seems to support the fill keyword, and they all "fill" by default, with no option to "not fill."

THE LOWDOWN ON THE `border-image` PROPERTY

The `border-image` property is part of the Backgrounds and Borders module, found at www.w3.org/TR/css3-background. It's a shorthand property, but you can't use the individual properties right now, since no browser supports them declared outside of the shorthand `border-image` property.

In the `border-image` property, you specify an image, how far in from each edge you want the browser to slice the image, and how to repeat each image (except the corners) across its border.

You can use one to four slice values, depending on whether each side needs to be sliced differently. One value applies the same slice offset to all four sides; two values applies the first to the top and bottom and the second to the right and left; three values applies the first to the top, second to the right and left, and third to bottom; and four values applies each to an individual side, starting at the top edge and going clockwise. See Figure 3.15 for a diagram of where the browser slices a border image.

The repeat value can be set to `stretch`, `repeat`, `round`, or `space`. Using one repeat value will apply the value to all four sides, while two repeat values applies the first value to the top and bottom borders and the second value to the left and right sides. A value of `repeat` will tile all four edges plus the center; `stretch` will stretch them to fill the area; `round` will tile and scale them so each fits a whole number of times; and `space` will tile them so each fits a whole number of times and then evenly distribute the extra space between the tiles.

Remember to always set `border-width` in conjunction with `border-image` to create a border area for the image to draw onto. There is also a `border-image-width` property, but no browser currently supports it, nor does any browser currently support `border-image-outset`.

Sadly, border images don't conform to curved borders created by `border-radius`.

Other than creating a torn-edge look, you might want to use `border-image` for:

- Buttons; see http://ejohn.org/blog/border-image-in-firefox
- Gradient backgrounds
- Scalloped edges to create the effect of a stamp or raffle ticket
- Graphic edges to create the effect of a picture frame or certificate; see www.norabrowndesign.com/css-experiments/border-image-frame.html
- A curved or angled edge of a box
- Box drop shadows that are curved or angled (`box-shadow` can do only straight drop shadows, but you can create an image of an irregular shadow and apply it as a border image)

TABLE 3.3 *border-image* **browser support**

IE	FIREFOX	OPERA	SAFARI	CHROME
No	Partial with -moz-, 3.5+	Partial, 10.5+	Partial with -webkit-	Partial

How exactly the browser applies these images depends on the third part of the border-image property: the repeat value. In this example, we're using a value of stretch, which will make the browser stretch all four border images, plus the center (but not the corners), to fill the available space (**Figure 3.16**). You can also set it to repeat (**Figure 3.17**), round (**Figure 3.18**), or space. (The round value is supported only by Firefox and Opera currently.) No browser currently supports the space value, so I can't show you a screenshot!

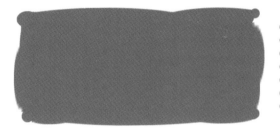

FIGURE 3.16 **This** border-image **has been stretched.**

FIGURE 3.17 **This** border-image **has been repeated.**

FIGURE 3.18 **This** border-image **has been rounded.**

APPLYING THE TORN-EDGE IMAGE

Let's put border-image to use in our page to apply the torn-paper edge image, shown in Figure 3.12, to the article div. We want to apply the image only to the left border, so we'll make that border 50 pixels wide—the width of the image—and set the other borders to zero:

```
#paper {
    float: left;
    margin: 40px;
    padding: 3.2em 1.6em 1.6em 1.6em;
    border-width: 0 0 0 50px;
    background: url(images/paperlines.gif) #FBFBF9;
    background: url(images/thumbtack.png) 50% 5px no-repeat,
                url(images/stains1.png) 90% -20px no-repeat,
                url(images/stains2.png) 30% 8% no-repeat,
                url(images/stains3.png) 20% 50% no-repeat,
                url(images/stains4.png) 40% 60% no-repeat,
                url(images/paperlines.gif) #FBFBF9;
    -moz-background-size: auto, auto, auto, auto, auto,
                          auto 1.6em;
    -webkit-background-size: auto, auto, auto, auto, auto,
                             auto 1.6em;
    background-size: auto, auto, auto, auto, auto,
                     auto 1.6em;
}
```

PLAYING WITH BORDER IMAGES

The border-image property is pretty confusing—I won't deny it. If, after walking through the examples provided, you're still feeling a little unsure, I highly recommend you check out these border image web tools:

- "border-image-generator" by Kevin Decker (http://border-image.com) allows you to upload any image to see how it will look when applied as a border image. You can change the slice offsets, border widths, and repeat method and instantly see how your border image changes.

- "Grokking CSS3 border-image" by Nora Brown (www.norabrowndesign.com/css-experiments/border-image-anim.html) uses five preset images and lets you change between a few preset border-image values to see how the images are affected.

Getting to change values on the fly and see how they affect the visual output is one of the best ways to learn how a piece of CSS works.

Next, we'll apply the border image, using the standard `border-image` property for Chrome and Opera and the prefixed properties for Firefox and Safari:

```
#paper {
    float: left;
    margin: 40px;
    padding: 3.2em 1.6em 1.6em 1.6em;
    border-width: 0 0 0 50px;
    -moz-border-image: url(images/edge.png) 0 0 0 50 round;
    -webkit-border-image: url(images/edge.png) 0 0 0 50
    ⌐ round;
    border-image: url(images/edge.png) 0 0 0 50 round;
    background: url(images/paperlines.gif) #FBFBF9;
    background: url(images/thumbtack.png) 50% 5px no-repeat,
                url(images/stains1.png) 90% -20px no-repeat,
                url(images/stains2.png) 30% 8% no-repeat,
                url(images/stains3.png) 20% 50% no-repeat,
                url(images/stains4.png) 40% 60% no-repeat,
                url(images/paperlines.gif) #FBFBF9;
    -moz-background-size: auto, auto, auto, auto, auto,
                    auto 1.6em;
    -webkit-background-size: auto, auto, auto, auto, auto,
                    auto 1.6em;
    background-size: auto, auto, auto, auto, auto,
                    auto 1.6em;
}
```

We've set each of the slice locations to zero except for the left one; we don't want to slice off any from the top, right, or bottom, but we do want to slice in from the left edge by 50 pixels so that the entire 50-pixel-width of the image is used for the left border.

For the repeat value, we've used `round` to repeat the image but keep it from ending in the middle of a hole. Since Safari and Chrome don't support this value, they treat it as `repeat` instead, which is an acceptable second choice.

USING `background-clip` TO POSITION IMAGES

Our edge image is now repeating down the left side of the `div`, but the background image is showing through it (**Figure 3.19**). That's because, by default, borders are drawn on top of the background area. You may have never noticed it before, because usually your borders are just solid lines, without any transparent pieces. But change your border-style to dashed and you'll see what I mean. Border images are placed the same way.

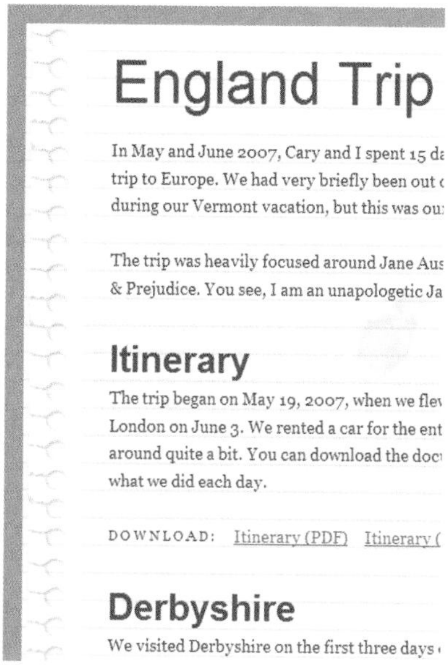

England Trip

In May and June 2007, Cary and I spent 15 da
trip to Europe. We had very briefly been out (
during our Vermont vacation, but this was ou:

The trip was heavily focused around Jane Aus
& Prejudice. You see, I am an unapologetic Ja

Itinerary

The trip began on May 19, 2007, when we fle\
London on June 3. We rented a car for the ent
around quite a bit. You can download the doc
what we did each day.

DOWNLOAD: Itinerary (PDF)   Itinerary (

Derbyshire

We visited Derbyshire on the first three days (

FIGURE 3.19 The torn-edge image repeats down the left side, but overlaps the background.

ORDER OF THE BACKGROUND PROPERTIES

Normally, the order I write the properties in each rule is irrelevant; it's just a standard order that I always use, and you can feel free to reorder the properties however you like. In the case of background-clip, however, make sure to write it *after* the shorthand background property, as shown, because background-clip can be included in the shorthand background property (see Figure 3.10). If you write background-clip separately first, and then write the background property without any background-clip information in it, you're effectively telling the browser you want to use the default value of border-box, overriding the earlier background-clip values.

So why not just include the background-clip value we want in the shorthand background property? We can't, for the same reasons we can't include the background-size values in the background property right now: some browsers need prefixes and don't yet understand the standard property, by itself or in the background shorthand property.

THE LOWDOWN ON THE
background-clip PROPERTY

The background-clip property is part of the Backgrounds and Borders module, found at www.w3.org/TR/css3-background. It controls under which sections of a box the background is painted.

The allowed values are border-box (the default value to paint backgrounds under borders), padding-box (to clip backgrounds at the outer edge of the padding area and not extend under borders), and content-box (to clip backgrounds at the outer edge of the content area and not extend under padding or borders). Firefox 3.6 and earlier don't support content-box, and use values of border and padding, not border-box and padding-box; Firefox 4 doesn't have these issues. Safari 5 supports the border-box and padding-box values in the standard background-clip property, but supports only content-box in the -webkit-background-clip property.

Webkit also supports a value of text, available only in the -webkit-prefixed property, which makes the text act like a mask on the background image, obscuring whatever parts of the background image are not behind the text. It's a cool effect, but probably won't make it into the spec. For more information and examples, see www.css3.info/webkit-introduces-background-cliptext, http://trentwalton.com/2010/03/24/css3-background-clip-text, and http://trentwalton.com/2010/04/06/css3-background-clip-font-face.

Other than moving a background out from under a border image, you might want to use background-clip for:

◆ Moving a background color or image out from under a dashed or dotted border

◆ Creating the appearance of a double border, one made from the actual border and one made from the padding, by using content-box

◆ Keeping the background color from bleeding outside the edges of rounded corners, as sometimes happens in Webkit-based browsers, by using padding-box; see http://tumble.sneak.co.nz/post/928998513/fixing-the-background-bleed

TABLE 3.4 `background-clip` **browser support**

IE	FIREFOX	OPERA	SAFARI	CHROME
Yes, 9+	Yes, 4+; Partial, 1+, with -moz-	Yes	Yes, 3+, with -webkit-; Partial, 5+	Yes

Luckily, we can change this default behavior with CSS3. CSS3 lets you control where backgrounds are placed relative to the borders with the new `background-clip` property. The default value, `border-box`, makes backgrounds extend under the borders as they've always done. Setting `background-clip` to `padding-box` starts the backgrounds inside the borders, under the padding area:

```
#paper {
    float: left;
    margin: 40px;
    padding: 3.2em 1.6em 1.6em 1.6em;
    border-width: 0 0 0 50px;
    -moz-border-image: url(images/edge.png) 0 0 0 50 round;
    -webkit-border-image: url(images/edge.png) 0 0 0 50
    ¬ round;
    border-image: url(images/edge.png) 0 0 0 50 round;
    background: url(images/paperlines.gif) #FBFBF9;
    background: url(images/thumbtack.png) 50% 5px no-repeat,
               url(images/stains1.png) 90% -20px no-repeat,
               url(images/stains2.png) 30% 8% no-repeat,
               url(images/stains3.png) 20% 50% no-repeat,
               url(images/stains4.png) 40% 60% no-repeat,
               url(images/paperlines.gif) #FBFBF9;
    -moz-background-size: auto, auto, auto, auto, auto,
                          auto 1.6em;
    -webkit-background-size: auto, auto, auto, auto, auto,
                            auto 1.6em;
    background-size: auto, auto, auto, auto, auto,
                    auto 1.6em;
    -moz-background-clip: padding;
    -webkit-background-clip: padding-box;
    background-clip: padding-box;
}
```

Chrome, Safari 5, Firefox 4, and Opera use the standard property, while Firefox 3.6 and earlier and Safari 4 and earlier use the prefixed versions. Note also that the `-moz-background-clip` property takes a value of `padding` instead of the standard `padding-box`.

Making this change moves the lines background image out from under the border image (**Figure 3.20**).

FIGURE 3.20
The background-clip
property moves the
background image
out from under the
border image.

WORKAROUNDS FOR NON-SUPPORTING BROWSERS

Browsers that don't support border-image won't know what they're missing, in this case, as they'll still see the regular lined-background image. If you must have the torn edge, you can go back to using a background image for it on an additional wrapper div, as described earlier.

If you do this, you'll either need to remove the border-image from all the other browsers, or you'll need to hide the background image from the browsers that support border-image. I like the second approach, as it allows you the extra flexibility of having border images without too much extra work. Simply use Modernizr or IE conditional comments to create a wrapper rule that only certain browsers can see. This rule would assign left padding and the edge background image:

```
#wrapper {
    padding-left: 50px;
    background: url(images/edge.png) repeat-y;
}
```

The other browsers wouldn't see this rule at all. They'd still see the wrapper div in the HTML, of course, but they wouldn't apply any styles to it.

Alternately, you could combine the lined paper image with the torn edge image and apply this merged image to the existing div named paper. That would allow you to do away with the extra wrapper div, but it may be more work-intensive to have to maintain different images for different browsers. Again, you'd need to make sure that browsers that do support border-image continue to use the two separate images—one as the background and one as the border image.

There are a few ways to make border-image work through scripting, rather than ditching it in favor of background images. However, the scripting solutions work only when you're stretching the border images, not repeating or rounding them, so a script won't do in our case. But if your own project just needs stretched border images, check out:

◆ PIE by Jason Johnston (http://css3pie.com), described in Chapter 2. PIE also includes limited support for the border-image property in IE 6 through 8.

◆ borderImage by Louis-Rémi Babé (http://github.com/lrbabe/borderimage), a jQuery plugin that emulates border-image using VML for IE and canvas for non-IE browsers. You can find more description of how to use it at www.lrbabe.com/sdoms/borderImage.

Adding a Drop Shadow

In Chapter 2, you learned about the box-shadow property to create drop shadows beneath boxes. Our notebook-paper article seems like a good place for it as well, so let's add it. But we have to be careful—the drop shadow won't conform to the ragged edge of the border image, but rather to the box as a whole. That means that if the drop shadow shows on the left side of the box, you'll end up with a strange-looking straight-edged shadow that's slightly offset from the jagged paper edge (**Figure 3.21**).

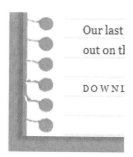

FIGURE 3.21
Drop shadows conform to the div's straight edge, not to any jagged lines within border or background images.

NOTE: The page with all the changes to this point is named paper_2. html in the exercise files that you downloaded for this chapter.

To avoid this problem, place the shadow far enough to the right to not peek out at all on the left edge. Add the following three lines to the `#paper` rule:

```
-moz-box-shadow: 6px 5px 3px hsla(0,0%,0%,.2);
-webkit-box-shadow: 6px 5px 3px hsla(0,0%,0%,.2);
box-shadow: 6px 5px 3px hsla(0,0%,0%,.2);
```

This creates a shadow below the right and bottom edges of the paper (**Figure 3.22**).

FIGURE 3.22 This drop shadow works better, showing on the right side of the div**.**

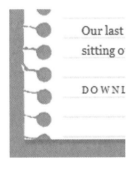

FIGURE 3.23 The drop shadow in Safari or Chrome might show up under an empty hole.

Since Safari and Chrome don't support round for the repeat value on the border image, it's possible to get a cut-off hole at the bottom of the paper, making the shadow underneath it look a little strange (**Figure 3.23**). It's not very noticeable, but if this really bothers you, remove the -webkit-box-shadow declaration. (Sometimes it's nice having each browser declared separately, isn't it!)

Of course, now the drop shadow will be gone in Webkit-based browsers. To create a drop shadow in Safari and Chrome without using -webkit-box-shadow, you could create an image of a shadow and apply it as a border image to the right and bottom borders, using the -webkit-border-image property.

Embedding Unique Fonts

We've done a lot of work on the background of the article so far. Now let's apply some extra styling to the actual content. We can use @font-face rules to make the headings look like they are handwritten—and this trick even lets IE in on the fun.

What is @font-face?

The @font-face rule is a way of linking to fonts on your server (just as you can link to images) that the browser downloads into its cache and uses to style the text on the page. It's often called *font embedding* (though the fonts aren't truly embedded anywhere), and the fonts that are "embedded" are called *web fonts*.

The @font-face rule was actually part of CSS 2 back in 1998, but was removed from the CSS 2.1 specification. It's now back, in CSS3, and finally has widespread browser support.

Until now, without web fonts, web designers have been limited to the small handful of common fonts installed on all users' computers, called *web-safe fonts*. Designers who didn't want to use just Arial, Verdana, or Georgia (among a few more) would have to resort to images, Flash, or scripting to create their text using unique fonts. These font-replacement techniques all suffer from accessibility and usability problems to varying degrees. They're also much more work-intensive to implement and maintain, and they can degrade the performance of your pages.

Using @font-face, on the other hand, keeps real text in the page. You don't have to depend on the user having the Flash plugin installed or JavaScript operating. You don't have to create any images or scripts, and your users don't have to download them. The work involved to implement it can be as simple as writing CSS like this:

```
@font-face {
    font-family: Raleway;
    src: url(fonts/raleway_thin.otf);
}
h1 {
    font-family: Raleway, "HelveticaNeueLt Std Thin",
    ¬"Helvetica Neue Light", "HelveticaNeue-Light",
    ¬"Helvetica Neue", Helvetica, Arial, sans-serif;
}
```

This tells the browser to use the raleway_thin.otf font file to render the text inside the h1 element (**Figure 3.24**). If the user's browser doesn't support @font-face or can't download the file for some reason, the browser simply works through the font stack for a fallback. The *font stack* is the list of fonts declared in the font-family property, which the browser tries to load from the user's machine, in order, until it finds a font it can use.

NOTE: For the considerations that should go into crafting a good font stack, as well as many links to proven font stacks and other resources, see http://nicewebtype.com/notes/2009/04/23/css-font-stacks.

> Always do right.
> This will gratify
> some people, and
> astonish the rest.
>
> - MARK TWAIN

As you might have suspected, however, using `@font-face` is more complicated in the real world.

Choosing Acceptable Fonts

One of the big issues with web fonts is that not every font ought to be used in web pages. Some fonts have licensing restrictions that forbid such a use, while others simply don't look good on the web.

LICENSING ISSUES

When choosing a font to use, read its license—often called an end-user license agreement (EULA) or terms of use—to see if it allows web font embedding. Many fonts' licenses don't, because when you use `@font-face`, the font file is downloaded into the user's cache, just like images. The user could go into her cache, take the font file, and install it on her system. Most font vendors are not interested in simply giving their products away to the thousands of people who browse your web site.

Of course, not many users are really going to go to this trouble. But Richard Fink describes the bigger problem font vendors have with font embedding in his article "Web Fonts at the Crossing" (www.alistapart.com/articles/fonts-at-the-crossing):

> The fear is that once fonts are on the web, they will become a commodity, the current model will break, and a devaluation of fonts, in general, will occur. The fear is that font designers will no longer be able to charge a print customer, say, $420 for a four-style font family with a 6–10 user license in a world where fonts are being delivered on web sites to virtually unlimited numbers of "users" who don't have to pay anything at all. What if the web drives down prices in the print sector and doesn't generate much revenue on its own?

Unfortunately, most fonts' licenses were not written with `@font-face` in mind, so when you read through a font's license, it may not say anything about not embedding fonts. Lack of a restriction doesn't mean you have a free pass to use the font. It's best to err on the side of caution and not use the font unless it explicitly says that web embedding or redistribution is OK.

This is the case even with free fonts. Just because the font vendor gave you the font for free doesn't mean you can redistribute it. Same thing with the fonts that came with your computer. Again, you have to check the license to be sure.

Luckily, there are many places online to find fonts whose licenses allow web font embedding:

NOTE: Although you still ought to look at each font's license to be sure, a general guide as to which foundries allow font embedding and font replacement methods is available at http://webfonts.info/wiki/index.php?title=Web_fonts_licensing_overview.

◆ **The League of Moveable Type** (www.theleagueofmoveabletype.com) is a small but growing collection of free, open-source fonts that are specifically provided for `@font-face` use. The Raleway font used in Figure 3.24 is one of these fonts.

◆ The Webfonts.info wiki has a page called **"Fonts available for @font-face embedding"** (http://webfonts.info/wiki/index.php?title=Fonts_available_for_%40font-face_embedding) that lists fonts (mostly free) whose licenses permit embedding. But like most wiki pages, it's not always as up-to-date and comprehensive as it could be.

◆ **Font Squirrel** (www.fontsquirrel.com) provides a large collection of free fonts whose licenses allow embedding. It also provides some handy tools for working with `@font-face`, as we'll talk about in a bit.

◆ Google has a library of free fonts for embedding called **Google Font Directory** (http://code.google.com/webfonts). You link to one of the fonts on their server using the Google Fonts API, which has a number of advantages (see http://mindgarden.de/benefit-of-the-google-font-api). But you can also download the fonts at http://code.google.com/p/googlefontdirectory/source/browse and host them yourself.

◆ Most of the fonts available at **Kernest** (www.kernest.com) are free, and all are specifically provided for `@font-face` use. Some are hosted by Kernest, but most you can download and host yourself.

◆ **exljbris** (www.josbuivenga.demon.nl) and **Fontfabric** (http://fontfabric.com) both provide a number of fonts for free that can be embedded on the web, as long as you provide attribution according to the terms in the EULAs.

NOTE: As you can imagine, the list of resources shown here is likely to change and grow. To see the most up-to-date list of web font sources, go to www.stunningcss3.com/resources.

- All of the fonts at **Fonthead** (www.fonthead.com) are allowed to be used with `@font-face` as well as other text replacement methods.

- **FontSpring** (www.fontspring.com/fontface) sells fonts that can be used both in a traditional way on your computer and in print work, as well as embedded on the web with `@font-face`.

- FontShop has created web versions of several fonts, called **Web FontFonts** (www.fontshop.com/fontlist/n/web_fontfonts), that you can buy separately from the traditional versions.

LETTING OTHERS DO THE HEAVY LIFTING

All the sources I listed for `@font-face`-ready fonts are places where you can download fonts to host on your own servers and then do the coding yourself. Another option is to let others do all this work for you using a font-embedding service, also called a type delivery service or font hosting and obfuscation service (FHOS).

These services offer a collection of fonts that their distributors have approved for web use through the service, getting around the licensing issues of `@font-face`. These fonts are hosted by the service, making them difficult or impossible to download and redistribute.

Font-embedding services are easy to use because they provide all the different font file formats needed for different browsers, as well as the code for you to add the fonts to your sites. This code may include JavaScript in addition to CSS in order to make the real fonts impossible to reuse or speed up their rendering. Most of these services are not free, though some have free options, and the pricing models vary, such as subscribing to a collection or paying per font and per site.

These services are popping up all over the place—many type vendors are creating their own services for their fonts only—but here are the major players:

- Typekit (http://typekit.com) is a subscription-based service where you pay yearly for access to a collection of fonts, which come from multiple foundries. The smallest collection is free, but has other use restrictions.

◆ Fontdeck (http://fontdeck.com) is a subscription-based service, but you pay for each font you want per year and per site, instead of paying a yearly fee for a collection of fonts. The fonts come from multiple foundries.

◆ Kernest (www.kernest.com) has a subscription model similar to Fontdeck, but nearly all of the fonts are free. The fonts come from multiple foundries. Some are hosted by Kernest, and most you can download and host yourself.

◆ Ascender offers two services: Web Fonts from Ascender (www.ascenderfonts.com/webfonts) and FontsLive (www.fontslive.com). Both have a subscription model similar to Fontdeck, and the fonts come from multiple foundries.

◆ WebINK (www.extensis.com/en/WebINK) has a subscription model similar to Typekit, but you pay a monthly fee based on the fonts' pricing tier and your bandwidth usage. The fonts come from multiple foundries.

◆ Webtype (www.webtype.com) has a subscription model similar to Fontdeck, but pricing varies based on the bandwidth you use. The fonts come from multiple foundries. You can also purchase traditional versions of the fonts to download and use on your desktop.

◆ Typotheque (www.typotheque.com/webfonts) offers a service for fonts from only its foundry, where you pay a one-time fee per font.

◆ Just Another Foundry (http://justanotherfoundry.com/webfonts) also offers a service for fonts from its foundry only, but you pay a yearly subscription fee.

◆ Fonts.com Web Fonts (http://webfonts.fonts.com) has a subscription model similar to Typekit, but you pay monthly. The highest-priced plan allows you to also download fonts to use on your desktop, but you can use the installed font only so long as it's being used in a web site through their service.

If you're thinking about using one of these services, read and use the list of buyer considerations at the end of the article "Web Fonts at the Crossing" at www.alistapart.com/articles/fonts-at-the-crossing before choosing. To see the most up-to-date list of font-embedding services, go to www.stunningcss3.com/resources.

READABILITY AND RENDERING ISSUES

Once you've cleared the licensing hurdle, don't go crazy and start loading up your pages with all sorts of bizarre fonts. Every time you choose to use a web font, have a specific reason for picking that font, beyond just that it looks cool. Make sure that the font truly enhances the text and doesn't make it less readable.

TIP: The Soma FontFriend bookmarklet (http://somadesign. ca/projects/fontfriend) lets you easily test out the fonts in your font stacks, including web fonts, so you can quickly see how each one will look on your page.

Test your web fonts with your actual content to make sure they will work. The Raleway font shown in Figure 3.24 might work well for large headings but be too thin to render well and be readable for body copy. Most commercial fonts were not designed to be viewed at small sizes on a screen, so in many cases it makes the most sense to reserve `@font-face` for headings and continue to use web-safe fonts like Georgia and Lucida for body copy.

Another aspect of web fonts that can affect legibility is how they are anti-aliased and hinted. Right now, web fonts are generally more jagged around the edges than traditional fonts, even when anti-aliased, usually because most were not designed to be viewed on screen. Higher quality fonts, as well as fonts that were designed for the web, have better *hinting*, which, in a nutshell, is a set of instructions in the font file that adjusts the edges of the characters to line up better with the pixel grids of our computer screens so they look better to the human eye. Font format plays a role in this too; TrueType fonts are generally better hinted than OpenType CFF fonts. The degree of jaggedness depends not only on the font but on the operating system and sometimes the browser; Mac is generally smoother than Windows, but can look blurry. Windows XP in particular can look quite bad if the user hasn't enabled ClearType (Microsoft's current technology for improving text rendering on screen).

NOTE: It's possible to force differently sized fonts to match up in size using the `font-size-adjust` property, but currently only Firefox supports it. See http:// webdesignernotebook. com/css/the-little-known-font-size-adjust-css3-property, as well as the links at the end of the article, for more information.

Not only is the readability of your web fonts important, but so too is the readability of the fallback fonts in your font stacks. Make sure to test the fallback fonts so that if the web font doesn't load, the user still gets readable and attractive text. You usually want to choose fallback fonts that have similar proportions to the web font you're putting at the front of your font stack. That way, the font size, weight, and other styles you apply to the text will work well with whatever font the user sees.

MORE ON FONT HINTING AND ANTI-ALIASING

Font hinting and anti-aliasing is a big, technical topic beyond the scope of this book, but if you'd like to learn more about it, check out these articles:

- "The Ails Of Typographic Anti-Aliasing" by Thomas Giannattasio (www.smashingmagazine.com/2009/11/02/the-ails-of-typographic-anti-aliasing) gives a good overview of anti-aliasing, hinting, sub-pixel rendering, and how various operating systems and browsers handle rendering web fonts.

- "Font Hinting Explained By A Font Design Master" by Richard Fink (http://readableweb.com/font-hinting-explained-by-a-font-design-master) and "Font Hinting" by Peter Bil'ak (www.typotheque.com/articles/hinting) give more detail on how hinting works.

- "Font smoothing, anti-aliasing, and sub-pixel rendering" by Joel Spolsky (www.joelonsoftware.com/items/2007/06/12.html) compares Apple and Microsoft's methods for smoothing on-screen text.

- "Browser Choice vs Font Rendering" by Thomas Phinney (www.thomasphinney.com/2009/12/browser-choice-vs-font-rendering) explains how browsers' text rendering is dependent on the operating system.

- Webkit-based browsers let you control the anti-aliasing mode using their proprietary `-webkit-font-smoothing` property. See "-webkit-font-smoothing" by Tim Van Damme (http://maxvoltar.com/archive/-webkit-font-smoothing) for examples and "Font Smoothing" by Dmitry Fadeyev (www.usabilitypost.com/2010/08/26/font-smoothing) for an argument against the property.

NOTE: Luckily, web font rendering is improving. For instance, IE 9 uses Microsoft's DirectWrite API to handle text rendering, making web fonts look very smooth; Firefox has said it will use DirectWrite in its Windows versions as well. Also, more and more font vendors are now selling web fonts, so as `@font-face` grows in popularity we will undoubtedly see more fonts for sale that are hinted aggressively for web use.

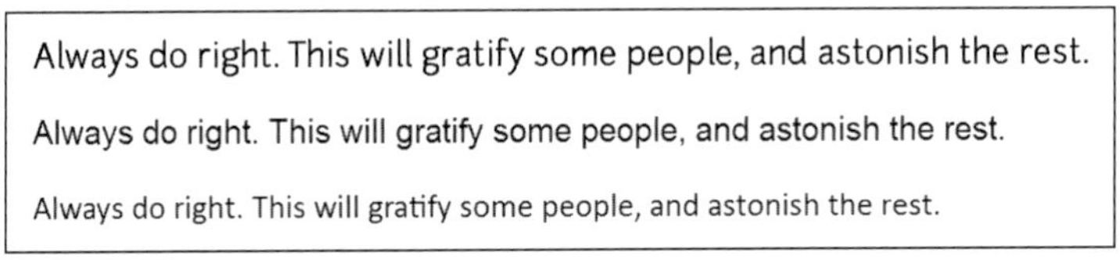

FIGURE 3.25 **Arial
(center) and Calibri
(bottom) are too small
to be the best fall-
backs for the Junction
(top) web font.**

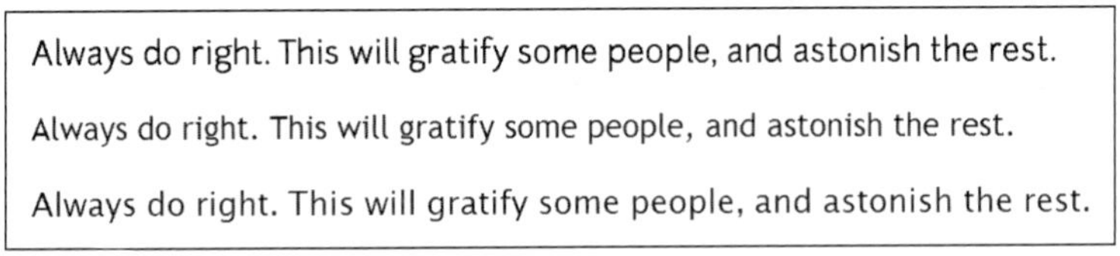

Always do right. This will gratify some people, and astonish the rest.

Always do right. This will gratify some people, and astonish the rest.

Always do right. This will gratify some people, and astonish the rest.

FIGURE 3.26
**Trebuchet MS matches
up well with Junction,
with Lucida Sans
Unicode being a
good runner-up.**

Always do right. This will gratify some people, and astonish the rest.

Always do right. This will gratify some people, and astonish the rest.

Always do right. This will gratify some people, and astonish the rest.

Browser Support

So once you've chosen a font that has the correct license and is legible on the web, all you need to do is link to it in an `@font-face` rule as shown earlier and you're done, right? Well, not quite. The `@font-face` rule has good browser support, but different browsers want you to use different font file types.

TrueType (TTF) and OpenType (OTF) font files, such as the ones you probably already have on your computer, work in most browsers.

IE supports `@font-face` as far back as version 4, but IE 4 through 8 support it only if you use a proprietary font format called Embedded OpenType (EOT). EOT is technically not a font format; it's a compressed copy of a TTF font that uses digital rights management (DRM) to keep the font from being reused.

NOTE: For more information on SVG fonts, see "About Fonts in SVG" by Divya Manian (http://nimbupani.com/about-fonts-in-svg.html).

The only type of font file that works on Safari on iOS (the browser on the iPhone, iPod Touch, and iPad, and often called "Mobile Safari") is SVG (Scalable Vector Graphics). SVG also works on Chrome, desktop Safari, and Opera, but not Firefox. You're probably most familiar with SVG as a vector graphics format, but an SVG file can contain font information too—after all, each character in a font is really just a vector drawing.

Using these three formats—TTF or OTF, EOT, and SVG—will make your unique fonts show up in every browser that supports `@font-face`. But you should also include a fourth format, WOFF, for future compatibility.

NOTE: Learn more about WOFF at www.w3.org/Fonts/WOFF-FAQ.

WOFF, which stands for Web Open Font Format, was introduced in 2009. Like EOT, WOFF is not technically a font format, but rather a compressed wrapper for delivering TTF or OTF fonts. Unlike EOT, however, WOFF contains no DRM. So far, the only browsers that support WOFF are Firefox 3.6 and later, Chrome 6, and IE 9, but the other major browsers are all working on adding support for it, and many font vendors have also expressed support. The WOFF specification became a W3C working draft in July 2010, so it's now officially on its way to becoming the standard web font format. Going forward, it's the one to use.

But don't get too overwhelmed by all these acronyms and browsers. As you'll learn in the next section, it's easy to create all the different formats you need. Check out Table 3.5 for a summary of which browsers support which font types.

NOTE: The compression in EOT and WOFF files is lossless. These fonts should look just as good as their TTF or OTF originals.

NOTE: This is a rapidly changing area of CSS support. See http:// webfonts.info/wiki/ index.php?title=%40font-face_browser_support and www.stunningcss3.com/resources for the latest information.

TABLE 3.5 @font-face **file types browser support**

	WOFF	OTF	TTF	SVG	EOT
IE	9	no	9	no	4
Firefox	3.6	3.5	3.5	no	no
Opera	no	10	10	10	no
Opera Mobile	no	9.7	9.7	9.7	no
Safari	no	3.1	3.1	3.1	no
Chrome	6	4*	4*	0.3	no
Safari on iOS	no	no	no	3.1	no

* Chrome 3 supported OTF and TTF fonts, but not by default—you had to do a command-line switch to enable it.

Each browser version number noted in Table 3.5 is the earliest—not the only—version of that browser to support that type.

Converting Fonts

Some providers of @font-face-ready fonts supply you with all the different font formats you need for the different browsers. For instance, Font Squirrel offers something they call "@font-face kits," each of which includes the original TTF or OTF font, an SVG version, a WOFF version, an EOT version, and a sample style sheet and HTML page showing the @font-face rules you need to place in your CSS. You can download these kits at www.fontsquirrel.com/fontface.

Even better is Font Squirrel's @font-face Kit Generator (www. fontsquirrel.com/fontface/generator). You can upload your font and convert it to whichever formats you wish. You can also control the CSS syntax it outputs, subset the characters to reduce file size, and use more options to fine-tune the fonts (**Figure 3.27**).

FIGURE 3.27
Font Squirrel's
@font-face Kit
Generator

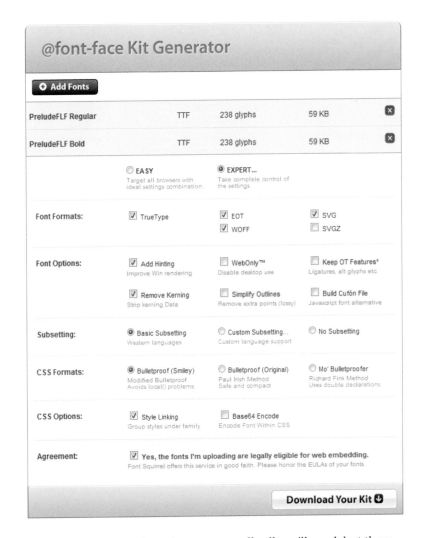

The files Font Squirrel produces are usually all you'll need, but there are a couple of other tools worth mentioning that will optimize your EOT and SVG files even further. EOTFAST is free desktop software (download at http://eotfast.com) that converts TTF files into compressed but lossless EOT files; the EOT files that Font Squirrel produces are not compressed. The command-line tool ttf2svg (http://xmlgraphics.apache.org/batik/tools/font-converter.html) converts TTF files into same size or smaller SVG files; you need to have Java and the Java SVG toolkit Batik installed on your system to run it.

Using @font-face

Let's finally put @font-face to use in our page. Since it looks like note-book paper, a font that simulates handwriting seems appropriate. I picked Prelude, a casual cursive font, for the headings (**Figure 3.28**). We're not going to apply a casual cursive font to the body copy, how-ever, as that kind of font at small sizes doesn't look very good and decreases legibility.

FIGURE 3.28
The Prelude font on
the Font Squirrel site

In the exercise files for this chapter, you'll find a folder named "fonts" that contains all the eight versions of Prelude that we'll need for our page: EOT, SVG, TTF, and WOFF files for both the regular and bold weight of the font. I created these versions using Font Squirrel's Generator tool, using the set-tings shown in Figure 3.27. I then remade the EOT files using EOTFAST to cut the file size of each EOT roughly in half.

LINKING TO THE FONTS WITH THE @font-face RULES

You may notice in Figure 3.27 that there are three choices in the Font Squirrel Generator for CSS Formats. These refer to three variations of the @font-face syntax used in the CSS. As with almost everything in CSS, there are multiple ways to code @font-face to get the same effect; all three syntaxes use valid, standards-compliant CSS and will work in the same browsers.

The rationale behind each of these three syntaxes is too complicated to fully explain here, and not terribly important. Any of the three will work for our purposes, and the choice really boils down to personal preference. My preference is the "Bulletproof Smiley" version.

Here's what the Bulletproof Smiley syntax for the Prelude font looks like:

> **NOTE:** If you want the details, click the blue links under each CSS format name in the Font Squirrel Generator to read the three articles explaining all the whys and hows.

```
@font-face {
    font-family: 'Prelude';
    src: url('fonts/preludeflf-webfont.eot');
    src: local('☺'),
        url('fonts/preludeflf-webfont.woff') format('woff'),
        url('fonts/preludeflf-webfont.ttf')
        ¬format('truetype'),
        url('fonts/preludeflf-webfont.svg#webfont')
        ¬format('svg');
}
@font-face {
    font-family: 'Prelude';
    src: url('fonts/preludeflf-bold-webfont.eot');
    src: local('☺'),
        url('fonts/preludeflf-bold-webfont.woff')
        ¬format('woff'),
        url('fonts/preludeflf-bold-webfont.ttf')
        ¬format('truetype'),
        url('fonts/preludeflf-bold-webfont.svg#webfont')
        ¬format('svg');
    font-weight: bold;
}
```

Put this Bulletproof Smiley syntax before any of the other CSS rules; it will work anywhere you put it, but you'll learn later in the chapter how putting it at the top of your styles can improve your page's performance." You can copy and paste it from paper_final.html in the exercise files.

These two `@font-face` rules group the regular and bold font faces into a single font family by declaring them with the same `font-family` name, Prelude. Each `@font-face` rule gives the path to the font files and, optionally, the style characteristics of an individual face (such as `font-weight: bold` or `font-style: italic`).

Let's look at just the first `@font-face` rule for now and go through it line by line.

The first part of the rule—`font-family: 'Prelude';`—assigns a name to the font you're linking to so that you can later refer to this font in your font stacks. You can make the name whatever you want; it's just a shorthand way of referring to a whole bunch of font information at once.

The second part of the rule—`src: url('fonts/preludeflf-webfont. eot');`—gives the path to the EOT version of the font for IE 8 and earlier. This is separated out from the other versions of the fonts because IE can't understand a `src` descriptor with multiple comma-separated values. It thinks it's one big path, preventing it from noticing the EOT and being able to use it when grouped with the other files.

The next part of the rule is a second `src` value that lists all the font files for non-IE browsers. Each browser will go through the list until it finds a format it can use, and then download that file, and only that file, to display the text. Each font includes a path to the font file, such as `url('fonts/preludeflf-webfont.woff')`, and a format hint, such as `format('woff')`. The format hint is optional, but including it alerts the browsers about the format of each font to keep them from downloading ones they can't use, which would waste bandwidth and slow page loading.

> **NOTE:** There are more nitty-gritty details about how this syntax works in Paul Irish's original article at http:// paulirish.com/2009/ bulletproof-font-face-implementation-syntax. They're not essential to know, but are interesting if you're a web geek like me.

> **NOTE:** The WOFF format is listed first because it's the standard that we want all browsers to use when they can. It's also the smallest file, so you want to make sure browsers that can use it see it first and therefore do use it.

HITTING THE SERVER

All browsers but IE8 and earlier don't actually download any font files until one is called for in a font stack elsewhere in the CSS. So you can declare lots of `@font-face` rules in your style sheet, but if one particular page doesn't have elements that use most of those fonts, for instance, you won't incur the hit of a bunch of extra HTTP requests.

IE8 and earlier, on the other hand, download every EOT file as soon as they encounter it. While you're testing font embedding, it's common to include a lot of extra `@font-face` rules in your style sheet so you can compare fonts. Be sure to remove any `@font-face` rules that you don't end up using so IE 8 and earlier don't download the EOT files unnecessarily.

But you probably noticed that at the start of the second `src` value is `local('☺')`. What in the world does this smiley face do?

The `local('☺')` part of the `src` value is there to protect IE. Without it there, IE would try to read the second `src` descriptor as one big path, as explained earlier, which would lead it to get a 404 error. While this doesn't stop `@font-face` from working—IE can still use the separate EOT—it's an extra, pointless hit on your server that you don't want. IE doesn't understand the `local()` syntax, and putting it at the start of the `src` value stops it from moving any further into the `src` value, seeing the `url()` value, and then trying to parse the path.

PROBLEMS WITH `local()`

Letting users skip downloading a font they already have installed sounds like such a good and helpful idea—so why not put the real font name in `local()` instead of a smiley face character? This is certainly an option. It's what Paul Irish's original "Bulletproof @font-face syntax" did, and you can still choose to download this syntax from the Font Squirrel Generator.

But before you use the real font name in `local()`, you should be aware of a few problems you might run into:

* Different fonts sometimes have the same names. It's possible that the user will end up seeing a completely different font from the one you intend. (See http://typophile.com/node/63992 for a discussion of this.) It's a very small chance, but some argue that, regardless, giving control over type to the user's machine and browser is not wise.

* In Chrome, all characters might be displayed as As in boxes if the local font that you're referring to was installed on the user's system using the font management software FontExplorer X. (Go to http://snook.ca/archives/html_and_css/font-face-in-chrome to see a screenshot of this weirdness.)

* In Safari, the user might get a dialog box asking permission to use the local font if it's being managed by FontExplorer X.

None of these problems are likely to happen very often, but if they do happen, the effect could be pretty bad. Many web font experts recommend never using `local()`, or using it only when the font file you're trying to keep the user from downloading is particularly large.

The local() syntax is perfectly valid CSS, by the way. Its real purpose in a @font-face rule is to point to a locally installed version of the font on the user's machine, so that if the user has the same font as you're embedding, he doesn't have to download the extra file. That's why Paul Irish, who came up with the syntax, recommends using a smiley face: we don't want to call for a font that might actually exist, and it's very unlikely that anyone will ever release a font named ☺.

The second @font-face rule declares the bold versions of the Prelude font family. It gives the paths to all the bold font files and also sets the font-weight to bold inside the rule. But the font-family name is Prelude (not PreludeBold or some other variation), matching the first @font-face rule. Assigning the same name tells the browser that the file is the bold version of the same Prelude font family. Now, any time the browser needs to have bold Prelude text (because of a strong element in the HTML or font-weight: bold in the CSS), it doesn't have to synthesize the boldness by making the characters thicker, but can instead use the true bold font files. Using a true bold or italic font face looks better than having the browser simulate it for you.

NOTE: IE doesn't always handle this font style switching within the @font-face rules correctly. IE 8 and earlier don't use the font when font-style: italic is in the @font-face rule. IE 9 does, but it synthesizes italic rendering anyway, even if the font you're calling isn't actually italic.

DECLARING THE FONT

Adding @font-face rules to your CSS doesn't actually make the fonts show up anywhere; it simply links them, so they're ready to be downloaded and used when you need them. Let's call them up in our h1 and h2 elements. Add Prelude, the name of the font we assigned in the @font-face rule, to the start of the existing font-family values in the h1 and h2 rules:

```
h1 {
    margin: -.3em 0 .14em 0;
    color: #414141;
    font-family: Prelude, Helvetica, "Helvetica Neue",
                 Arial, sans-serif;
    font-size: 3.5em;
    font-weight: normal;
}
h2 {
    clear: left;
    margin: 0 0 -.14em 0;
    color: #414141;
    font-family: Prelude, Helvetica, "Helvetica Neue",
                 Arial, sans-serif;
    font-size: 2.17em;
    font-weight: bold;
}
```

The sans-serif fallback fonts in the font stacks don't look anything like the cursive Prelude script, of course. I chose to do this because there aren't really any cursive web-safe fonts we can rely on as fallbacks. If someone is using a browser that can't do font embedding, I'd rather they see some nice, clean Helvetica or Arial text than whatever random cursive font they might have on their computers.

Note that the h1 rule sets the `font-weight` to `normal` and the h2 rule sets it to `bold`. This tells the browser to use the regular member of the Prelude font family (the first `@font-face` rule) for the h1 elements and the bold member of the Prelude font family (the second `@font-face` rule) for the h2 elements (**Figure 3.29**).

FIGURE 3.29
The cursive Prelude font in the headings on our page

We now have handwritten cursive text showing in our headings that is resizable, selectable, and indexable. There are differences in the anti-aliasing and hinting of the text between browsers and between Windows and Mac, but the advantages of real text outweigh the inconvenience of its slight jaggedness in some browsers (**Figure 3.30**).

TABLE 3.6 `@font-face` **browser support**

IE	FIREFOX	OPERA	SAFARI	CHROME
Yes	Yes, 3.5+	Yes, 10+	Yes	Yes

England Trip 2007

In May and June 2007, Cary and I spent 15 days travelin
to Europe. We had very briefly been out of the USA the y
Vermont vacation, but this was our first significant out-o

The trip was heavily focused around Jane Austen sites, b
Prejudice. You see, I am an unapologetic Janeite, and I h

Itinerary

The trip began on May 19, 2007, when we flew into the M

England Trip 2007

In May and June 2007, Cary and I spent 15 days traveling
Europe. We had very briefly been out of the USA the year
vacation, but this was our first significant out-of-country

The trip was heavily focused around Jane Austen sites, bc
You see, I am an unapologetic Janeite, and I have a very u

Itinerary

The trip began on May 19, 2007, when we flew into the M

FIGURE 3.30 Different platforms and browsers, such as Firefox 3.6 (left) and IE 9 (right), display the anti-aliasing of the headings differently.

THE LOWDOWN ON THE @font-face RULE

The @font-face rule is part of the Fonts module, found at www. w3.org/TR/css3-fonts.

A @font-face rule gives a font family name (using the font-family descriptor) that you make up and the path to one or more font files (using the src descriptor). Optionally, it can also include the style characteristics of an individual face (using font-weight, font-style, and font-stretch). You can use multiple @font-face rules with the same font-family name to group faces into one family.

To access the fonts in your @font-face rules, simply add each font family name to your font stacks in the font-family property.

Other than making text look like handwriting, you might want to use @font-face for:

◆ Creating a look and feel not possible with standard web-safe fonts

◆ Keeping branding consistent between printed materials (such as a logo or brochure) and their related web site

◆ Displaying text using non-Latin characters, which often don't render well in browser default fonts. Using a font designed for the language ensures all the characters display correctly.

A tempting use of @font-face is to use dingbat fonts to create icons without images. But this has serious accessibility problems. See http:// filamentgroup.com/lab/dingbat_webfonts_accessibility_issues and http://jontangerine.com/log/2010/08/web-fonts-dingbats-icons-and- unicode for a discussion of the problems and potential solutions.

IMPROVING PERFORMANCE

If you view your page in a browser now, you may notice a lag between when most of the page loads and when the handwritten font displays. Webkit-based browsers don't show the `@font-face`-styled text until they've finished downloading the font file (**Figure 3.31**).

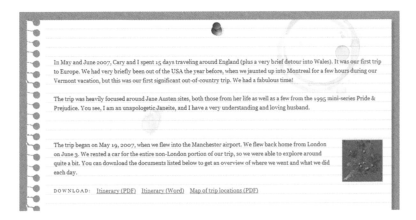

In Firefox and Opera, the fallback fonts show for a moment while the font file is downloaded, and then the browser re-renders the text with the new font. This is called the Flash of Unstyled Text, or FOUT, a term quippishly coined by Paul Irish.

These font-loading lags are usually a minor annoyance, but in some cases they can be quite noticeable and problematic. Fonts for non-Western languages, such as Chinese and Japanese, can contain thousands of characters and be several megabytes in size; these huge font files take a long time to download, of course. Also, users on mobile devices in areas with poor coverage, or at hotels with notoriously slow connection speeds, may be left waiting for the web fonts to appear for quite a while.

TIP: The font-size-adjust property, mentioned earlier, doesn't lessen the FOUT, but it makes it less noticeable because it makes the size of the fallback font match up better with the web font. Again, though, it works only in Firefox.

There are a number of things you can do to minimize or do away with the FOUT or the invisible text problem in Webkit:

♦ Keep your font file sizes as small as possible to begin with. Subsetting the characters within each font to include only the characters that you need can really help in this regard; the Font Squirrel Generator lets you do this.

♦ Put your `@font-face` rules at the top of your style sheets. This increases the chance that the browser will download them before the other files called for in your CSS, such as background images.

◆ Get the browser to download the font file as soon as possible by, for instance, calling it on a hidden element at the very start of your page. You can adapt many image preloading techniques, such as the many listed at http://perishablepress.com/press/tag/preload-images, to work with font files.

◆ Host your fonts elsewhere. By serving your fonts from one common location, you increase the chance that the visitor already has the font file in his or her cache, instead of having to download the same exact font file again from a new location. The font-embedding services listed earlier allow you to do this, as does Google's Font Directory, but you can also upload fonts you personally own to the TypeFront service (http://typefront.com). TypeFront hosts the fonts you give it, converts them to all the needed formats, and serves them only to the sites you specify.

◆ Set the Expires header in .htaccess to a date far in the future so that when a font is downloaded once, it's cached by the browser and not requested again for a very long time. This doesn't help with the initial page load when the browser first downloads the font, but it should help on subsequent loads. (See "HTTP Caching" by Steve Lamm at http://code.google.com/speed/articles/caching.html for more information.)

◆ Gzip your font files. Stoyan Stefanov found average file-size savings to be from 40 to 45 percent (see www.phpied.com/gzip-your-font-face-files). But he also found that this doesn't really help WOFF files, which are already very compressed, so this may not help you much with the FOUT in Firefox (see www.phpied.com/font-face-gzipping-take-ii). However, gzipping should help Opera avoid or minimize the FOUT and Safari and Chrome show the text sooner.

◆ Use scripting to hide all the content for a couple seconds while the browser downloads the fonts. This doesn't actually speed up downloading the fonts, of course, but it keeps the user from ever seeing the FOUT's disorienting shift in fonts. Paul Irish provides two different JavaScript options to do this, one of which uses Google's WebFont Loader JavaScript library (http://paulirish.com/2009/fighting-the-font-face-fout).

Our font files already use a subset of all characters and are called at the top of the CSS, so we've covered the most basic `@font-face` performance best practices. It's beyond the scope of this book to add any of the scripting or server-side techniques to our page, but this gives you a number of things to try if you're having trouble with web font loading times.

The Finished Page

We've completed all the styling for the article to make it look like a piece of notebook paper. In any up-to-date, non-IE browser, you should see something like **Figure 3.32**. Compare it to Figure 3.1.

FIGURE 3.32
The page with all CSS3 applied, shown here in Firefox 3.6.

England Trip 2007

In May and June 2007, Cary and I spent 15 days traveling around England (plus a very brief detour into Wales). It was our first trip to Europe. We had very briefly been out of the USA the year before, when we jaunted up into Montreal for a few hours during our Vermont vacation, but this was our first significant out-of-country trip. We had a fabulous time!

The trip was heavily focused around Jane Austen sites, both those from her life as well as a few from the 1995 mini-series Pride & Prejudice. You see, I am an unapologetic Janeite, and I have a very understanding and loving husband.

Itinerary

The trip began on May 19, 2007, when we flew into the Manchester airport. We flew back home from London on June 3. We rented a car for the entire non-London portion of our trip, so we were able to explore around quite a bit. You can download the documents listed below to get an overview of where we went and what we did each day.

DOWNLOAD: Itinerary (PDF)   Itinerary (Word)   Map of trip locations (PDF)

Derbyshire

We visited Derbyshire on the first three days of our trip. We stayed at a B&B called Bassett Wood Farm in the little village of Tissington, where the annual well dressing happened to be occuring at the same time. The landscape of Derbyshire was gorgeous; I can see why Elizabeth Bennet was so impressed. My highlights were visiting the two houses used for Pemberley in the Pride & Prejudice mini-series. I even got to see the little pond where Colin Firth's famous wet shirt scene occurs.

DOWNLOAD: Cary riding a horse for the first time (MOV)
Zoe at Lyme Park   Cary and Zoe in Dovedale Valley
Zoe at Sudbury Hall

Cotswolds

The next seven days were spent traveling all around the Cotswolds and the surrounding area. We stayed at a cottage in the famously picturesque village of Bibury. We explored more than a dozen other Cotswolds villages.

One of our favorite towns in the Cotswolds was Cirencester, because of the great food we had there and the Corinium Museum. The collection of Roman (and earlier) artifacts at the museum was much larger than we expected and quite fascinating.

The more ancient something is, the better Cary loves it, especially if it's all in ruins. So, Cary's highlights in the Cotswolds were not just the Roman museum but also the unearthed Chedworth Roman Villa and the ruins of Minster Lovell Hall. One of our favorite memories from the area was our wet, cold trek to the Belas Knap burial mound, built around 2500 BC. Drying out and warming up in the pub afterwards was lovely, and the whole thing was just so English.

DOWNLOAD: Zoe and Cary in a field of sheep   Zoe in Bibury   Cary at Minster Lovell Hall

Day-trips from the Cotswolds

While staying in Bibury, we took a couple trips out of the Cotswolds proper.

One day-trip was to Bath to see the Jane Austen sites and, of course, the Roman Baths (which are also Jane Austen related, incidentally). On the way back from Bath, we stopped at the village of Lacock, which was used for Meryton in the Pride & Prejudice mini-series (along with a bunch of other movies).

Another day-trip took us into Wales to see the ruins of Chepstow Castle. This was one of Cary's highlights during the trip. It was very large and quite impressive. On the way to Wales, we successfully hunted down the private

The preview version of IE 9 doesn't show the torn paper edge, but otherwise looks like Figure 3.32. IE 8 and earlier are missing most of the graphic effects, but since they show the lined background image and the handwritten font, the overall appearance is still attractive and notebook-paper-like (**Figure 3.33**). Also, in this case, all versions of IE up to 8 display almost identically—even 5.5 looks like the screenshot shown in Figure 3.33.

NOTE: The completed page showing all of these effects is named paper_final.html in the exercise files for this chapter.

FIGURE 3.33
IE (version 8 shown here) doesn't show all the CSS3 graphic effects, but does show the handwritten fonts.

England Trip 2007

In May and June 2007, Cary and I spent 15 days traveling around England (plus a very brief detour into Wales). It was our first trip to Europe. We had very briefly been out of the USA the year before, when we jaunted up into Montreal for a few hours during our Vermont vacation, but this was our first significant out-of-country trip. We had a fabulous time!

The trip was heavily focused around Jane Austen sites, both those from her life as well as a few from the 1995 mini-series Pride & Prejudice. You see, I am an unapologetic Janeite, and I have a very understanding and loving husband.

Itinerary

The trip began on May 19, 2007, when we flew into the Manchester airport. We flew back home from London on June 3. We rented a car for the entire non-London portion of our trip, so we were able to explore around quite a bit. You can download the documents listed below to get an overview of where we went and what we did each day.

DOWNLOAD: Itinerary (PDF)   Itinerary (Word)   Map of trip locations (PDF)

Derbyshire

We visited Derbyshire on the first three days of our trip. We stayed at a B&B called Bassett Wood Farm in the little village of Tissington, where the annual well dressing happened to be occuring at the same time. The landscape of Derbyshire was gorgeous; I can see why Elizabeth Bennet was so impressed. My highlights were visiting the two houses used for Pemberley in the Pride & Prejudice mini-series. I even got to see the little pond where Colin Firth's famous wet shirt scene occurs.

DOWNLOAD: Cary riding a horse for the first time (MOV)   Zoe at Lyme Park
Cary and Zoe in Dovedale Valley   Zoe at Sudbury Hall

Cotswolds

The next seven days were spent traveling all around the Cotswolds and the surrounding area. We stayed at a cottage in the famously picturesque village of Bibury. We explored more than a dozen other Cotswolds villages.

One of our favorite towns in the Cotswolds was Cirencester, because of the great food we had there and the Corinium Museum. The collection of Roman (and earlier) artifacts at the museum was much larger than we expected and quite fascinating.

The more ancient something is, the better Cary loves it, especially if it's all in ruins. So, Cary's highlights in the Cotswolds were not just the Roman museum but also the unearthed Chedworth Roman Villa and the ruins of Minster Lovell Hall. One of our favorite memories from the area was our wet, cold trek to the Belas Knap burial mound, built around 2500 BC. Drying out and warming up in the pub afterwards was lovely, and the whole thing was just so English.

DOWNLOAD: Zoe and Cary in a field of sheep   Zoe in Bibury   Cary at Minster Lovell Hall

Styling Images and Links by Type

There's hardly a page on the web that doesn't have several links and images on it. Those links might target several different types of documents besides other web pages, such as PDFs or video files. Those images might be of several different types, like photos, illustrations, and charts. Styling images and links based on their unique type is quite possible without CSS3, but involves more time, work, and markup. New selectors in CSS3 allow you to target each link or image type individually in a more specific, streamlined way. Once again, CSS3 comes to the rescue to improve the efficiency of both your development habits and your pages.

The Base Page

The page that we'll be using as our starting point is the finished page from Chapter 3 (**Figure 4.1**). It contains a lot of links to different types of files, but all of these links are styled the same right now. It would be nice if links to certain file types were styled differently, to give the user a visual cue to the type of document they're about to open. The page also contains several images, most of which are photos, but one of which is a thumbnail of a map. Again, it would be nice to style photos differently than other images, but right now all these images are styled the same way.

FIGURE 4.1 All of the links are styled the same as each other, as are all of the images.

What are Attribute Selectors?

We can add type-based styling to the links and images using *attribute selectors*. Attribute selectors are so powerful and useful because they allow you to target specific elements without needing IDs or classes in the HTML. Instead, attribute selectors target an element based on the existence or value of a specific attribute on that element.

For instance, the selector `img[alt]` is made up of the type selector `img` followed by the attribute selector `[alt]`. All attribute selectors are designated by square brackets, but what goes in the brackets depends on what you're trying to target. The `img[alt]` selector targets all `img` elements that have an `alt` attribute present. Using this selector while testing your pages, you could give all images that have `alt` attributes a bright green outline, so you could see at a glance which images don't have the outline and need `alt` attributes added.

```
img[alt] {
    border: 3px solid #0C0;
}
<img src="photos/poe.jpg" width="320" height="241"
¬alt="My cat Poe">
<img src="photos/dog.jpg" width="320" height="240">
```

NOTE: An attribute selector doesn't have to be used in conjunction with only type selectors. You can use it with any type of simple selector. For instance, `.warning[title]` combines a class selector with an attribute selector. You can also use it by itself; a selector of `[title]` would select every single element that has a title attribute on it.

Lorem ipsum dolor sit amet, consectetur adipiscing elit. Suspendisse id neque elit. Vestibulum sodales, eros nec mattis auctor, ligula nunc facilisis arcu, eget ultricies nulla dui ac est. Vestibulum in placerat nibh. Proin vel pharetra orci. Sed dictum lectus a eros hendrerit blandit. Fusce aliquam bibendum mollis. Cum sociis natoque penatibus et magnis dis parturient montes, nascetur ridiculus mus. Suspendisse ut eros tortor. Suspendisse pulvinar augue vel ipsum facilisis vel volutpat est pretium. Donec vel leo enim. Curabitur quis tincidunt orci. Sed tempor porta erat ac malesuada. Curabitur faucibus, dui ut condimentum volutpat, odio massa sodales massa, a laoreet sem ante vitae nisl. Quisque sollicitudin, tellus nec consequat vulputate, arcu elit blandit mauris, eu congue massa diam eu lectus. Vivamus hendrerit lacus sed tortor cursus fringilla.

Duis non ante a mi feugiat ullamcorper. Morbi pharetra quam in justo pretium feugiat. Aenean ut turpis ut nulla pellentesque ultrices aliquet sed leo. Nunc accumsan eros at justo interdum lobortis scelerisque odio imperdiet. Nunc at risus magna. Maecenas non mauris eget dui accumsan porta. Curabitur nec erat urna. Nulla facilisi. Donec elementum mattis augue, a bibendum lorem viverra sit amet. Nam non ipsum vel velit pretium mattis. Nam a risus nulla, et condimentum tellus.

Sed varius quam sed ligula tempor euismod. Donec et felis leo, ac fringilla nibh. Fusce vestibulum tincidunt consequat. Pellentesque pretium tincidunt velit, consectetur consequat sapien viverra nec. Suspendisse a enim id est tempor sollicitudin sed non diam. Aliquam porttitor rhoncus felis sit amet fringilla. Integer consequat gravida condimentum. Praesent quis leo nec nulla volutpat viverra sit amet id est. Sed

FIGURE 4.2 The image of the cat has an `alt` **attribute on its** `img` **element, so it has a green outline. The image of the dog doesn't have an** `alt` **attribute.**

The img[alt] selector is an example of the simplest type of attribute selector—one that checks only for the presence of an attribute, regardless of its value. It's one of the four types of attribute selectors that are in the CSS 2.1 spec (which are shown in Table 4.1).

TABLE 4.1 CSS 2.1 Attribute Selectors

ATTRIBUTE SELECTOR	FUNCTION
[attr]	Matches an element with an attr attribute present, regardless of its value.
[attr=val]	Matches an element with an attr attribute whose value is exactly val.
[attr~=val]	Matches an element with an attr attribute whose value is a space-separated list of words, one of which is exactly val.
[attr|=val]	Matches an element with an attr attribute whose value is either exactly val or begins with val immediately followed by a hyphen.

The W3C calls these CSS 2.1 attribute selectors *attribute presence and value selectors*.

CSS3 introduces three new attribute selectors that offer even more fine-grained control over what you're trying to target.

TABLE 4.2 CSS3 Attribute Selectors

ATTRIBUTE SELECTOR	FUNCTION
[attr^=val]	Matches an element with an attr attribute whose value starts with val.
[attr$=val]	Matches an element with an attr attribute whose value ends with val.
[attr*=val]	Matches an element with an attr attribute whose value contains val somewhere within it.

The W3C calls these CSS3 attribute selectors *substring matching attribute selectors* because they match a part of a value instead of the whole thing.

Attribute selectors are easiest to understand with live examples, so let's add them to our page now to see how they work and start getting ideas for what their practical uses might be.

TIP: If you start getting confused when writing a complex selector, plug it into the SelectORacle at http://gallery.theopalgroup.com/selectoracle for a plain English (or Spanish) translation of what the selector will target.

NOT MATCHING

A really handy attribute selector to have would be one for "not match-ing" that could style all the elements that don't match the value given. For instance, you could use it to create a rule that says "find all `input` elements that don't have the `type` attribute set to `submit`," in order to target and style all non-submit-button `input` elements.

Unfortunately, there's no such attribute selector, but there is a way to emulate its behavior using the `:not` selector, a new pseudo-class in CSS3. It targets elements that do not match whatever you put into it. So the selector `input:not([type=submit])` tells the browser "find all `input` elements that don't have their `type` attribute set to `submit`." The `:not` selector is supported by all major browsers except IE 8 and earlier. Learn more about it at http://kilianvalkhof.com/2008/css-xhtml/the-css3-not-selector.

If you're using a JavaScript framework, it may include this sort of "not matching" attribute selector; for instance, see http://api.jquery.com/attribute-not-equal-selector for jQuery and http://mootools.net/docs/core/Utilities/Selectors for MooTools.

Indicating File Types with Dynamically Added Icons

To get started, download the exercise files for this chapter at www.stunningcss3.com and open selectors_start.html in your code editor of choice. Its CSS is contained in a `style` element in the head of the page. This is the same page used in Chapter 3, so you can also use your final page from Chapter 3 as your starting point here.

Throughout the page, there are links to documents to download, in these file types:

- PDF
- DOC
- MOV
- JPG

In some cases, I've indicated the file type to the user by putting it in parentheses at the end of the link text, such as "Map of trip locations (PDF)." I want to give users a heads-up that clicking on certain links might launch additional applications, like Acrobat Reader, or prompt them to save a file. But I'm a human being—I may not remember to add this file-type notice at the end of every link that could benefit from it. Or what if this page was part of a content-management system (CMS), and my non-technical client was adding links? He might be even less likely to remember to add these friendly file-type warnings.

A more foolproof way to add some sort of file-type indicator is to use attribute selectors, which would have the browser take care of it automatically. Every link ends with a file-type extension, so we can use the "end of the value" attribute selector to examine the extension and add the appropriate icon as a background image on the *a* element.

First, prepare the *a* elements inside the file-download lists to have background images added to them:

```
ul a {
    display: block;
    min-height: 15px;
    padding-left: 20px;
    background-repeat: no-repeat;
    background-position: 0 3px;
}
```

This makes the links block elements with a minimum height matching the height of the icon images, so the icons won't ever get cut off. It also adds left padding to create empty space for each icon to sit in. Each icon background image will display only once (no-repeat) and be positioned three pixels down from the top of the link (0 3px) to align it with the top of the text.

WHEN TO ADD QUOTATION MARKS?

You need quotation marks around the value of an attribute selector only when it's a string. If the value is an identifier, you don't need the quotation marks, but they don't hurt either. The difference between identifiers and strings basically comes down to identifiers being more limited in the characters they can contain and start with. See www.w3.org/TR/CSS21/syndata.html#value-def-identifier for the definition of an identifier and www.w3.org/TR/CSS21/syndata.html#strings for the definition of a string.

If you don't want to have to remember all this, play it safe by always putting quotation marks around your attribute selector values.

Now we can add the attribute selectors to target each file type extension:

```
a[href$=".pdf"] {
    background-image: url(images/icon_pdf.png);
}
a[href$=".doc"] {
    background-image: url(images/icon_doc.png);
}
a[href$=".mov"] {
    background-image: url(images/icon_film.png);
}
a[href$=".jpg"] {
    background-image: url(images/icon_photo.png);
}
```

NOTE: These icons came from the free famfamfam Silk icon set by Mark James at www.famfamfam. com/lab/icons/silk.

The href$= part of each attribute selector tells the browser "find every href attribute that ends with," and then the values in quotation marks, such as .pdf, give the ending attribute value to match against. When the browser finds a match, it applies the background image indicated, adding appropriate icons to all the links (**Figure 4.3**).

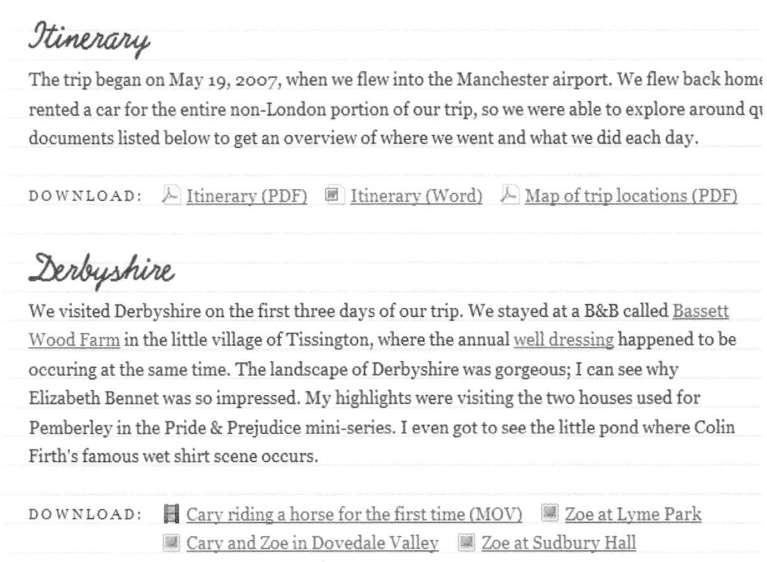

FIGURE 4.3
Each link now has an icon beside it to match its file-type extension.

Itinerary

The trip began on May 19, 2007, when we flew into the Manchester airport. We flew back home rented a car for the entire non-London portion of our trip, so we were able to explore around qu documents listed below to get an overview of where we went and what we did each day.

DOWNLOAD: Itinerary (PDF)   Itinerary (Word)   Map of trip locations (PDF)

Derbyshire

We visited Derbyshire on the first three days of our trip. We stayed at a B&B called Bassett Wood Farm in the little village of Tissington, where the annual well dressing happened to be occuring at the same time. The landscape of Derbyshire was gorgeous; I can see why Elizabeth Bennet was so impressed. My highlights were visiting the two houses used for Pemberley in the Pride & Prejudice mini-series. I even got to see the little pond where Colin Firth's famous wet shirt scene occurs.

DOWNLOAD: Cary riding a horse for the first time (MOV)   Zoe at Lyme Park   Cary and Zoe in Dovedale Valley   Zoe at Sudbury Hall

NOTE: The page with all the changes to this point is named selec-tors_l.html in the exercise files that you down-loaded for this chapter.

SCALING THE ICONS

Instead of using `min-height` on the links to ensure that their background icons never get cut off, you could use `background-size` to scale the icons with the text. The rule might look like this:

```
ul a[href] {
    display: block;
    padding-left: 20px;
    background-repeat: no-repeat;
    background-position: 0 3px;
    -moz-background-size: 1.2em;
    -webkit-background-size: 1.2em;
    background-size: 1.2em;
}
```

I haven't added this CSS to the page because when the browser scales the icons, they look a little blurry—even when the browser is making them smaller, not bigger. I don't think it's a good idea to use browser-based scaling on crisp-edged images like these particular icons. But keep this technique in mind for times when you're using images with less well-defined edges, where some blurriness won't be noticeable.

Alternative Icon Ideas

We're finished with the styling for the link icons, but you could take attribute selectors even further if you wanted to.

SAY IT INSTEAD OF SHOWING IT

The icons are a nice little hint to help your users, but if you wanted to be even more obvious and explicit, you could use generated content to write out the file-type extension at the end of each link instead of or in addition to the icons.

You'd first need to make sure that this information wasn't already manually written in each link. Then, you could add the following rule, for example, to write out "(PDF)" after each link to a PDF file:

```
a[href$=".pdf"]:after {
    content: " (PDF)";
}
```

COMBINING MULTIPLE ATTRIBUTE SELECTORS

As with almost any other type of selector, you can combine multiple attribute selectors into one to give you even more fine-grained control over what you want to target. For instance, what if you wanted to show the photo icon for links to PNG images, but a chart icon for links to PNG images that also happened to be charts? Depending on how your images are named, this selector would work:

```
a[href$=".png"][href*="chart"] {
    background-image: url(images/icon_chart.png);
}
```

This selector tells the browser "find all links that have '.png' at the end of their href attributes and have 'chart' somewhere in the href attribute." So all of the following links would get matched:

```
<a href="images/chart_locations.png">
<a href="images/piechart.png">
<a href="charts/travel.png">
```

Fixing IE 6

IE 6 is the only major browser that doesn't support attribute selectors and doesn't show the icons. The only way to work around this is to add a script that provides support for attribute selectors.

ADDING AN IE-FIXING SCRIPT

One such script that makes the advanced selectors already present in your CSS work is Dean Edwards' script, confusingly named IE7 (http://code.google.com/p/ie7-js). You can download the script and link to that local copy, or you can link to the public copy hosted on Google Code. Linking to the public copy has the advantage that visitors to your page may already have the script in their cache if they've visited another site linking to it, making the page load faster for them.

Add a link to the public copy of the script in the head of the page, inside an IE 6-only conditional comment:

```
<!--[if IE 6]>
<script src="http://ie7-js.googlecode.com/svn/
version/2.1(beta4)/IE7.js"></script>
<![endif]-->
```

The script makes IE 6 understand the attribute selectors so the icons show up, but it does weird things to the spacing and wrapping of the links. To fix these issues, we need to make the links `inline-block` and set `white-space` to `nowrap`, but this causes minor problems in other browsers. So, we'll use the same conditional comments `html` tag trick that we used in Chapter 2 to create a rule that only IE 6 can read.

Go to the opening `html` tag of the page, and change it to the following HTML:

TIP: If you don't want to type all this by hand, open selectors_final. html from this chapter's exercise files, and copy and paste it from there.

```html
<!--[if lt IE 7 ]><html lang="en" class="ie6"><![endif]-->
<!--[if IE 7 ]><html lang="en" class="ie7"><![endif]-->
<!--[if IE 8 ]><html lang="en" class="ie8"><![endif]-->
<!--[if IE 9 ]><html lang="en" class="ie9"><![endif]-->
<!--[if gt IE 9]><html lang="en"><![endif]-->
<!--[if !IE]>--><html lang="en"><!--<![endif]-->
```

Now you can add an IE 6-only rule:

```css
.ie6 ul a {
    display: inline-block;
    white-space: nowrap;
}
```

IE 6 now displays like the other browsers—as long as JavaScript is enabled. If an IE 6 user has JavaScript off, she won't see the icons. This is fine—they're an enhancement, not necessary pieces of content. But with JavaScript off, IE 6 will still read the `ul a` rule, which adds extra padding to each link, creating unnecessary empty space between the links in IE 6. To get rid of this, add an `[href]` attribute selector to both the `ul a` and `.ie6 ul a` rules:

```css
ul a[href] {
    display: block;
    min-height: 15px;
    padding-left: 20px;
    background-repeat: no-repeat;
    background-position: 0 3px;
}
.ie6 ul a[href] {
    display: inline-block;
    white-space: nowrap;
}
```

NOTE: The page with all the changes to this point is named selectors_2.html in the exercise files for this chapter.

These rules now target all `a` elements that have `href` attributes inside the `ul` elements—and since *all* the `a` elements have `href` attributes, the rules match exactly the same links as before the attribute selector part was added. But when JavaScript is off and IE 6 doesn't understand attribute selectors, it will ignore both rules completely now, getting rid of the extra padding and other styling that they add.

USING A JAVASCRIPT LIBRARY

An alternative to using the IE7 script as we've just done is to use a JavaScript library or framework that has attribute selectors built into it, and then write them into your own script to accomplish whatever effect you want. The downside to this is that your script wouldn't take into account the attribute selectors already present in your CSS and make them work; you'd have to recreate them in your script instead. But if you're already writing a script to take care of some other effects in your pages, it might be better to throw in the selectors you need instead of adding on the IE7 script to your pages.

The article "Selecting and Styling External Links, PDFs, PPTs, and other links by file extension using jQuery" (http://dabrook.org/blog/articles/selecting-and-styling-external-links-or-pdf-ppts-and-other-files-by-extensi) gives an example of how to use the attribute selectors available in jQuery to create a custom script to add icons to links. Most major JavaScript libraries, such as jQuery and MooTools, have attribute selectors built in, and there are a few JavaScript libraries exclusively devoted to selectors. These include:

◆ YUI Selector Utility (http://developer.yahoo.com/yui/selector)

◆ Sizzle (http://sizzlejs.com)

◆ Sly (http://github.com/digitarald/sly)

There are also some scripts that sit on top of a JavaScript library to take advantage of its advanced selectors without requiring you to write your own selectors—they simply detect the selectors you already have in your CSS and make them work. Keith Clark's Selectivizr script (http://selectivizr.com) mentioned in Chapter 1 is a great option. Simply add the script to your page, plus one of the seven corresponding JavaScript libraries, and attribute selectors will work in IE. If you're using jQuery, another option is the jQuery SuperSelectors plugin (http://github.com/chrispatterson/jquery-super-selectors).

Styling Full-size Photos and Thumbnails Differently

Another great use of attribute selectors in our page is to give the photos a different style than the map thumbnail. To do this without CSS3, we could simply give the thumbnail a class and apply unique styles to this class. This would be quite easy in this particular page. But using classes is not always so simple in the real world.

The Trouble with Classes

While classes have many legitimate uses, they do have some problems that make them difficult to use in some situations.

- **Classes add bulk to your HTML.** In our example, adding one class isn't going to hurt anyone, but in much larger pages and sites with more complex styles, a lot of extra classes could be necessary, adding a good chunk to the file size. Any time you can avoid adding classes and IDs to the HTML and use another way to reliably target elements instead, you should do so.

- **Markup may be controlled by a CMS or plugin,** making it impossible for you to add classes to the HTML.

- **Your client may be the one adding content,** and you can't count on him to remember to assign the proper classes.

- **You may not be allowed to touch the HTML** if you're just the CSS developer on a project, or if you've been brought into an existing project just to make a few style updates.

- **Classes can be time-consuming** to add to an existing site with tons of pages, if you're trying to go back and add new styles. It's much easier to write CSS that takes advantage of whatever HTML is already there, without your having to go back and add extra style hooks into the HTML.

PLANNING FOR ERRORS

While there's a possibility that whoever is creating pages might save images in the wrong folders, I think it's far more likely that a client would neglect to assign a class than save an image in a new place away from the rest of the images. If you want to be extra sure, you can assign classes as a backup, and then apply the styles to both the classes and the attribute selectors. That way, if someone forgets to assign a class, the attribute selector takes care of it, and if someone forgets to save something in the right place, the class takes care of it. It's extra work, but it's a fail-safe method in cases where you might not be able to count on either the attribute or the class always being correct. Also, IE 6 will be able to use the class if you're not using a script to give it support for attribute selectors.

If you do group together a class selector and an attribute selector, be aware that IE 6 will ignore the entire rule, even though it should be able to read and use the class selector portion. (This doesn't apply if you're using a script to give IE 6 support for attribute selectors, of course.) In order to work around this, you'd need to separate each out into its own rule, like so:

```
img[src*=thumbnails] {
    float: left;
    margin: 0 20px 10px 0;
}
img.thumbnail {
    float: left;
    margin: 0 20px 10px 0;
}
```

It's redundant, but if you have to support IE 6 without scripting, it's your only option. We're not going to do it in this example page, not only because we're using scripting instead, but also because we're using attribute selectors for a decorative, non-essential effect, which I'm fine with IE 6 users missing out on. But if you're using attribute selectors for something more important—or just want to provide a fail-safe—this is an option you can consider using.

THE LOWDOWN ON ATTRIBUTE SELECTORS

The attribute selector is part of the Selectors module found at www.w3.org/TR/css3-selectors. There are seven attribute selectors:

♦ [attr] matches an element with an attr attribute present, regardless of its value.

♦ [attr=val] matches an element with an attr attribute whose value is exactly val.

♦ [attr~=val] matches an element with an attr attribute whose value is a space-separated list of words, one of which is exactly val.

♦ [attr|=val] matches an element with an attr attribute whose value is either exactly val or begins with val immediately followed by a hyphen.

♦ [attr^=val] matches an element with an attr attribute whose value starts with val.

♦ [attr$=val] matches an element with an attr attribute whose value ends with val.

♦ [attr*=val] matches an element with an attr attribute whose value contains val somewhere within it.

The first four are called *attribute presence and value selectors* and are part of CSS 2.1. The last three are called *substring matching attribute selectors* and are part of CSS3.

The values in attribute selectors can be identifiers or strings; strings must be enclosed in quotation marks.

Attribute selectors have the same specificity as class and pseudo-class selectors.

Other than link icons and type-based image styling, you might want to use attribute selectors for:

♦ Styling different form-field input types uniquely (using input[type=submit], for instance); see http://dev.opera.com/articles/view/styling-forms-with-attribute-selectors

◆ Varying the styling of phrases in different languages (using [lang|=en], for instance)

◆ Adding a visual indication to elements that have title attributes set (using [title])

◆ Removing bullets from lists within navigation divs (using div[id^=nav] to match <div id="nav-primary"> and <div id="nav-secondary">, for instance)

◆ Styling email links (using a[href^=mailto]); see http://css-tricks. com/better-email-links-featuring-css-attribute-selectors

◆ Styling links that go to external sites (using a[href^=http] or a[rel=external]), that are secure (using a[href^=https]), that go to a specific URL (such as a[href*="paypal.com"]), that open in new window (using a[target="_blank"]), or that go to your own home page (using a[href="http://myurl.com"] or a[href="/index.html"])

◆ Checking for empty links before launching a site; see http://fuelyourcoding.com/unconventional-css3-link-checking

◆ Displaying the access key of a link (using a:after { content: '[' attr(accesskey) ']' })

◆ Displaying the citation source of a blockquote (using blockquote[cite]:after { content: ' - ' attr(cite) })

◆ Styling blockquotes differently based on the value of their cite attributes

◆ Displaying an image's alternative text as its caption (using img[alt]:after { content: attr(alt) })

◆ Creating a user style sheet to hide ads on web pages; see http:// 24ways.org/2005/the-attribute-selector-for-fun-and-no-ad-profit

◆ Hiding rules from IE 6

TABLE 4.3 **Attribute selectors browser support**

IE	FIREFOX	OPERA	SAFARI	CHROME
Yes, 7+*	Yes	Yes	Yes	Yes

* IE 7 and later support all the attribute selectors, but are sometimes buggy. Test well.

Using Attribute Selectors to Target by Type

NOTE: The -4px part of the box-shadow property is the spread radius, which Safari 4 (including the version on iOS 3 and earlier) doesn't support, making the shadow fail to appear in those browsers. You could remove the spread radius to fix this, but that would make the shadow look not quite as nice in Safari 5 and Chrome, which do support it. It's up to you!

As long as there is some reliable difference between the HTML used for the thumbnails and the photos, we can tap into that difference with attribute selectors. In this case, the distinction is that the map thumbnail is saved in the folder named "thumbnails" and the photos are saved in the folder named "photos." The folder name is part of the path in the `src` attribute, so we can use attribute selectors to target each image type independently via particular `src` attribute values.

Let's start by floating the map thumbnail left instead of right:

```
img[src*=thumbnails] {
    float: left;
    margin: 0 20px 10px 0;
}
```

The * attribute selector tells the browser "find every `src` attribute that has 'thumbnails' somewhere within it." This matches the map image:

```
<img src="thumbnails/map.png" width="100" height="100"
¬alt="">
```

FIGURE 4.4 The map thumbnail is now floating left, instead of right like the other images.

Now let's add some styling to the photos to make them look like Polaroid pictures. Add the following new rule:

```
img[src*=photos] {
    padding: 5px 5px 30px 5px;
    background: #fff;
    -moz-box-shadow: 3px 6px 8px -4px #999;
    -webkit-box-shadow: 3px 6px 8px -4px #999;
    box-shadow: 3px 6px 8px -4px #999;
    -moz-transform: rotate(2deg);
    -o-transform: rotate(2deg);
    -webkit-transform: rotate(2deg);
    transform: rotate(2deg);
}
```

Now all the photos have a white border around them, a drop shadow behind them, and a slight angle (**Figure 4.5**).

FIGURE 4.5 The photos now have unique styling to make them look Polaroid-esque.

The Finished Page

We've completed all the styling on the links and images in our page. Check out your work in a browser, and compare **Figure 4.6** to Figure 4.1. IE 7 and later support attribute selectors, and we've given IE 6 a script to provide it with support, so most of the changes we made are visible in IE. The only bits it doesn't see are the drop shadows and rotation of the photos.

NOTE: The completed page showing all of these effects is named selectors_final. html in the exercise files for this chapter.

FIGURE 4.6 The final page with unique styling on the links and images, thanks to CSS3 attribute selectors.

England Trip 2007

In May and June 2007, Cary and I spent 15 days traveling around England (plus a very brief detour into Wales). It was our first trip to Europe. We had very briefly been out of the USA the year before, when we jaunted up into Montreal for a few hours during our Vermont vacation, but this was our first significant out-of-country trip. We had a fabulous time!

The trip was heavily focused around Jane Austen sites, both those from her life as well as a few from the 1995 mini-series Pride & Prejudice. You see, I am an unapologetic Janeite, and I have a very understanding and loving husband.

Itinerary

 The trip began on May 19, 2007, when we flew into the Manchester airport. We flew back home from London on June 3. We rented a car for the entire non-London portion of our trip, so we were able to explore around quite a bit. You can download the documents listed below to get an overview of where we went and what we did each day.

DOWNLOAD: Itinerary (PDF)   Itinerary (Word)   Map of trip locations (PDF)

Derbyshire

We visited Derbyshire on the first three days of our trip. We stayed at a B&B called Bassett Wood Farm in the little village of Tissington, where the annual well dressing happened to be occuring at the same time. The landscape of Derbyshire was gorgeous; I can see why Elizabeth Bennet was so impressed. My highlights were visiting the two houses used for Pemberley in the Pride & Prejudice mini-series. I even got to see the little pond where Colin Firth's famous wet shirt scene occurs.

DOWNLOAD: Cary riding a horse for the first time (MOV)
                       Zoe at Lyme Park
                       Cary and Zoe in Dovedale Valley
                       Zoe at Sudbury Hall

Cotswolds

The next seven days were spent traveling all around the Cotswolds and the surrounding area. We stayed at a cottage in the famously picturesque village of Bibury. We explored more than a dozen other Cotswolds villages.

One of our favorite towns in the Cotswolds was Cirencester, because of the great food we had there and the Corinium Museum. The collection of Roman (and earlier) artifacts at the museum was much larger than we expected and quite fascinating.

The more ancient something is, the better Cary loves it, especially if it's all in ruins. So, Cary's highlights in the Cotswolds were not just the Roman museum but also the unearthed Chedworth Roman Villa and the ruins of Minster Lovell Hall. One of our favorite memories from the area was our wet, cold trek to the Belas Knap burial mound, built around 2500 BC. Drying out and warming up in the pub afterwards was lovely, and the whole thing was just so English.

DOWNLOAD: Zoe and Cary in a field of sheep   Zoe in Bibury   Cary at Minster Lovell Hall

Improving Efficiency Using Pseudo-classes

5

In the last chapter, you learned how to use attribute selectors to target individual links and images without having to add IDs or classes to your HTML. In this chapter, you'll learn about more CSS3 selectors that can help you keep your code clean and lean, as well as avoid the need for JavaScript or Flash. We'll use them to apply more visual enhancements to both the speech bubbles and article page, and then top it off with some CSS-controlled animation and transitions to enhance usability.

WHAT YOU'LL LEARN

We'll create alternating styles for the speech bubbles and the photos in the article page, as well as create a table of contents that highlights the current section of the article, and we'll do it using these pieces of CSS3:

◆ The `:nth-child()` pseudo-class to select alternating elements

◆ The `:nth-of-type()` pseudo-class to select alternating elements of a certain type

◆ The `:last-child` pseudo-class to style the last element of a list differently

◆ The `:target` pseudo-class to style the target of a URL containing a fragment identifier

◆ Transitions to change the value of a property gradually instead of abruptly

◆ Animations to control more complex visual changes

Targeting Specific Elements Without Using IDs or Classes

Just like attribute selectors, pseudo-classes and pseudo-elements can be used to select specific elements in the HTML without assigning those elements IDs or classes, keeping your markup cleaner. Pseudo-classes and pseudo-elements target pieces of HTML that either don't exist as standalone elements, or do exist but have a unique characteristic that you can't target with the other simple selectors. For instance, you can use the `:first-line` pseudo-element to format the first line of a paragraph, even though that first line doesn't have HTML tags wrapped around it. In this way, some pseudo-classes and pseudo-elements are even more powerful than attribute selectors, because they allow you to target elements that could never have an ID or class added to them to begin with.

Pseudo-classes and pseudo-elements as a whole are not new, or particular, to CSS3, but CSS3 added several individual pseudo-classes that allow us even more precise control over what parts of the document we want to target. Many of these new selectors are structural pseudo-classes.

WHAT'S THE DIFFERENCE BETWEEN A PSEUDO-CLASS AND A PSEUDO-ELEMENT?

The simplest way to remember the difference is this: pseudo-classes select HTML elements that could have classes added to them, while pseudo-elements select things that aren't HTML elements at all.

The four pseudo-elements in CSS are ::first-line, ::first-letter, ::before, and ::after. All of these are fragments of other HTML elements, not individual elements themselves. They're not part of the document tree, so the only way to target them is with pseudo-element selectors.

In terms of syntax, in CSS3, pseudo-classes start with one colon and pseudo-elements start with two. (They used to both have one, and this syntax still works.) You can have only one pseudo-element per selector, and it has to come at the end (for instance, #article p::first-line); pseudo-classes don't have these restrictions.

New Structural Pseudo-classes

CSS3 introduces the concept of "structural pseudo-classes" to target elements in the document tree based on unique characteristics of the elements, such as relative placement. For instance, the :first-child pseudo-class targets an element that is the first child element of its parent element. This child element is a standalone HTML element in the document tree, but what makes it unique is that it's first, and it's this unique characteristic that we want to be able to select by, without having to add a class or ID.

All of the structural pseudo-classes are based on the document tree, also called the document object model (DOM), so let's have a quick refresher on what that is. The *document tree* is the hierarchical structure of the HTML page, made up of elements, attributes, and text, each called a *node*. It contains multiple levels because elements are nested inside each other (**Figure 5.1**). Elements nested directly inside other elements are called *children* of those outer elements; they're also *descendants*, along with elements that are nested further down. The outer elements are called *parents* (if one level up) or *ancestors* (if two or more levels up). Elements that are nested at the same level with each other—in other words, they have the same parent—are called, predictably, *siblings*. An element can be many or all of these things at once, just like you can be someone's child and someone else's parent at the same time; the terms are all relative to where a certain element is in relation to a certain other element.

FIGURE 5.1 A sample document tree, showing ancestor, descendant, parent, child, and sibling elements

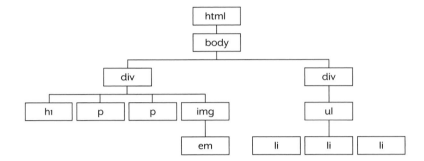

Now that we've gotten all that terminology down, we can see all the ways we can establish relationships among the elements. Table 5.1 shows the structural pseudo-classes.

TABLE 5.1 Structural pseudo-classes

PSEUDO-CLASS	DESCRIPTION
:root	Selects the element that is the root of the document. In HTML, this is always the html element.
:nth-child()	Selects based on position within the list of its parent's children.
:nth-last-child()	Same as :nth-child(), but the counting for the position number is done from the last child upward instead of the first child downward.
:nth-of-type()	Selects based on position within the list of its parent's children, but only counting children of a certain type (such as p, img, etc.).
:nth-last-of-type()	Same as :nth-of-type(), but counting from the last child of the specified type instead of the first.
:first-child	Selects the first child of a parent element. (In Figure 5.1, the h1 element is a first child.)
:last-child	Selects the last child of a parent element. (In Figure 5.1, the img element is a last child.)
:first-of-type	Selects the first sibling of its own type in a parent element. (In Figure 5.1, the first p element would be selected by p:first-of-type.)
:last-of-type	Selects the last sibling of its own type in a parent element.
:only-child	Selects an element that is the only child of its parent. (In Figure 5.1, the ul element is an only child.)
:only-of-type	Selects the only element of its own type in the parent element.
:empty	Selects elements that have no children elements or text inside them.

Other than the `:first-child` pseudo-class, which is part of CSS 2.1, all of these structural pseudo-classes are new to CSS3. They offer us a whole host of new ways to target elements very precisely.

Back to the Speech Bubbles: Alternating Colors

We can use the `:nth-child()` pseudo-class to make every other speech bubble in our comments page from Chapter 2 have a different background color. And we'll do this without using classes or JavaScript.

HOW `:nth-child()` WORKS

One of the most powerful and useful structural pseudo-classes is `:nth-child()`. I already mentioned that it selects an element based on its position within the list of its parent's children; in other words, it selects an element based on how many siblings it has before it.

You write the position number of the element you want to select inside the parentheses of the selector, such as `li:nth-child(5)`. This selector would match the fifth `li` element in a list. In addition to numbers inside the parentheses (the selector's *argument*), you can also use the keyword odd or even to select every other element in a row, such as the second, fourth, sixth, and so forth. But where `:nth-child()` gets really powerful is when you use a formula as its argument, allowing you to create more complex alternating patterns or even select specific blocks of sequential children at a time. The formula has the syntax an+b, where a is a cycle size that you pick, n is a counter starting at zero, and b is an offset value that you pick. Here's an example:

> `li:nth-child(3n+1)`

Since n starts at zero and then increases by one each cycle, this selector would match:

$(3 \times 0) + 1 = 1 = $ 1st list item

$(3 \times 1) + 1 = 4 = $ 4th list item

$(3 \times 2) + 1 = 7 = $ 7th list item

$(3 \times 3) + 1 = 10 = $ 10th list item

And so on!

While you could certainly add classes to the first, fourth, seventh, and tenth list items, it's time-consuming to do so, easy to forget to do, adds to the weight of your pages, and—probably most importantly—is a pain to maintain. If you ever want to add another list item in between existing ones, you have to re-class all the list items from that point forward, as their position numbers will have all changed. Using the :nth-child() pseudo-class that keeps track of the position numbers for you and matches accordingly is far more efficient and mistake-proof.

Don't let the math scare you off from using :nth-child(). There are some great online tools that can help you get a better sense for how :nth-child() works by letting you play around with values to see how they affect the styles of the page immediately. My favorite of these tools is at http://leaverou.me/demos/nth.html, by Lea Verou, which allows you to test not only :nth-child() but also :nth-last-child(), :nth-of-type(), and :nth-last-of-type().

ZEBRA STRIPING

One of the most ubiquitous uses of :nth-child() is to make every other row of a table a different color. This is commonly called "zebra striping." It can often be more than just an aesthetic enhancement; it can increase usability by making it easier to scan across a long table without losing your place.

NOTE: There's a little research that suggests that zebra striping isn't as helpful as you might think—still useful, but not a huge boon. Read more about this in "Zebra Striping: More Data for the Case" by Jessica Enders (www.alistapart.com/articles/zebrastripingmoredata forthecase).

Without :nth-child(), you zebra stripe a table by applying a class to every other row, called something like "even" or "alt", and then give this class a different background color. You have to either apply these classes manually or have a piece of JavaScript do it for you. Neither solution is as efficient as :nth-child().

You can use :nth-child() formulas to zebra stripe; the formula 2n would match all the even rows, for instance. But the keywords even and odd are shortcuts that are easier to use. We'll use the even keyword in our blog comments page to make every other speech bubble a different color.

To get started, download the exercise files for this chapter at www.stunningcss3.com and open alternate_start.html in your code editor of choice. Its CSS is contained in a style element in the head of the page. This is the same page used in Chapter 2, so you can also use your final page from Chapter 2 as your starting point here.

Right now, all the speech bubbles in this page are the same shade of greenish-blue (**Figure 5.2**). This color has the value hsla(182,44%,76%,.5). Since we're using HSLA, it's easy to tweak the values to get a slightly different shade for our alternating color. Remember that hue values run from 0 to 360, along the spectrum from red to purple. So if you wanted to make the alternating color a little more green, you simply use a slightly lower hue value, such as 160 instead of 182. If you wanted to make the alternating color a little more blue, use a higher hue value, such as 200.

FIGURE 5.2 All of the comments have the same greenish-blue background color.

Let's use a bluer shade for our alternating color. I'll use 210 for the hue value to make the color difference more obvious. Add this new rule to the CSS in the head of the page:

```
li:nth-child(even) blockquote {
    background-color: hsla(210,44%,76%,.5);
}
```

Save the page, and view it in an up-to-date browser. You'll see that the second and fourth comments are blue, while the first and third are still greenish-blue (**Figure 5.3**).

This new shade of blue doesn't look as good at the same muted saturation level that the greenish-blue shade uses, so let's bump up the saturation value to brighten it, and also increase the lightness value a bit to improve the contrast with the black text:

```
li:nth-child(even) blockquote {
    background-color: hsla(210,70%,82%,.5);
}
```

NOTE: The completed page showing these changes is named alternate_final.html in the exercise files for this chapter.

Now the alternate color is a brighter shade of blue (**Figure 5.4**). HSLA made it easy to pick a complementary color, and :nth-child() made it easy to apply that color to every other speech bubble. While alternating the color of blog comments like this doesn't really have a usability benefit, as zebra striping table rows often does, you can see how efficient it is to use :nth-child() for selecting elements in a pattern.

FIGURE 5.3 The even-numbered speech bubbles now have a muted blue background color.

FIGURE 5.4 Quickly tweaking the HSLA values results in a brighter shade of blue on the even-numbered speech bubbles.

TABLE 5.2 :nth-child() **browser support**

IE	FIREFOX	OPERA	SAFARI	CHROME
Yes, 9+	Yes, 3.5+	Yes*	Yes	Yes

* Opera supports :nth-child(), but doesn't correctly update the styles if more elements are added to the page, using JavaScript, after it's loaded. This bug can be fixed by added a :last-child declaration to the page. See www.quirksmode.org/css/nthchild.html for a demo of this and more information.

THE LOWDOWN ON THE :nth-child() PSEUDO-CLASS

The :nth-child() pseudo-class is part of the Selectors module found at www.w3.org/TR/css3-selectors. It's a structural pseudo-class that selects an element based on how many siblings precede it within the same parent element.

Inside the parentheses of :nth-child(), you write either a number (to select one particular child), the keyword odd or even (to select every other child, either odd-numbered or even-numbered), or a formula in the syntax an+b (to select a particular combination of children you want). In this formula, a is a cycle size, n is a counter that starts at zero, and b is an offset value.

Negative values are allowed for a and b. If a is 1, you can omit it (so 1n+3 is the same as n+3). If b is 0, or if a and b are equal, you can omit the b value (so 2n+0 and 2n+2 are the same as 2n). For more details on this, see http://reference.sitepoint.com/css/understandingnthchildexpressions.

Other than zebra striping, you might want to use :nth-child() for:

◆ Styling the first two or more paragraphs of an article differently (using -n+2, if styling just the first two)

◆ Giving the first ten items in a top-100 list a larger font size (using -n+10)

◆ Making older blog posts or Tweets in a list have a smaller font size or fainter color as you move down the list

◆ Creating the appearance of randomness (for instance, making every third feature box have one background color, every fourth have another, and so on)

◆ Forcing a line break or margin change at every fourth image thumbnail, for instance, to create an image gallery with multiple rows of thumbnails all in the same HTML list; see http://mondaybynoon.com/2010/03/18/css3-center-thumbnail-galleries

◆ Styling specific table columns differently (for instance, making the third column, which contains numbers, have right-aligned text)

◆ Changing the width of side-by-side items based on how many are there, to always fill the available space; see http://andr3.net/blog/post/142

WORKAROUNDS FOR IE

IE 8 and earlier do not support `:nth-child()`; IE 9 does. In this case, the alternating colors are a minor visual enhancement that users of IE 8 and earlier can do without. IE simply ignores the new rule and keeps all the speech bubbles the same color as before. Nothing looks broken, incomplete, or ugly.

If you do want to provide a workaround for IE 8 and earlier, however, you'll need to use JavaScript. If you're zebra striping, there are a myriad of scripts that will add the alternating classes for you. The one that will be best for you will depend on your project, so Google "zebra stripe JavaScript" or "zebra stripe PHP" or whatever suits your needs.

Alternately, you can use a script that adds support for advanced selectors to IE, and then simply use those selectors to accomplish whatever effect you want, including but not limited to zebra striping. One such script is Dean Edwards' IE7.js that we used in the last chapter (http://code.google.com/p/ie7-js), but you have to upgrade to the IE9.js version of the script in order to get pseudo-classes to work; the IE7.js version only makes attribute selectors and a few other selectors work. Another great script that adds pseudo-class support is Selectivizr (http://selectivizr.com), but as mentioned in Chapter 4 it also requires the use of one of several separate JavaScript libraries like jQuery, MooTools, or DOMAssistant in order to work. Both of these scripts make IE identify the selectors present in your CSS and render whatever styles they define.

Also, as explained in Chapter 4, many JavaScript libraries have advanced selectors like `:nth-child()` built in, which you can write into your own scripts to get `:nth-child()` functionality in IE. This route wouldn't take into account the `:nth-child()` selectors already present in your CSS; you'd have to recreate them in your script. See the "Using a JavaScript Library" section in Chapter 4 for links to JavaScript libraries you can use.

Back to the Photos: Random Rotation

Now that we've enhanced our speech bubbles with `:nth-child()`, let's return to the article page we worked on in Chapters 3 and 4 to see how we can achieve alternating styles on the photos within the page. Right now, all the photos are rotated in order to make them appear more realistic. But since they're all rotated the same amount, they look very uniform (**Figure 5.5**). It would be nice to be able to use

`:nth-child()` to rotate different photos different amounts to enhance the appearance of randomness and realism.

FIGURE 5.5 All the photos are rotated slightly to the right.

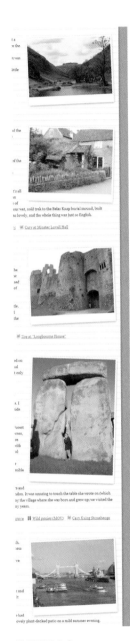

FIGURE 5.6

**The photos now alter-
nate between left
and right rotation,
to look more realistic.**

However, if you used the selector img[src*=photos]:nth-child(even) to rotate all the even-numbered images to the left instead of the right, you might be surprised to find that the last two images *both* rotate right, instead of alternating. This is because the :nth-child() pseudo-class selects *all* children of the same parent. The img elements are siblings with all the p and h2 elements, so all of these elements are counted for :nth-child(). Even though img is included in the selector, all that the selector is saying is "Find all the images that have 'photos' in their src attribute. Then apply these styles to the ones that are even-numbered children." If you count all the img, p, and h2 elements in the parent div, you'll find that the second-to-last photo is child number 29 of the div, and the last photo is child number 37. Thus, the :nth-child() rule selecting even-numbered children doesn't apply to either of them, and they stay rotated to the right.

What we really need is a selector like :nth-child() but that counts only elements of a particular type. Lucky for us, CSS3 provides such a selector: the :nth-of-type() pseudo-class. It works exactly the same as :nth-child(), but it counts only whatever element you specify in front of it.

Let's put it to use in our page. Open rotate_start.html from the exercise files for this chapter (or use your final page from Chapter 4). Add the following new rule to the styles in the head of the page:

```
img[src*=photos]:nth-of-type(even) {
    -moz-transform: rotate(-2deg);
    -o-transform: rotate(-2deg);
    -webkit-transform: rotate(-2deg);
    transform: rotate(-2deg);
}
```

Save your page, and view it in a browser to see that every other photo is now rotated to the left instead of the right (**Figure 5.6**). The last two images aren't angled the same way; they alternate rotation.

You might notice in Figure 5.6 that the first, third, and fifth photos are rotated to the left, even though the selector says to rotate even-numbered ones to the left. That's because there's another img element before all the photos on the page: the map thumbnail. This img element makes the first, third, and fifth *photos* the second, fourth, and sixth *images* overall. The :nth-of-type() pseudo-class only cares about the element type when doing its counting—in this case, that element type is img. What the full selector is saying is "Find all the images that have 'photos' in their src attribute. Then apply these styles to those that are even-numbered img element children."

THE POWER OF `:nth-of-type()`

If you want to see what heavy lifting `:nth-of-type()` can do (along with some other advanced selectors), check out http://csswizardry. com/2010/04/building-sites-without-using-ids-or-classes by Harry Roberts for an example of a multiple-column page laid out without using a single ID or class value. All of the `div`s are targeted with advanced selectors instead. It's not a practical effect, just a demonstration of what's possible and a good learning tool for how these selectors work.

THE LOWDOWN ON THE `:nth-of-type()` PSEUDO-CLASS

The `:nth-of-type()` pseudo-class is part of the Selectors module found at www.w3.org/TR/css3-selectors. It's a structural pseudo-class that selects an element based on how many siblings of the same type come before it within the same parent element. It takes the same sorts of values as `:nth-child()` for its argument (inside the parentheses).

Other than rotating photos, you might want to use `:nth-of-type()` for:

- Creating the appearance of randomness in some way other than varying the rotation

- Alternating images within an article floating left and right

- Styling the first one or more paragraphs of an article differently; if other elements might prevent those paragraphs from reliably being the first children, such as an h2 or `img` that sometimes comes first, `:nth-child()` won't work

- Alternating styles on terms within a definition list; since each `dt` element may have only one or multiple `dd` elements following it, you can't use `:nth-child()`

- Alternating styles on `blockquote` elements within an article

> **NOTE:** IE support for `:nth-of-type()` is exactly the same as for `:nth-child()`, and the JavaScript workarounds are the same as well.

> **NOTE:** The completed page showing these changes is named rotate_final. html in the exercise files for this chapter.

TABLE 5.3 `:nth-of-type()` **browser support**

IE	FIREFOX	OPERA	SAFARI	CHROME
Yes, 9+	Yes, 3.5+	Yes*	Yes	Yes

* Opera has the same bug with `:nth-of-type()` as it does with `:nth-child()`.

FIGURE 5.7
The rotation is now
more varied, to
look more random
and realistic.

There's no way in CSS3 to make the browser count only img elements that have particular attributes. Any other img elements mixed in with the photos are going to be used for counting and calculating the child number. In the case of our page, we're just trying to make the photos look random, so having other images interrupt our pattern isn't a bad thing. The :nth-of-type() pseudo-class works for our purposes, even if it can't select exactly what we might like.

In fact, let's make the photos look even more random by adding another :nth-of-type() rule:

```
img[src*=photos]:nth-of-type(3n) {
    -moz-transform: rotate(1deg);
    -o-transform: rotate(1deg);
    -webkit-transform: rotate(1deg);
    transform: rotate(1deg);
}
```

This makes every third image angled to the right by one degree. The photos have a fairly random-looking pattern of rotation now: the first is rotated negative -2deg, the second 1deg, the third negative -2deg, the fourth 2deg, and the fifth 1deg (**Figure 5.7**).

Even though the :nth-of-type() selector may not do exactly what you expect and want, it still provides a heap of control over what elements you want to target without having to resort to classes or IDs.

Dynamically Highlighting Page Sections

You've now seen two examples of how CSS3's structural pseudo-classes can add visual enhancements to your pages while keeping your code free of classes and IDs, and without using JavaScript. Other CSS3 pseudo-classes can also add much more dynamic-looking effects to your pages, such as highlighting the current section when you use a within-page link to jump down the page. This is not only a visual enhancement, but a usability one, as it helps orient the viewer to where they are in the page.

For instance, when you click on a citation number in a Wikipedia article, the page jumps down to that note at the end of the page. Wikipedia highlights the note you clicked on so you don't have to locate it among the potentially hundreds of other notes (**Figure 5.8**).

FIGURE 5.7
The rotation is now
more varied, to
look more random
and realistic.

This is especially helpful in orienting the viewer when the selected item is too close to the bottom of the page to be brought all the way up to the top of the browser window.

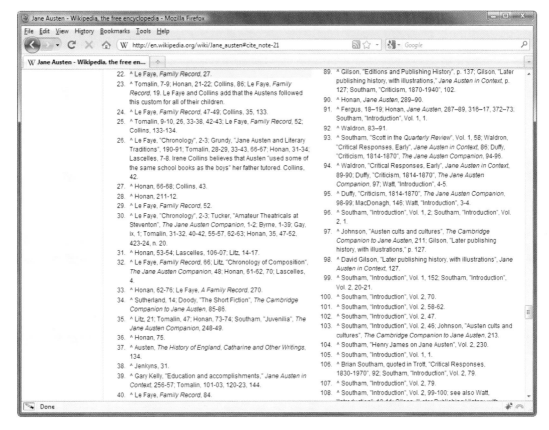

FIGURE 5.8 Wikipedia uses the `:target` **pseudo-class to highlight the selected footnote in blue.**

You can highlight the selected footnote, heading, or section on a page with JavaScript. But it's so much more efficient—both in terms of your development time and in terms of page loading speeds—to do it with the CSS3 `:target` pseudo-class.

The `:target` Pseudo-class

Some URLs have *fragment identifiers*, represented by an octothorp (the character #, commonly called a pound sign, number sign, or hash mark) followed by an anchor name or element ID, to link to a certain element in the page. The URL http://en.wikipedia.org/wiki/

Jane_austen#cite_note-21 shown in Figure 5.8 is an example of this type of URL. The `:target` pseudo-class selects the element being linked to, and lets you style it.

On Wikipedia, when you click a footnote number, the li element for the footnote you're taken to becomes the target. Here's how Wikipedia styles those footnote targets:

```
ol.references > li:target, sup.reference:target, span.
citation:target {
    background-color: #DEF;
}
```

We can also use the `:target` pseudo-class for a similar effect in our article page.

Adding the Table of Contents

Right now, the article page doesn't have any fragment identifiers we can link to. Let's add IDs to all of the subheads in the page, since they naturally divide it up into sections.

If you've been working along with the rotate_start.html file, you can continue making changes to it now, or you can open the file target_start.html from the exercise files for this chapter; both should be the same. In your page, add id attributes to each h2 element, starting with the "Derbyshire" one, with the values shown:

```
<h2 id="derbyshire">Derbyshire</h2>
<h2 id="cotswolds">Cotswolds</h2>
<h2 id="daytrips">Day-trips from the Cotswolds</h2>
<h2 id="winchester">Winchester and Surrounding Area</h2>
<h2 id="london">London</h2>
```

Now add a table of contents to the top of the page that will link to each of these h2 elements. Add the following list right before the "Itinerary" h2 element:

```
<ul id="toc">
    <li><a href="#derbyshire">Derbyshire</a></li>
    <li><a href="#cotswolds">Cotswolds</a></li>
    <li><a href="#daytrips">Day Trips from the Cotswolds
    ¬</a></li>
    <li><a href="#winchester">Winchester and Surrounding
    ¬Area</a></li>
    <li><a href="#london">London</a></li>
</ul>
```

Save the page, and view it in a browser. The links in the table of contents should take you down to the corresponding subheading in the page. We haven't yet given any special styles to the targeted or current subheading, but before we do that, let's style the table of contents itself.

NOTE: The page with all the changes to this point is named target_1.html in the exercise files that you downloaded for this chapter.

STYLING THE TOC

The table of contents list already has some non-standard styling because of the existing rules for ul and a elements; the links are all on one line and spaced out from each other (**Figure 5.9**). Let's enhance the styles further.

FIGURE 5.9 The table of contents before any special styling is applied

Add a background image of a hand-drawn arrow to the list:

```
#toc {
    background: url(images/arrow.gif) no-repeat top right;
    padding-top: 1.6em;
}
```

Next, get rid of the left padding on the li and a elements and use right padding instead, so the list as a whole is aligned on the left side:

```
#toc li {
    padding: 0 1.2em 0 0;
}
#toc a {
    padding-left: 0;
}
```

This is also a good opportunity to use another CSS3 pseudo-class. The :last-child pseudo-class lets you apply unique styles to the last child of a parent element. Here, we can use it to remove the right padding from the last list item:

```
#toc li:last-child {
    padding-right: 0;
}
```

Removing this right padding decreases the amount of space the last list item takes up, reducing the chance that it will drop down onto a second line before it really needs to. The `:last-child` pseudo-class is very handy for removing padding, margins, borders, or other styles from the last item in a list, `div`, or table row.

Figure 5.10 shows the results of our styles thus far. The list looks better, but is still quite plain. How about we add a little icon or number in front of each item in the list?

FIGURE 5.10 The table of contents now has a background image and better spacing between links.

CREATING NUMBER "ICONS" WITH PURE CSS

To create numbers in front of the list items, we could use an ordered list (`ol` element) instead of an unordered list (`ul` element). But there's no way to directly style the list marker numbers that the browser adds. There are ways to hack around this, but they limit the looks we can achieve and add junk to the markup.

Another option is to use background images of numbers. This has the disadvantage, though, of adding five more HTTP requests to the page. To minimize this, you could use a technique called "CSS sprites" where you combine all the images into one and then use background positioning to reveal the portion of this big image that you want to show on each list item. But even using sprites, you still have to deal with one extra HTTP request that you don't really need, plus some complicated CSS to make the technique work.

Instead of using images, let's use generated content like we did in Chapter 2 to insert the numbers for us. But we'll take it a step further this time. Instead of hard-coding the actual numbers in the `content` property—which would require five different rules for the five different list items—we'll use CSS counters, a CSS 2.1 feature, to dynamically generate and increment the numbers.

To use counters, you must first create a set of counters with a name of your choosing, using the `counter-reset` property:

```
#toc {
    background: url(images/line.png) no-repeat top right;
    padding-top: 1.6em;
    counter-reset: list;
}
```

MORE ON SPRITES

Although CSS3 makes it possible to do away with many of the images for which you've previously needed sprites, there are still going to be times when using the sprites background image technique will come in handy. Here's where you can learn more:

◆ "CSS Sprites: What They Are, Why They're Cool, and How To Use Them" by Chris Coyier (http://css-tricks.com/css-sprites)

◆ "CSS Sprites Workflow" by Chris Coyier (http://css-tricks.com/css-sprites-workflow)

◆ "CSS Sprites: Useful Technique, or Potential Nuisance?" by Louis Lazaris (www.smashingmagazine.com/2010/03/26/css-sprites-useful-technique-or-potential-nuisance)

This establishes a set of counters, arbitrarily named "list," that you can now apply to a sequence of elements. (You can also set a base value to start counting from in the `counter-reset` property, but it's zero by default, which is what I want, so I haven't included a number here.) The elements we want to apply the "list" set of counters to are the sequence of `li` elements inside the table of contents list. To apply the counters, use the `counter-increment` property in the `#toc li` rule:

```
#toc li {
    padding: 0 1.2em 0 0;
    counter-increment: list;
}
```

This tells the browser that you want to increment the counter on each `li` element, but it doesn't actually display the counter. You need to use the `content` property to do that. Create a new rule using the `:before` pseudo-class on the `li` elements to make the counters display before each list item's content:

```
#toc li:before {
    content: counter(list);
}
```

This tells the browser that the content you want to display is a counter, and the name of that counter is "list." And with that, the numbers magically appear before each list item, starting at one and incrementing by one on each new list item (**Figure 5.11**).

> **NOTE:** So remember: to use counters, you need to use three different properties: `counter-reset`, `counter-increment`, and `content`. For more on counters, read "Automatic numbering with CSS Counters" by David Storey at http://dev.opera.com/articles/view/automatic-numbering-with-css-counters.

We can style these numbers just like any other pieces of content in our
pages. First, let's get them on the same line as the text, by floating both
the numbers and text and adding a little left padding to the list items:

```
#toc li:before {
    content: counter(list);
    float: left;
}
#toc a {
    float: left;
    padding-left: 5px;
}
```

Now let's give each number a circular background using border-
radius, in the same shade of blue as the links, but semitransparent:

```
#toc li:before {
    content: counter(list);
    float: left;
    width: 1.6em;
    height: 1.6em;
    -moz-border-radius: .8em;
    -webkit-border-radius: .8em;
    border-radius: .8em;
    background: #87B3CE;
    background: hsla(203,78%,36%,.5);
}
```

NOTE: IE 9 does sup-
port border-radius,
but appears not to
on generated content
(as of this writing), so
the numbers will have
square instead of circu-
lar backgrounds in IE 9.

As explained in the "Creating ovals and circles with border-radius"
sidebar in Chapter 2, you can turn blocks into circles by setting the
same width and height (here, 1.6em) and then setting the border-
radius to half of this value (.8em).

Figure 5.12 shows that the numbers do indeed have circular backgrounds now, but the text needs some further alignment within those
circles. Add these new declarations to the #toc li:before rule:

```
color: #fff;
font-family: Arial, Helvetica, "Helvetica Neue",
sans-serif;
font-weight: bold;
text-decoration: none;
text-shadow: 0 1px 0 hsla(0,0%,0%,.6);
text-align: center;
```

FIGURE 5.12 Using `border-radius` gives circular backgrounds to the numbers.

Now the numbers look positively image-like (**Figure 5.13**). We've created the appearance of icons without needing any images or touching the HTML.

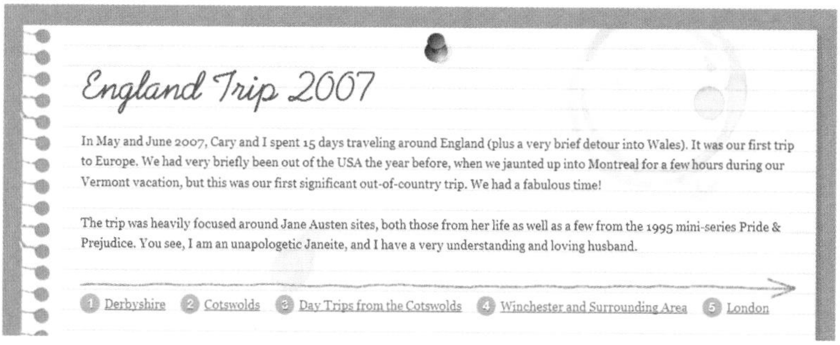

FIGURE 5.13 With some CSS3 styling, the numbers look like image icons.

Browsers that don't understand generated content will not see the numbers, let alone their styles (**Figure 5.14**). In this case, the numbers are decorative, not essential content, so this is an acceptable instance of progressive enhancement.

NOTE: The page with all the changes to this point is named target_2.html in the exercise files for this chapter.

FIGURE 5.14 IE 6 and IE 7 (top) don't show the numbers, while IE 9 and IE 8 (bottom) do, but without all of their styling.

Changing Background Color on the Jumped-to Section

All of this work on the table of contents was just a prelude to what we really came here to do: highlight the section of the page that you jump to when you click one of the links in the table of contents. The element that is targeted when you click a link is an h2 element, so the selector we need is h2:target. Create a new rule with this selector, and assign it a background color of the same shade of blue used for the number icons, but at a more semitransparent level:

```
h2:target {
    background-color: hsla(203,78%,36%,.2);
}
```

It's as simple as that. Save the page, view it in a browser, and click on one of the links. The corresponding heading will display a semitransparent light blue background (**Figure 5.15**).

FIGURE 5.15
The browser not only brings the targeted heading to the top of the window, but also applies a background color.

To spruce up the appearance a bit, you can add some left padding and a shadow to the text:

```
h2:target {
    padding-left: 10px;
    background-color: hsla(203,78%,36%,.2);
    text-shadow: 1px 1px 2px #fff;
}
```

We now have a noticeable but not obtrusive highlight on the current heading to help orient the user when the focus jumps down the page (**Figure 5.16**). The style also applies when you enter the page with the fragment identifier in the URL to begin with.

NOTE: The page with all the changes to this point is named target_3.html in the exercise files for this chapter.

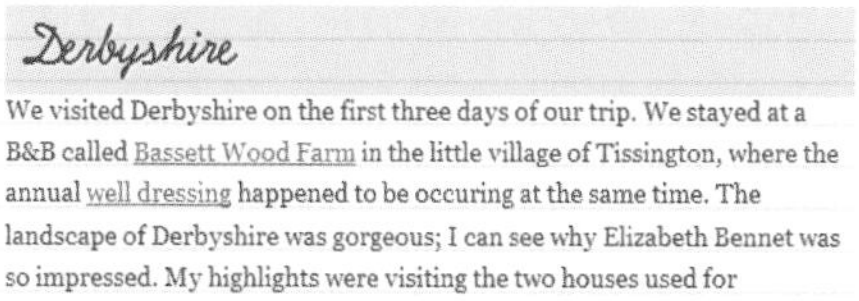

Derbyshire

We visited Derbyshire on the first three days of our trip. We stayed at a B&B called Bassett Wood Farm in the little village of Tissington, where the annual well dressing happened to be occuring at the same time. The landscape of Derbyshire was gorgeous; I can see why Elizabeth Bennet was so impressed. My highlights were visiting the two houses used for

FIGURE 5.16 The highlighted heading now has a subtle text shadow and padding to move it away from the left edge of the background strip.

HIGHLIGHTING THE WHOLE SECTION

In our example page, highlighting the whole section of the article instead of just that section's heading would be overkill, but this can be effective in other instances. To do this, you'd need some element wrapped around the section, such as a div or section element (naturally!). Give this wrapper element an ID, and then target this ID with the :target pseudo-class.

An alternate way to do it would be to use an adjacent sibling selector in conjunction with the :target pseudo-class, such as dt:target + dd. This only works, however, if you know how many elements will follow the target, and their types. The example selector given will style one dd element after the targeted dt, for instance, but wouldn't style any subsequent dd elements that might exist under that dt element.

THE LOWDOWN ON THE :target PSEUDO-CLASS

The :target pseudo-class is part of the Selectors module found at www.w3.org/TR/css3-selectors. It allows you to select an element that is the target of a referring URL with a fragment identifier in it.

Other than highlighting the heading of the current page section, you might want to use :target for:

◆ Highlighting footnotes

◆ Revealing explanatory text next to a targeted heading, so the user gets more context for where she is in the page; see http://web-graphics.com/mtarchive/001454.php

◆ Bringing an item to the front of a stack of overlapping boxes or images; see http://virtuelvis.com/archives/2003/07/target-fun

◆ Tabbed content boxes; see http://css-tricks.com/css3-tabs

◆ Accordion menus or expanding and collapsing content boxes; see www.paulrhayes.com/2009-06/accordion-using-only-css and www.thecssninja.com/css/accordian-effect-using-css

◆ Slideshows; see www.dinnermint.org/css/using-css3s-target-pseudo-class-to-make-a-slideshow and www.nealgrosskopf.com/tech/thread.php?pid=45

◆ Image galleries; see www.tobypitman.com/pure-css-sliding-image-gallery, www.ie7nomore.com/fun/scroll, and www.ie7nomore.com/fun/slideshow

◆ Modal windows or lightboxes; see http://sixrevisions.com/css/semantic-css3-lightboxes and www.thecssninja.com/css/futurebox2

Please note that some of these techniques are probably better controlled with JavaScript than CSS, due to potential accessibility and usability problems with pure CSS versions. That said, they might be useful in certain limited circumstances or provide you with ideas for other ways to use :target effectively, so I've included them here as a jumping off point for your inspiration.

TABLE 5.4   :target **browser support**

IE	FIREFOX	OPERA	SAFARI	CHROME
Yes, 9+	Yes	Partial*	Yes	Yes

* Opera supports :target, but doesn't remove the :target styling when you use the Back or Forward buttons to navigate away from the target.

WORKAROUNDS FOR IE

IE 8 and earlier don't support the `:target` pseudo-class; the table of contents links will still work to jump IE users to the corresponding headings, of course, but the headings won't be highlighted. Since this is how most in-page links work, there's little chance that users of IE 8 and earlier are going to suspect something is missing. Nor is it likely that users who don't see the highlight are going to get very disoriented in our page of limited content.

In a real page with far more content, however, the highlight could be a much more important usability feature. Think about the Wikipedia example with hundreds of footnotes—that highlight really comes in handy. Or what if the section being jumped to is so close to the bottom of the page that the browser can't bring it all the way up to the top of the viewport—this can be pretty disorienting, too. If your page does warrant an IE workaround, you'll need to use JavaScript. Here are a few scripts that would work:

- "Suckerfish :target" by Patrick Griffiths and Dan Webb (http://www.htmldog.com/articles/suckerfish/target)

- "Improving the usability of within-page links" by Bruce Lawson (http://dev.opera.com/articles/view/improving-the-usability-of-within-page-l)

- "Fragment Highlight" by David Dorward (http://dorward.me.uk/software/frag)

Animating the Change with Pure CSS

Another nice enhancement to our heading highlight would be to either fade in or fade out the background color; the "movement" created by the gradually changing color might direct the viewer's attention even more effectively than the abrupt change.

You can do this with JavaScript. One popular implementation of such an effect is called the "Yellow Fade Technique." It was named and started by 37signals in their popular web app Basecamp. When you made a change, that change would be highlighted with a yellow background for a moment, and then the yellow color would fade away. This brought more attention to the item that was changed, enhancing the usability goal of helping the user orient herself or notice the most important information on the page. See http://37signals.com/svn/

archives/000558.php for 37signals' blog post explaining the Yellow Fade Technique.

And yes, of course, we can accomplish a similar effect using CSS3 instead of JavaScript. Webkit-based browsers, Opera, and Firefox 4 support transitions, and Webkit-based browsers also support animations created with pure CSS. Transitions can be used here to fade in the color when the heading is targeted, and then fade it out again when the target is removed. Animations can be used to either fade in or fade out the color—or both, in succession—when the heading is targeted. Let's check out both options.

WAIT A MINUTE. THIS IS MAKING ME UNCOMFORTABLE.

Before we go any further, let me pause and assuage your potential anxiety. I know that CSS transitions and animations make some people uneasy.

For one thing, they don't have great browser support. At the time of this writing, transitions are supported only in Webkit-based browsers, Opera 10.5 and later versions, and Firefox 4—a small chunk of overall browser user-share. Animations are supported only in Webkit-based browsers. Because of this, I think you should use them more sparingly than most of the other pieces of CSS3. But I don't think poor browser support should keep you from using them entirely, as long as you're certain that the effects you're using them for are truly non-essential enhancements. That way, adding them doesn't hurt anyone, and only costs you a little bit of time and effort. Plus, as soon as support does improve, your pages—and your CSS skills—will be ahead of the curve.

Another concern some people have with CSS transitions and animations is that both—but particularly animation—tread into the territory of "behavior," not "style." Thus (some argue) these effects should not be included in CSS; they're the job of JavaScript, other scripting or programming languages, or Flash.

I agree with this argument to a point. Animation is very often behavior. But it's very often style, too. Think about a button with a glow that pulses. Is this pulsing glow a behavior of the button? Or is it simply a *visual* effect—a visual *style*? Jimmy Cuadra, in his article "CSS3 transitions and animation: Presentation or behavior?" (www.jimmycuadra.com/blog/12-css3-transitions-and-animation-presentation-or-behavior), calls these sorts of effects "presentational behavior." I like the distinction he makes between presentation and behavior:

Instead of thinking of presentation as what things look like and behavior as what things do, we should think of presentation as anything that doesn't fundamentally alter the page, and behavior as anything that manipulates document structure or data, or that facilitates explicit user interaction.

Elliot Swan, in a comment at http://mondaybynoon.com/2009/05/04/ covering-the-implication-and-basics-of-css-animation/#comment-9099, offers another way to define or describe transitions and animations:

I see transitions/animations as neither styles nor behaviors, but as effects (or you could also argue that an effect is the result of style and behavior combined).

This idea of "presentational behavior" or "effects" is not new to CSS3. CSS 2.1 has a taste of behavior-like styles using the :hover, :focus, and :active pseudo-classes. A button that changes color when you hover over it is displaying a behavior, but the behavior is a decorative and usability enhancement, not essential to the content or functionality of the page. CSS3 simply extends this further, giving you the ability to control a wider range of dynamic stylistic effects with CSS. I think it makes sense and is acceptable to have simple, decorative animations controlled by a styling language; the more complex or behavioral animations should stay in the domain of scripting languages or Flash.

Yes, CSS animation can be abused. It shouldn't be used for essential behaviors, or for very complex animations that something like Flash could handle more gracefully and efficiently, although a few people will likely use it in these ways. That's a shame, but it's a fact of life with just about *any* CSS technique. Evil web designers can always twist virtuous CSS into work on their dastardly web sites.

Don't worry about what evil web designers might do with CSS animations and transitions. Just worry about using them responsibly and effectively yourself. After all, they're not without their benefits.

BENEFITS OF CSS TRANSITIONS AND ANIMATIONS

One of the greatest advantages to you of CSS transitions and animations is that once you know the syntax, they can be a lot easier to implement and later modify than equivalent effects in JavaScript or Flash. (Just make sure you're using CSS3 animations appropriately— a very complex animation is going to be easier to create in Flash, but you shouldn't be using CSS3 animation for something complex anyway.) CSS is also free, whereas using Flash for creating animations is definitely not free.

In terms of benefits to your users, CSS transitions and animations don't rely on having JavaScript enabled or the Flash plugin installed; the effects run off built-in browser functionality. Some users have JavaScript disabled, and Flash does not and apparently never will work on the iOS for iPhone, iPod Touch, and iPad. So although browser support is poor for CSS animation now, in the future, when support has increased, it may be the best way to show the widest possible audience your simple decorative effects.

CSS3 transitions and animations can also have performance benefits. You don't need any external JS or SWF files to run them, so there are less HTTP requests. They also sometimes take less of the user's machine's performing power to run, at least compared to a JavaScript version. But this largely depends on the particular animation and the alternate technology you're comparing it to—Flash is often less processor-intensive than the CSS3 equivalent. So again, be sure to use transitions and animations only on relatively simple effects and to test them well.

> **NOTE:** See an interesting comparison of ads created with Flash versus with CSS3 at www.sencha.com/blog/2010/07/20/html5-family-css3-ads-versus-flash-ads.

I'm not suggesting that CSS transitions and animations are a magic bullet, or that they have no disadvantages. But they're another great tool that we can use carefully in appropriate situations. Let's see how to do that now.

FADING IN THE COLOR USING CSS TRANSITIONS

The first option for fading in the background color of the current heading is to use transitions. These are essentially the simplest type of CSS animation. Transitions let you ease the change between two different styles of an element gradually and smoothly, instead of seeing an immediate and abrupt difference in style when an element is hovered, targeted, or has its state otherwise changed.

> **NOTE:** You can view how each of the transition timing functions works with the helpful demo at http://css3.bradshawenterprises.com.

You apply a transition by telling the browser which property you want to gradually change (using `transition-property`) and how long the change should take in seconds (using `transition-duration`). You can optionally add a delay to the start of the transition (`transition-delay`) and vary the speed of change over the duration of the transition (`transition-timing-function`).

All of these properties can also be combined into the shorthand `transition` property. Add it, and the three browser-specific equivalents, to the h2 rule:

```
h2 {
    clear: left;
    margin: 0 0 -.14em 0;
    color: #414141;
    font-family: Prelude, Helvetica, "Helvetica Neue",
                 Arial, sans-serif;
    font-size: 2.17em;
    font-weight: bold;
    -moz-transition: background-color 1s ease-out;
    -o-transition: background-color 1s ease-out;
    -webkit-transition: background-color 1s ease-out;
    transition: background-color 1s ease-out;
}
```

Here, we've told the browsers that any time the `background-color` value of an h2 element changes, we want it to make that change happen gradually over the course of one second. We've also specified a `transition-timing-function` of `ease-out` so that the animation will slow down slightly at the end.

Transitions are hard to illustrate in a static book, but **Figure 5.17** shows the gradual change in color when a heading is targeted. The transition runs in reverse, from blue to transparent, when you use the Back button in your browser to remove the target from the heading.

FIGURE 5.17 Over the one-second course of the transition, the background of the heading darkens from fully transparent to blue.

WHAT CAN YOU TRANSITION?

Not all properties can be transitioned. The W3C calls those that can "animatable properties" and lists them at www.w3.org/TR/css3-transitions/#animatable-properties-. That's why I've used background-color in the h2:target rule instead of the background shorthand property; background-color can be transitioned and background can't. Or at least, it *shouldn't* be able to be transitioned. Webkit and Firefox don't obey this, but Opera does, so the transition wouldn't work in Opera if we used background instead of background-color.

NOTE: To try out this transition yourself, view the file target_4.html, included in the exercise files for this chapter, in one of the transition-supporting browsers. The file contains all the changes from the chapter to this point.

We could have put the transition on the h2:target rule instead of the h2 rule. But if we did this, the transition would run only when a heading became targeted; it wouldn't run in reverse when the target is removed, but would instead abruptly change back to transparent. Also, currently, Opera supports transitions only when you place them on the original state of the element, not on the changed state, so the transition wouldn't work in Opera if it were applied to the h2:target rule. This seems to be incorrect behavior, but the in-progress W3C spec doesn't make this clear.

In addition to the background color transition, we can make the left padding added to the highlighted headings transition too, to create the appearance that the text is sliding to the right. You can do this by simply writing the padding transition in the same transition property, separated by a comma:

```
h2 {
    clear: left;
    margin: 0 0 -.14em 0;
    color: #414141;
    font-family: Prelude, Helvetica, "Helvetica Neue",
                Arial, sans-serif;
    font-size: 2.17em;
    font-weight: bold;
    -moz-transition: background-color 1s ease-out,
                padding-left .5s ease-out;
    -o-transition: background-color 1s ease-out,
                padding-left .5s ease-out;
    -webkit-transition: background-color 1s ease-out,
                padding-left .5s ease-out;
    transition: background-color 1s ease-out,
                padding-left .5s ease-out;
}
```

THE LOWDOWN ON THE transition PROPERTY

The transition property is part of the Transitions module found at www.w3.org/TR/css3-transitions. It's shorthand for the transition-property, transition-duration, transition-timing-function, and transition-delay properties. It allows you to gradually change from one value of a property to another upon an element's state change.

The necessary pieces of a transition are transition-property (to specify the property of the element you want to gradually change) and transition-duration (to specify over how long the change should take—the default is zero if you leave it off). The other properties are optional.

Multiple properties of an element can be transitioned simultaneously; write each property's transition in the same transition property, separated by commas. You can also use a value of all for transition-property to specify that all of the element's properties should transition.

Not all properties can be transitioned; see www.w3.org/TR/css3-transitions/#animatable-properties- for a list of those that can. All of the transition-supporting browsers support transitioning *most* of these properties; there are various exceptions that would take up too much space to list here.

See www.webdesignerdepot.com/2010/01/css-transitions-101 and http://thinkvitamin.com/design/sexy-interactions-with-css-transitions for more transition syntax details and examples.

Other than fading in a background color change, you might want to use transition for:

- Gradually changing between hover/focus and non-hover/focus states of buttons, tabs, or links

- Making images appear to light up or brighten when hovered (by transitioning opacity)

- Fading between images that are stacked on top of each other (such as a black and white version that gets swapped with a colored version, or before and after images); see http://trentwalton.com/2010/03/30/css3-transition-delay and http://css3.bradshawenterprises.com

- Making image icons appear to gradually change color when hovered (by having transparent areas within them through which a background color shows, and you then transition the background color); see www.ackernaut.com/tutorials/rocking-icons-with-css

- Gradually making tooltips or informational boxes appear; see www.zurb.com/playground/drop-in-modals

- Creating the appearance that something is growing or shrinking (by transitioning its width, height, or transform scale value); see www.zurb.com/playground/css3-polaroids and www.marcofolio.net/css/animated_wicked_css3_3d_bar_chart.html

- Making elements slide into view (by transitioning width, height, positioning, or transforms), such as in an image gallery, accordion menu, or featured content slider; see www.nealgrosskopf.com/tech/thread.php?pid=45, http://dev.opera.com/articles/view/css3-show-and-hide, www.impressivewebs.com/animated-sprites-css3, and http://css3.bradshawenterprises.com

- Creating a moving background image; see www.paulrhayes.com/2009-04/auto-scrolling-parallax-effect-without-javascript

TABLE 5.5 `transition` **browser support**

IE	FIREFOX	OPERA	SAFARI	CHROME
No	Yes with -moz-, 4+	Yes with -o-, 10.5+	Yes with -webkit-	Yes with -webkit-

Now the padding change from zero to ten pixels happens gradually along with the gradual background color change (**Figure 5.18**). How smoothly both of these transitions run depends a bit on your browser (Webkit seems to be the smoothest and Firefox the most jerky), but all the supporting browsers perform well on these simple effects.

FIGURE 5.18 Over the course of the transition, the background of the heading darkens and its text moves ten pixels to the right.

FADING OUT THE COLOR USING CSS ANIMATIONS

I think briefly showing the background color on the current heading and then fading it out would be even more effective and attractive than fading it in. It would be great if we could use transitions to do this, as transitions have better browser support than animations (remember, only Webkit supports animation right now). Unfortunately, transitions won't work here, because we need each heading to go from transparent (before it's targeted) to blue (when it's targeted) to transparent again (a second after its targeted). That's three points of change, and transitions can only handle changing between two values.

CSS3 animations can change between as many values as you want. They do this by letting you set up a series of *keyframes*, or points in time within the animation, each with its own set of styles. The browser then smoothly transitions between the keyframes in order, gradually changing all the properties included in each one.

To create an animation in CSS, you first need to give it a name of your choosing and define what it will do at each keyframe. You do this using an @keyframes rule, but since only Webkit supports it right now, we need to create two rules, one with the -webkit- browser prefix and one without, for future compatibility. Add this new rule to CSS in the page:

```
@-webkit-keyframes fade {
    0% {background: hsla(203,78%,36%,.2);}
    100% {background: none;}
}
@keyframes fade {
    0% {background: hsla(203,78%,36%,.2);}
    100% {background: none;}
}
```

This assigns a name of "fade" to our animation and specifies two keyframes: one zero percent of the way through the duration (in other words, at the very beginning) and one 100 percent of the way through the duration (in other words, at the very end). We could also have used the keywords from and to in place of 0% and 100% to denote the starting and ending states.

Now that we've defined what we want our animation to do, we need to apply it to an element. We want the animation to occur on targeted h2 elements, so create a new h2:target rule and place it under the existing one (soon you'll see why we don't want to add on to the existing h2:target rule):

```
h2:target{
    padding: 0;
    background: none;
    -webkit-animation-name: fade;
    -webkit-animation-duration: 2s;
    -webkit-animation-iteration-count: 1;
    -webkit-animation-timing-function: ease-in;
}
```

This tells the browser that the animation we want to run on this element is named "fade" (using -webkit-animation-name). We want the animation to take two seconds (the -webkit-animation-duration value) and run only once (the -webkit-animation-iteration-count value). We've also told the browser we want the animation to ease in, making it slightly slower at the beginning than the end.

You can combine all these properties into the animation shorthand property. Combine the -webkit- prefixed properties into the -webkit-animation property, and also add the non-prefixed animation property to the h2:target rule:

```
h2:target{
    padding: 0;
    background: none;
    -webkit-animation: fade 2s ease-in 1;
    animation: fade 2s ease-in 1;
}
```

This second h2:target rule also removes the left padding and background color declared in the first one. If we didn't remove the background, the animation would run once, and then once it was over, it would display the static background color of the h2, popping back to blue suddenly and staying blue. We need the heading to have no background so the animation can control the background entirely; once the animation is over, we want the heading to remain transparent.

Removing the padding, on the other hand, is optional. I've chosen to remove it because it doesn't make sense to have the heading text indented once the background color has faded away. To fix this, it's possible to animate the padding, having it decrease from ten pixels to zero, just as we transitioned the padding in the opposite direction, but I found the padding movement to be more distracting in this case—it looked good with the fade-in, but I didn't like it with the fade-out. I opted for simplicity and decided to nix the padding altogether.

Save the page, and view it in Safari or Chrome. When you click on a link, the background of the selected heading will immediately become blue and then fade away smoothly. (This looks just like the sequence in Figure 5.17, but in reverse.)

What would be even nicer is if the blue color stayed in place for a moment, and then faded away. The animation-delay property allows you to delay the beginning of the animation, but that's not appropriate in this case, because the heading has no background color to start with. Before the animation starts, the user would not see blue, but just a lack of any background at all.

GETTING MORE COMPLEX

In this example, we're changing only the background color in each keyframe, but you can add as many properties to a keyframe as you want. You simply write them between the curly brackets of the keyframe like you would in any other CSS rule. For instance, if you wanted to change the font size as well as the background color, you could do this:

```
@-webkit-keyframes fade {
    0% {
        background: hsla(203,78%,36%,.2);
        font-size: 100%;
    }
    100% {
        background: none;
        font-size: 120%;
    }
}
```

It's also possible to assign more than one animation to a single element, so you could break each of the above property changes out into its own animation:

```
@-webkit-keyframes fade {
    0% {background: hsla(203,78%,36%,.2);}
    100% {background: none;}
}
@-webkit-keyframes scaletext {
    0% {font-size: 100%;}
    100% {font-size: 120%;}
}
```

Then declare both animations on one element:

```
h2:target {
    -webkit-animation-name: fade, scaletext;
    -webkit-animation-duration: 2s;
    -webkit-animation-iteration-count: 1;
    -webkit-animation-timing-function: ease-in;
}
```

Defining the animations separately takes more code, but may make it easier to keep track of what's happening at which points in complex animations, and it allows you to control the duration, iteration, and other properties of each independently. Another advantage is that you can reuse each animation on other elements. For instance, you might want both the fade and text scaling to happen on the h2 elements, but on h3 elements you may only want the text to scale. Since the animations are separate, you can reuse the "textscale" animation instead of having to create a whole new animation for the h3 elements.

THE LOWDOWN ON THE animation PROPERTY

The animation property is part of the Animations module found at www.w3.org/TR/css3-animations. It's shorthand for animation-name, animation-duration, animation-timing-function, animation-delay, animation-iteration-count, and animation-direction (in that order).

Before using the above properties to apply an animation to an element, you first name the animation and define what it does using an @keyframes rule. The keyframes are multiple points in time through the duration of the animation, indicated with percentages; the keywords from and to correspond to 0% and 100%, respectively. Each keyframe contains style rules that should apply at that point in time. The browser gradually changes the styles from one keyframe to the next.

Other than fading out a background color, you might want to use animation for:

◆ Pulsing glow on buttons; see www.zurb.com/playground/radioactive-buttons

◆ Loader spinners; see http://24ways.org/2009/css-animations

◆ Flash cards; see http://line25.com/articles/super-cool-css-flip-effect-with-webkit-animation

◆ Making elements roll into view; see www.zurb.com/playground/sliding-vinyl

There are loads of more complex, movie-like effects people have created with CSS animations, but I've tried to limit my examples here to some of the more practical ones. Still, it's fun to see what can be done; Google "CSS3 animation" to get a taste.

TABLE 5.6 animation **browser support**

IE	FIREFOX	OPERA	SAFARI	CHROME
No	No	No	Yes with -webkit-	Yes with -webkit-

Instead of using animation-delay to put off the start of the animation, we can create a delay within the animation itself by adding another keyframe to the animation that keeps the color the same shade of blue:

```
@-webkit-keyframes fade {
    0% {background: hsla(203,78%,36%,.2);}
    20% {background: hsla(203,78%,36%,.2);}
    100% {background: none;}
}
@keyframes fade {
    0% {background: hsla(203,78%,36%,.2);}
    20% {background: hsla(203,78%,36%,.2);}
    100% {background: none;}
}
```

Now the animation will start immediately by displaying a blue background, keep showing that background until 20 percent of the way through the animation's duration (.4 seconds), and then start fading to transparent.

WORKAROUNDS FOR NON-SUPPORTING BROWSERS

The fade-out animation is now working great in Safari and Chrome, but what about other browsers? We had to remove the background color from the targeted h2 elements to make the animation work, so now nothing changes in non-Webkit browsers when you click on one of the table of contents links; they just remain transparent.

What we need is a way to let browsers that don't support CSS animations see the first h2:target rule with the blue background color, and browsers that do support CSS animations see the second h2:target rule with the transparent background color. We can do this using the Modernizr script described in Chapter 1.

This script is included in the exercise files you downloaded for this chapter, so add a link to it in the head of the page:

```
<script src="scripts/modernizr-1.6.min.js"></script>
```

This script adds classes to the html element of the page the correspond to what the browser does and doesn't support. So, for instance, Modernizr will add a class of "cssanimations" to the html element in Safari and Chrome, and all other browsers will get a class of "no-css-animations". This allows us to change the second h2:target selector to apply only when the cssanimations class is present:

```
.cssanimations h2:target{
    padding: 0;
    background: none;
    -webkit-animation: fade 2s ease-in 1;
    animation: fade 2s ease-in 1;
}
```

NOTE: To try out this animation yourself, view the file target_5.html, included in the exercise files for this chapter, in Safari or Chrome. The file contains all the changes from the chapter to this point.

NOTE: The version of Modernizr included with the exercise files is 1.6, the latest version at the time of this writing. But there may be a newer version by the time you read this, which you should use instead. Check at www.modernizr.com.

> **NOTE:** The completed page showing these effects that you can compare in different browsers is named target_final.html in the exercise files for this chapter.

Save your page, and view it in both a Webkit-based browser and a non-Webkit browser. In the former, you'll see the fade-out animation run when a heading is targeted. In the latter, you'll see the fade-in transition run when a heading is targeted. In browsers that don't support either transitions or animations, but do support `:target` (such as IE 9 and Firefox 3.6 and earlier), you'll see the blue background immediately appear on the targeted heading. And finally, in browsers that support none of the above (such as IE 8 and earlier), you'll see nothing special happen when you click a table of contents link.

The table of contents links will still work, of course—they'll still jump people down the page, just as we're all used to, so there's no reason users of less capable browsers will know anything is missing. If you really must have a fade effect on the targeted heading in these browsers, you have a couple workaround options:

- Use an animated GIF. Yes, it's a bit old-school, but it's still a perfectly valid technique. Be aware that this works only on browsers that support `:target`. All you have to do is add an animated GIF of the color change as the background image in the h2:target rule. You can read an entire tutorial about this method in "Star on :target" by Brian Suda at http://thinkvitamin.com/dev/stay-on-target.

- Use a script. This will work regardless of whether or not the browser supports `:target` (as long as the user has JavaScript enabled, of course, and as long as the script was written to support that user's browser). Providing such a script is beyond the scope of this book, but you may want to check out www.marcofolio.net/css/css3_animations_and_their_jquery_equivalents.html and http://weston.ruter.net/projects/jquery-css-transitions for some scripts that can make all sorts of transitions and animations work. Also consider Googling "javascript animation framework." Finally, if you're just interested in a fade technique, Google "yellow fade technique" and you'll find a bunch of scripts—some standalone, some related to a particular framework—that you can choose from.

In either of these options, remember to hide the extra CSS or scripts from browsers that don't need them, using either IE conditional comments or Modernizr.

6

Different Screen Size, Different Design

It's no secret or surprise that the variety of ways people browse the web is increasing. People may view your web pages on widescreen TVs, desktop computers, netbooks, mobile phones—even a refrigerator. While you can't make a site that looks identical on every single device at every screen size and text size, you can make a site that adapts to the users' settings so that it looks good and works well in the screen space available. In this chapter, you'll learn how to use CSS3 media queries to tailor a web page's design to various screen sizes on the fly, making your web pages more dynamic, responsive, and usable.

WHAT YOU'LL LEARN

We'll be restyling an entire page layout to work with different screen sizes and devices using these pieces of CSS3:

◆ Media queries to apply styles selectively based on the visitor's device properties

◆ Multi-columns to flow text into side-by-side columns

The Base Page

Figure 6.1 shows a layout for a fictional bakery. The layout is liquid (also known as fluid) so that it adjusts to the width of the browser window, making it work at a variety of screen sizes without generating horizontal scrollbars or causing elements to overlap. But it certainly looks better at some screen sizes than at others. On very wide or very narrow windows, the design is still usable and looks OK, but it's not as attractive as it is within the 800- to 1200-pixel range (**Figure 6.2**).

FIGURE 6.1
The fictional Little Pea Bakery home page, as seen in a browser window that's 1024 pixels wide.

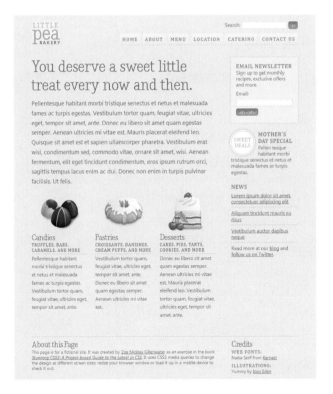

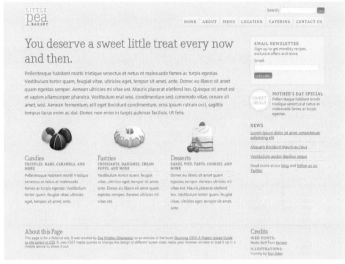

FIGURE 6.2 **The design looks OK, but not great, in very narrow and very wide windows.**

In Chapter 2 of my book *Flexible Web Design: Creating Liquid and Elastic Layouts with CSS*, I show that flexible layouts don't have to be plain or ugly to work at a variety of screen sizes. You can build pages with flexible images, reasonable text-line lengths, and creative use of space to make sure the design works well at a large range of widths. But I don't deny that it's impossible to create a design that looks every bit as good condensed into 300 pixels as it does stretched out to 2000 pixels. I've always advocated using `min-width` and `max-width`, as well as separate styles for mobile devices, in order to get around this problem.

Since the writing of *Flexible Web Design* in 2008, however, a new tool for creating layouts that work at any ridiculously large range of sizes you want has gained good browser support: media queries.

What are Media Queries?

NOTE: All the available media features are listed and described fully at www.w3.org/TR/css3-mediaqueries/#media1. The ones you'll probably need most often are min-width, max-width, min-device-width, max-device-width, orientation (portrait or landscape), color, and resolution.

Media queries let you customize styles based on the characteristics of the user's device or display, such as the viewport width, whether it's in portrait or landscape mode, or whether it shows color. This is different from the media types, such as screen and print, that you can specify for your style sheets in CSS 2.1. With media queries, you specify not only the media type to which you want to apply a set of styles, but also one or more characteristics of the user's display. Here's an example:

```
@media screen and (max-width: 600px) {
    body {
        font-size: 88%;
    }
    #content-main {
        float: none;
        width: 100%;
    }
}
```

TIP: If you want to use the media type all in your media query, you can make your CSS shorter by leaving out the media type entirely, as well as the word and, like so: @media (max-width:600px).

The above media query starts with the @media rule, and then specifies a media type (in this case, screen). Next there's the word and, followed by the characteristic we want to match against, called the *media feature*. This particular media feature, max-width: 600px, tells the browser that the styles for this media query, which are contained within a set of curly brackets for the media query as a whole, should apply only up to a maximum width of 600 pixels. If the viewport width exceeds 600 pixels, the browser will ignore the styles inside the media query.

This media query can be dropped right into your main style sheet, keeping all your styles in one place for easy debugging and maintenance, as well as saving an HTTP request. If you want, however, you can apply media queries to separate style sheets on the link element or @import rule:

```
@import url(narrow.css) only screen and (max-width:600px);
```

```
<link rel="stylesheet" media="only screen and
¬(max-width:600px)" href="narrow.css">
```

Here, I've added the keyword only in front of the media type screen to keep some older browsers that don't understand media queries from downloading and applying the style sheets universally. Most non-supporting browsers will not use the sheet anyway, but this is extra insurance. The only keyword isn't needed when you place the @media rule directly in your main style sheet.

Whether embedded with other CSS or in separate sheets, media queries are a powerful new tool in web design. We can use them to customize and fine-tune our styles to each user's device and settings with more precision than we've ever been able to before. This can improve not only the attractiveness of our web pages, but also their usability. We can change text line lengths, leading, and font sizes to make sure the text remains readable at different widths. We can rearrange columns and resize or remove images on small screens to make better use of the space and let users get right to the content they want. We can make links larger on touch-screen mobile devices to make them easier for people to activate with their fingers. And we can do all this without having to involve complicated scripting for browser sniffing, feature detection, or style-sheet switching. You just continue to use the CSS that you already know to write different styles for different scenarios.

Let's use media queries now on our example page to customize the design to large screens, small screens, and mobile devices.

Changing the Layout for Large Screens

We'll start with the styles for large screens. Download the exercise files for this chapter at www.stunningcss3.com, and open media-queries_start.html in your code editor. Its CSS is contained in a style element in the head of the page.

The design of this example page starts looking a bit stretched out at around 1200 pixels wide, so let's add a media query that will apply only when the window is 1200 or more pixels wide. Add the following CSS after all the existing styles in the style element in the head:

```
@media screen and (min-width: 1200px) {
}
```

This media query has to be at the end of the styles so that it will override the earlier styles, using the cascade of CSS. It tells the browser that we want the styles within this media query to apply to screen media types, but only if the user's viewport width is 1200 pixels at a minimum. Of course, right now there are no styles in the media query, just empty brackets waiting to be filled. Since we have so much extra space in viewports over 1200 pixels wide, how about we fill those brackets with styles to change the layout from two columns to three?

To do this, we'll change the positioning of the navigation div, as well as the widths and margins of the two content divs. Here are the current styles of these three divs, outside the media query:

```
#nav-main {
    float: right;
    margin: 40px 0 0 0;
}
#content-main {
    overflow: hidden;
    float: left;
    width: 70%;
    margin-bottom: 40px;
}
#content-secondary {
    float: right;
    width: 25%;
    margin-bottom: 40px;
}
```

NOTE: Opera 10.6 has a strange bug that makes the navigation div disappear when you first expand the window past 1200 pixels. When you hover over the area where it should be, it shows up. There's no workaround for this right now; hopefully the Opera team will fix this bug soon.

Modify these styles for viewports over 1200 pixels wide by adding new rules within the media query you just created:

```
@media screen and (min-width: 1200px) {
    #nav-main {
        position: fixed;
        top: 136px;
        width: 13%;
        margin: 0;
    }
    #content-main {
        width: 58%;
        margin-left: 18%;
    }
    #content-secondary { width: 20%; }
}
```

This positions the navigation div under the logo, creating a third column. To make room for it, it was necessary to decrease the width of the content-secondary div from 25 percent to 20 percent, decrease the width of the content-main div from 70 percent to 58 percent, and add a left margin to content-main.

Let's also change the widths of the about and credits divs in the footer to match the widths of the columns above them. Add their IDs onto the #content-main and #content-secondary rules in the media query:

```
#content-main, #about {
    width: 58%;
    margin-left: 18%;
}
#content-secondary, #credits { width: 20%; }
```

Now all the page elements are better positioned to work well in the width available (**Figure 6.3**). Save your page, and view it in an up-to-date browser. Resize your window to see how the layout automatically changes when you get past 1200 pixels wide.

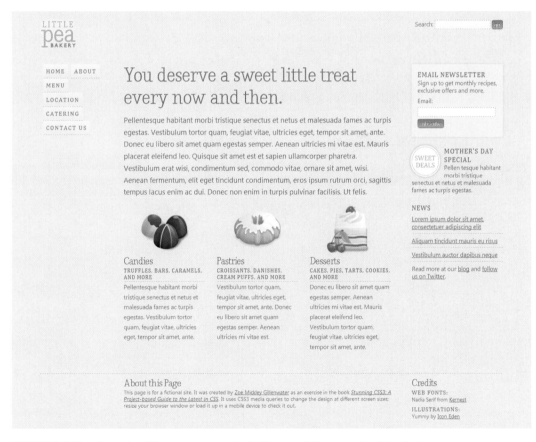

FIGURE 6.3 **The elements of the page now make better use of the space in wide windows.**

THE LOWDOWN ON MEDIA QUERIES

Media queries are described in a module of the same name, found at www.w3.org/TR/css3-mediaqueries. They let you customize styles based not only on media type, such as `screen` and `print`, but also on characteristics of the user's display, such as viewport width. These characteristics, called media features, are listed at www.w3.org/TR/css3-mediaqueries/#media1; not all browsers that support media queries support all of them.

A media query can be written within a style sheet, using the `@media` rule, followed by the media type and one or more media features. Media queries can also be written onto `link` elements and `@import` rules, omitting the `@media` rule.

You can include more than one media feature in a single media query, such as `@media screen and (min-width:320px) and (max-width:480px)`. You can also include more than one media query in the same `@media` rule, separated by commas, such as `@media screen and (color), projection and (color)`, similar to a grouped selector.

You can write the word `not` at the start of a media query to apply its styles only when the media query is not true, such as `@media not print and (max-width:600px)`.

Other than changing layout at different screen sizes, you might want to use media queries for:

- Adjusting text size and leading to keep text more readable at different line lengths; see http://forabeautifulweb.com/blog/about/proportional_leading_with_css3_media_queries

- Increasing text size of buttons, tabs, and links on mobile devices to make these elements easier to activate with your finger on touch screens

- Decreasing body-text size on small mobile screens since the user is effectively zoomed in, making the text seem larger than on desktop screens

- Revealing in-page links to jump to content down the page on small mobile screens

- Swapping in higher resolution images on high-resolution devices, such as the iPhone 4; see http://dryan.com/articles/posts/2010/6/25/hi-res-mobile-css-iphone-4 as well as the example later in this chapter

- Swapping in differently sized images for different viewport sizes

- Applying different print styles for different sizes of paper

TABLE 6.1 Media queries browser support

IE	FIREFOX	OPERA	SAFARI	CHROME
Partial, 9+	Partial, 3.5+	Partial	Partial	Partial

I've listed all of these browsers as having partial support because they don't support all the available media features. The details for each browser are too long and, well, detailed to cover here; however, all listed browsers support most of the media features, including the ones you are most likely to use regularly.

From Horizontal Nav Bar to Vertical Menu

Although everything is now in the place we want it, some of the page elements could use further cosmetic updates. For instance, the li elements in the nav-main div are floated and have left margins in order to align them all horizontally and space them out from each other, but this keeps them from stacking on top of each other, only one to a line, as we want in a vertical menu. They also have slightly rounded top corners, which looks good when they're horizontal, but not when they're sitting right on top of each other. We no longer need these styles now that we're styling the links as a vertical menu, so we'll override them with new styles within the media query:

```
#nav-main li {
    float: none;
    margin: 0;
}
#nav-main a {
    -moz-border-radius: 0;
    -webkit-border-radius: 0;
    border-radius: 0;
}
```

Now each link is on its own line and takes up the full width of the menu (**Figure 6.4**).

Next, let's apply some styling to the menu as a whole to make it look more similar to the email newsletter box on the other side of the page, which has a semitransparent background, slightly rounded corners, and a soft drop shadow:

```
#nav-main {
    position: fixed;
    top: 136px;
    width: 13%;
    margin: 0;
    -moz-box-shadow: 0 0 8px hsla(0,0%,0%,.1);
    -webkit-box-shadow: 0 0 8px hsla(0,0%,0%,.1);
    box-shadow: 0 0 8px hsla(0,0%,0%,.1);
    -moz-border-radius: 3px;
    -webkit-border-radius: 3px;
    border-radius: 3px;
    background: hsla(0,0%,100%,.3);
    text-align: right;
}
```

FIGURE 6.4 **Each link now takes up the full width of the menu.**

Since the menu has its own background color now, tone down the semitransparent gradients on the links within it, so that the two colors layered over each other don't get too opaque:

```
#nav-main a {
    -moz-border-radius: 0;
    -webkit-border-radius: 0;
    border-radius: 0;
    background: -moz-linear-gradient(hsla(0,0%,100%,.3),
    ↪ hsla(0,0%,100%,0) 15px);
    background: -webkit-gradient(linear, 0 0, 0 15,
    ↪ from(hsla(0,0%,100%,.3)), to(hsla(0,0%,100%,0)));
}
#nav-main a:hover {
    background: -moz-linear-gradient(hsla(0,0%,100%,.6),
    ↪ hsla(0,0%,100%,.2) 15px);
    background: -webkit-gradient(linear, 0 0, 0 15,
    ↪ from(hsla(0,0%,100%,.6)), to(hsla(0,0%,100%,.2)));
}
```

FIGURE 6.5 **The menu in the left column has been restyled to resemble the newsletter subscription box in the right column.**

These changes complete the navigation's transformation from horizontal bar to vertical menu (**Figure 6.5**).

Multi-column Text

One of the main complaints people have with layouts that adjust to viewport width is that the length of lines of text can become either too short or too long to be read comfortably or look attractive. Some of this fear of "non-standard" line lengths is based on assumption and myth. In reality, there is no magic line length that is ideal for everyone; a person's age, reading level, native language, disability, and other factors all influence which line length he finds easiest to read.

NOTE: You can learn more about line length in Chapter 1 of *Flexible Web Design*, which you can download for free at www.flexiblewebbook.com/bonus.html.

However, it's true that line lengths on the extreme ends of the range don't work well for the majority of readers and don't always look very attractive. One way that we can now control line lengths is with the new multi-column properties in CSS3. These properties allow you to flow the content of a single HTML element into multiple columns, similar to a newspaper layout.

You create the columns using either the `column-count` or `column-width` properties; in the latter case, the browser will decide how many columns to make based on the available space. (You can also use both properties together, though you may get unexpected results; see "The lowdown on multi-columns" for more information.)

Let's break the introductory paragraph into two columns in both the regular layout and the wide layout. Find the existing h1 + p rule in the styles outside of the media query; it should be on line 102, about a third of the way down the `style` element. Add the `column-count` property, plus the three browser-specific versions, to the rule:

```
h1 + p {
    -moz-column-count: 2;
    -o-column-count: 2;
    -webkit-column-count: 2;
    column-count: 2;
    color: #7F4627;
    text-shadow: -1px -1px 0 hsla(0,0%,100%,.6);
    font-size: 120%;
}
```

Right now, no browser supports the non-prefixed `column-count` property, and Opera doesn't do anything with the `-o-column-count` property since it doesn't yet support multi-columns, but it's wise to include both for future compatibility.

The property tells supporting Mozilla- and Webkit-based browsers that you want to break the paragraph into two column-boxes. These column boxes are not actual elements in the document tree of the HTML, rather just virtual boxes that the browser creates to flow the content of the paragraph into. The paragraph is now what the W3C calls a *multicol element*—it's a container for a multiple-column layout.

You can control the space between the columns using the `column-gap` property. Set it to 1.5 ems in the h1 + p rule:

```
h1 + p {
    -moz-column-count: 2;
    -moz-column-gap: 1.5em;
    -o-column-count: 2;
    -o-column-gap: 1.5em;
    -webkit-column-count: 2;
    -webkit-column-gap: 1.5em;
    column-count: 2;
    column-gap: 1.5em;
    color: #7F4627;
    text-shadow: -1px -1px 0 hsla(0,0%,100%,.6);
    font-size: 120%;
}
```

If you don't set a `column-gap` value, each individual browser decides how much space to add by default, so it's best to standardize it by explicitly setting the value you want. Here, we've used a value in ems so that the gap will grow larger as the text grows larger, keeping the text more readable.

Now the introductory paragraph is broken into two columns in both the regular layout and the wide layout created with the media query (**Figure 6.6**). This completes all the styling for the wide version of the bakery page (**Figure 6.7**).

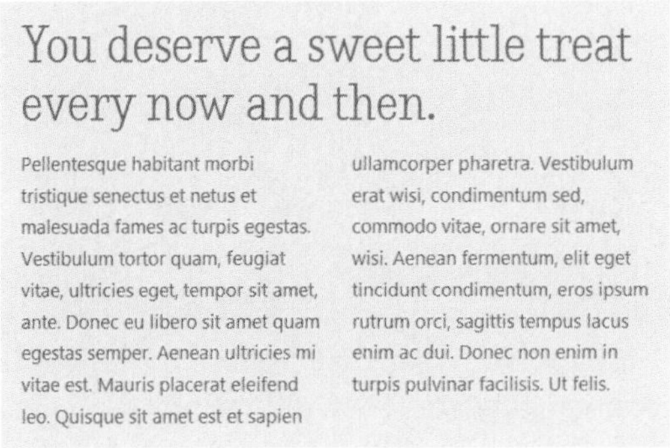

FIGURE 6.6 **The text of the introductory paragraph flows into two columns in Firefox, Safari, and Chrome.**

FIGURE 6.7
The completed design for wide viewports

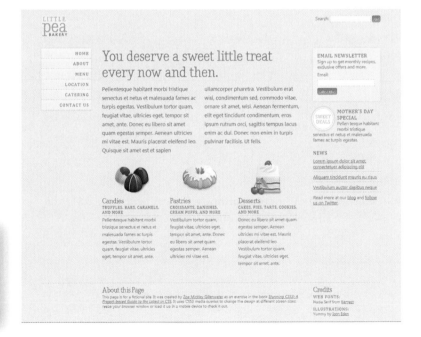

NOTE: The page with all the changes to this point is named media-queries_1.html in the exercise files for this chapter.

PROBLEMS WITH MULTI-COLUMNS

Although CSS3 multi-columns work well for the introductory paragraph in our bakery page, there are a number of problems with them that limit their usefulness, which you should be aware of before you use the feature. Some of these problems are technical in nature, so as the W3C refines the specification and browsers fix bugs and improve support, they should disappear or at least lessen. These problems include:

* **Balancing column heights.** If there's not enough content to fill each column equally, the browser has to decide which column gets the extra height. Different browsers choose differently, with sometimes unexpected results.

* **Flowing margin, padding, and borders across columns.** Webkit-based browsers allow margin, padding, and borders to be split across columns, creating a very strange appearance.

* **Breaking content across columns.** Being able to control where content breaks across columns is important, as you want to be able to ensure that a heading stays with its associated text, for instance. The column-break properties control this, but no browser supports them now.

* **Overflowing columns or content.** Browsers are currently inconsistent about how to handle overflow when not all of the content or columns can fit in the container (the multicol element); it may overflow to the right or below, or just be truncated. An individual piece of content that is too large to fit in a column box, such as an image that is wider than the column width, is supposed to be cut off in the middle of the column gap, but Firefox lets it overflow and Webkit cuts it off at the edge of the column, not within the gutter as the spec dictates.

* **Floating content within columns.** Floats within a multicol element are supposed to be positioned relative to the column box in which they appear. Firefox does this; Webkit, strangely, puts the float outside of the multicol element entirely.

* **Pagination when printed.** When a multicol element has to break across two or more pages when printed, the columns are not supposed to break across the pages. The content should run through the columns on the first page, then run through the columns on the second page, and so on. Older versions of Webkit-based browsers didn't follow this; current versions simply make the content go back to a single column when printed, avoiding the issue entirely.

NOTE: For a demo of the first two problems in this list, see http://zomigi.com/blog/deal-breaker-problems-with-css3-multi-columns.

But some problems with multi-columns are more inherent to the idea of columns on the web to begin with. Having to scroll down to read a column and then back up to read the next column, over and over again, is just plain annoying and tiresome. This isn't a technical problem—it's a usability problem with breaking up content that's taller than a constrained screen. Treating the web like print often doesn't work well. For more on the usability and design problems inherent to CSS3 multi-columns, see "Multicolumn layout considered harmful" by Roger Johanssen (www.456bereastreet.com/archive/200509/css3_multicolumn_layout_considered_harmful), "More on multi-column layouts" by Richard Rutter (www.clagnut.com/blog/1590), and "CSS3 Multi-Column Thriller" by Andy Clarke (www.stuffandnonsense.co.uk/archives/css3_multi-column_thriller.html).

Because of all of these problems, I strongly recommend only using multiple columns in a limited manner. I think they're fine for a couple paragraphs or a list, for instance. I don't think they work very well for long blocks of body copy or content that is complex, with several paragraphs, types of elements, or images within it. Just keep this in mind, and use multi-columns wisely.

WORKAROUNDS FOR NON-SUPPORTING BROWSERS

Multi-columns are a quintessential progressive enhancement technique, since browsers that don't support the multi-column properties simply see the text as it started out—in one column.

If you must provide a workaround for non-supporting browsers, there are several scripts that can flow content into multiple columns. The CSS3 Multi Column script by Cédric Savarese (www.csscripting.com/css-multi-column) is a nice one because it reads the multi-column properties already in your CSS and makes them work in non-supporting browsers. You may also want to check out:

- Columnizer jQuery plugin, by Adam Wulf (http://welcome.totheinter.net/columnizer-jquery-plugin)

- MooColumns MooTools class, by Jason J. Jaeger (http://greengeckodesign.com/moocolumns)

- Multi-column script, by Randy Simons (http://randysimons.nl/125,english/129,multi-column-text)

- Column script, by Michael van Ouwerkerk (http://13thparallel.com/archive/column-script)

THE LOWDOWN ON MULTI-COLUMNS

Multi-columns are described in the Multi-column Layout module found at www.w3.org/TR/css3-multicol. They're created using either the `column-count` or `column-width` properties (or both). You can set both using the `columns` shorthand property, but Firefox doesn't yet support it.

The `column-width` property lets the browser decide how many columns to make based on the space available. The value you set in `column-width` is actually more like a *minimum* width; for instance, if you set `column-width` to 100 pixels inside a 250-pixel-wide container, and you set the `column-gap` to zero, the browser will make two columns that are both 125 pixels wide.

The `column-count` property allows you to set the number of columns explicitly, with their widths determined by the space available. If you set both `column-count` and `column-width`, the `column-count` value acts as a *maximum* number of columns. For instance, in the same 250-pixel-wide container, if you set `column-width` to 100 pixels and `column-count` to 3, the browser will not make three columns but only two.

You can use the `column-gap` property to create spaces between the columns, and the `column-rule` property to create a vertical line within each gap as a visual separator. The `column-span` property allows elements to span across multiple columns, but is not yet supported by any browser.

The `break-before`, `break-after`, and `break-inside` properties control where content is broken across columns, but they are not yet supported by any browser.

Other than breaking short pieces of body text into multiple columns, as we've done in this chapter, I think the only safe use for multi-columns currently is to break a single list of short items into multiple columns; see http://trentwalton.com/2010/07/19/css3-multi-column-layout-column-count for an example.

TABLE 6.2 **Multi-columns browser support**

IE	FIREFOX	OPERA	SAFARI	CHROME
No	Partial	No	Partial	Partial

Changing the Layout for Small Screens

With the wide-screen variation completed, let's turn our attention now to smaller screens. First off, we'll add a second media query right below the first one you added, targeting viewports that are narrower than 760 pixels wide:

```
@media screen and (max-width: 760px) {
}
```

This tells the browser that we want the styles that we'll add within this media query to apply to screen media types in viewports up to a maximum width of 760 pixels. Why have I chosen 760 pixels? Because this width prevents these styles from being applied to either maximized windows on 800 by 600 resolution desktop monitors or to iPads, which have a screen size of 768 by 1024 pixels. In both of these cases, I want the normal styles to apply, as I think the layout looks fine at these sizes. But under 760, the layout starts looking squished, with an increasing possibility of content overflowing its containers.

Once again, let's start by changing the styles on the nav bar to better fit the available space. When the window is narrowed, the entire nav bar drops onto a line below the logo, which is fine, but it stays right-aligned, which doesn't look as good when it doesn't have the logo to its left. So let's change the styles on the nav bar to left-align it when it's on a line below the logo:

```
@media screen and (max-width: 760px) {
   #nav-main {
      clear: left;
      float: left;
   }
   #nav-main li { margin: 0 .5em 0 0; }
}
```

You can see the difference that these styles make in **Figure 6.8**. It's a small change, but it's a nice little bit of polish that only took a small bit of CSS to accomplish.

LITTLE
pea
BAKERY
Search:
go
HOME ABOUT MENU LOCATION CATERING CONTACT US
LITTLE
pea
BAKERY
Search:
go
HOME ABOUT MENU LOCATION CATERING CONTACT US

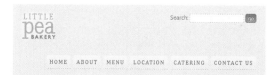

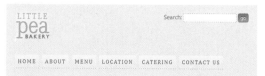

FIGURE 6.8 The nav bar can't fit beside the logo in narrow windows, so we switched it from the right side to the left using a media query.

Next, let's get rid of the two columns in the introductory paragraph—they're awkwardly narrow when the window is under 760 pixels (**Figure 6.9**). Change the column count to 1 in a new `h1 + p` rule in the second media query:

```
h1 + p {
   -moz-column-count: 1;
   -o-column-count: 1;
   -webkit-column-count: 1;
   column-count: 1;
}
```

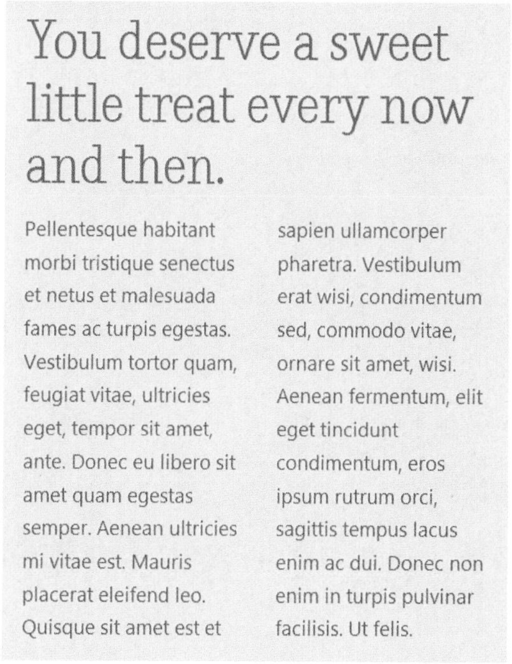

You deserve a sweet little treat every now and then.
Pellentesque habitant morbi tristique senectus et netus et malesuada fames ac turpis egestas. Vestibulum tortor quam, feugiat vitae, ultricies eget, tempor sit amet, ante. Donec eu libero sit amet quam egestas semper. Aenean ultricies mi vitae est. Mauris placerat eleifend leo. Quisque sit amet est et
sapien ullamcorper pharetra. Vestibulum erat wisi, condimentum sed, commodo vitae, ornare sit amet, wisi. Aenean fermentum, elit eget tincidunt condimentum, eros ipsum rutrum orci, sagittis tempus lacus enim ac dui. Donec non enim in turpis pulvinar facilisis. Ut felis.

FIGURE 6.9 The columns can fit only two or three words per line in narrow windows.

Now the line lengths are more reasonable in the introductory paragraph (**Figure 6.10**), but the three side-by-side columns underneath that paragraph are still extremely narrow (**Figure 6.11**). Let's fix them next.

FIGURE 6.10 Reducing the `column-count` back to 1 in narrow windows makes the introductory text better-looking and easier to read.

You deserve a sweet little treat every now and then.

Pellentesque habitant morbi tristique senectus et netus et malesuada fames ac turpis egestas. Vestibulum tortor quam, feugiat vitae, ultricies eget, tempor sit amet, ante. Donec eu libero sit amet quam egestas semper. Aenean ultricies mi vitae est. Mauris placerat eleifend leo. Quisque sit amet est et sapien ullamcorper pharetra. Vestibulum erat wisi, condimentum sed, commodo vitae, ornare sit amet, wisi. Aenean fermentum, elit eget tincidunt condimentum, eros ipsum rutrum orci, sagittis tempus lacus enim ac dui. Donec non enim in turpis pulvinar facilisis. Ut felis.

FIGURE 6.11
The featured product boxes are very narrow, having to sit side by side in a small viewport.

Candies
TRUFFLES, BARS, CARAMELS, AND MORE

Pellentesque habitant morbi tristique senectus et netus et malesuada fames ac turpis egestas. Vestibulum tortor quam, feugiat vitae, ultricies eget, tempor sit amet, ante.

Pastries
CROISSANTS, DANISHES, CREAM PUFFS, AND MORE

Vestibulum tortor quam, feugiat vitae, ultricies eget, tempor sit amet, ante. Donec eu libero sit amet quam egestas semper. Aenean ultricies mi vitae est.

Desserts
CAKES, PIES, TARTS, COOKIES, AND MORE

Donec eu libero sit amet quam egestas semper. Aenean ultricies mi vitae est. Mauris placerat eleifend leo. Vestibulum tortor quam, feugiat vitae, ultricies eget, tempor sit amet, ante.

Right now, each featured product box is a `div` that's floated to the left. Removing the floats will make them stack on top of each other instead, filling the whole width of the main content `div`. But when they're stacked on top of each other, the illustration that goes with each feature box doesn't look as nice positioned at the top of the box—it makes more sense to put the illustration on the left side of the box. So add this new rule to the media query:

NOTE: The three illustrations are part of the free Yummy icon set designed by Icon Eden (www.iconeden.com/icon/yummy-free-icons.html).

```
.feature {
    float: none;
    width: auto;
    margin: 0 0 1.6em 0;
    padding: 0 0 0 140px;
    background-position: top left;
}
```

This rule stops the feature boxes from floating and removes their percentage widths. It also removes the top padding from each box and replaces it with left padding, providing room for each illustration—a background image—to sit in on the left side of the box.

FIGURE 6.12 Having the featured product boxes stack, with their icons on the left instead of the top, looks better in the limited space of narrow windows.

Candies
TRUFFLES, BARS, CARAMELS, AND MORE
Pellentesque habitant morbi tristique senectus et netus et malesuada fames ac turpis egestas. Vestibulum tortor quam, feugiat vitae, ultricies eget, tempor sit amet, ante.

Pastries
CROISSANTS, DANISHES, CREAM PUFFS, AND MORE
Vestibulum tortor quam, feugiat vitae, ultricies eget, tempor sit amet, ante. Donec eu libero sit amet quam egestas semper. Aenean ultricies mi vitae est.

Desserts
CAKES, PIES, TARTS, COOKIES, AND MORE
Donec eu libero sit amet quam egestas semper. Aenean ultricies mi vitae est. Mauris placerat eleifend leo. Vestibulum tortor quam, feugiat vitae, ultricies eget, tempor sit amet, ante.

There's only one more change to make to the narrow version of the page. The right column is now fairly thin, increasing the chance that long words will overflow it. The headings in the column are in the greatest danger, since their all-caps style makes them take up so much room. We can lessen their chance of overflowing by decreasing their text size and letter spacing:

```
h3 {
    font-size: 100%;
    letter-spacing: 0;
}
```

You can see the change that this rule produces in **Figure 6.13**. Again, it's a subtle change, but it's a nice little piece of insurance to keep the text contained and thus more readable.

FIGURE 6.13 Reducing the size and spacing of the headings in the sidebar decreases the chance that text will overflow when the sidebar gets really narrow.

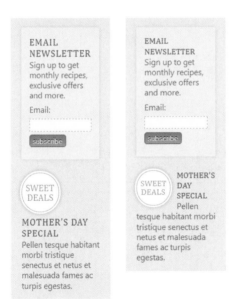

This completes the changes we're going to make for the narrow version of the bakery page (**Figure 6.14**). Save your page and view it in an up-to-date browser. Resize the window to see the design change at very narrow and very wide widths.

NOTE: The page with all the changes to this point is named media-queries_2.html in the exercise files for this chapter.

FIGURE 6.14 The completed design for narrow viewports

Changing the Layout for Mobile Devices

If you got very zealous in resizing your window to test the narrow-screen styles, you may have noticed that—even with the changes we made—the layout doesn't look very good at extremely narrow widths like the ones you find on mobile devices. Well, there's only one thing to be done: add another media query!

Media queries are a great way to customize the styles on mobile devices quickly and easily. But please be aware that I'm not suggesting they're the *only* way you should deal with mobile sites; you may need to add server-side scripting or other techniques to change the content and functionality on the mobile version of your site. While media queries may be enough customization for the mobile version of a small business's brochure site (such as our example bakery site), a big, complicated news site probably needs to use additional techniques to significantly change the content, navigation, and other functionality on their mobile site. Plus, hiding or swapping in different content extensively using media queries is not efficient—the browser may still download the content it doesn't need (see www.quirksmode.org/blog/archives/2010/08/combining_media.html for more on this). So don't think media queries are necessarily going to solve all your mobile web design problems—use media queries as *one* of your mobile optimization tools.

> **TIP:** If you want to target a particular device, you can look up its screen size at http://cartoonized.net/cellphone-screen-resolution.php.

When adding a mobile media query, what size should you target? Mobile phone screen sizes vary dramatically, but many of the most popular phones—including iPhones and many Android phones—have screens that are 320 by 480 pixels wide. Screens on other phones are rarely larger than this. But the design of our bakery page starts to break down around 550 pixels. So let's use 550 as the width to target with our third media query, which will work in 320 by 480 mobile phones as well as mobile phones with slightly larger screens.

Before we add this media query, however, let's talk a bit about device width.

What is Device Width?

One of the media features you can use in media queries is called `device-width`, along with `min-device-width` and `max-device-width`. *Device width* refers to the number of pixels available across the actual device or display, rather than within the viewport. This means that a desktop computer with its screen resolution set to 1280 by 800 has a device width of 1280 pixels. When you target `device-width` in your media queries, browsers ignore the size of the user's browser window and instead pay attention to the user's screen resolution.

Mobile phones generally don't use windows—the "window" is always the same size as the entire screen, so the idea of a viewport, as we traditionally think of it, doesn't really fit. Device width seems more relevant.

But there's a little catch. Apple doesn't always make its products' `device-width` equal to the number of pixels available across the width of the screen, as most other phones do. iPhones before version 4 and iPod Touches, though they both have screen sizes of 320 by 480 pixels, always have Mobile Safari report that the device width is 320 pixels, even when the user is viewing the device in landscape mode and is seeing 480 pixels of width. iPads work the same way—the device width is always reported as 768 pixels, despite the orientation of the iPad. This is even more confusing in the iPhone 4, which has a high-resolution screen of 640 by 960 pixels, but reports its device width as 320 pixels.

This doesn't mean you can't or shouldn't use `device-width`, but it does mean that you may find it more intuitive to use `min-width` and `max-width` instead of `min-device-width` and `max-device-width`. They both work the same way on mobile phones; the main difference is whether or not each applies on non-mobile devices too. For instance, a media query targeting a `max-width` of 550 pixels will apply to both mobile devices with screens under 551 pixels and desktop browser windows narrower than 551 pixels. But a media query targeting a `max-device-width` of 550 pixels has almost no chance of applying to anything other than mobile devices—I don't think there are many desktop computers with screen resolutions under 551 pixels wide! So neither one is inherently better or worse than the other—they're just different options that you can choose between depending on what you're trying to target.

The Third Media Query

Let's add the third media query now to apply to windows up to 550 pixels wide:

```
@media screen and (max-width: 550px) {
}
```

Make sure you add this *beneath* the second media query (the one targeting a maximum width of 760 pixels). That's because the second media query applies to mobile devices as well—a mobile device with a 480-pixel-wide screen is under the maximum width of 760 pixels. If you put the 550-pixel media query *before* the 760-pixel media query, the 760 one would override the styles in the 550 one. This is just how the CSS cascade works—rules that come later override rules of the same specificity that were declared earlier.

USEFUL MEDIA QUERIES FOR MOBILE

We're using `max-width: 550px` for our mobile media query, but there are all sorts of alternate media queries you could use instead, depending on which devices or user settings you're trying to target. Here are several examples to give you an idea of what's possible, so you can craft your own to suit your project's needs:

- `(min-device-width: 320px)` and `(max-device-width: 480px)` works in mobile phones with 320 by 480 resolution (like iPhones and Android devices) in both portrait and landscape orientations.
- `(max-width: 320px)` works in 320 by 480 mobile phones in portrait only.
- `(min-width: 321px)` works in 320 by 480 mobile phones in landscape only.
- `(min-device-width: 768px)` and `(max-device-width: 1024px)` works in iPads in both orientations.
- `(min-device-width: 481px)` and `(max-device-width: 1024px)` and `(orientation: landscape)` works in iPads in landscape only. It also works in desktop browsers that are wider than they are tall when on screens with a resolution width of 1024 or lower.
- `(min-device-width: 481px)` and `(max-device-width: 1024px)` and `(orientation: portrait)` works in iPads in portrait only. It also works in desktop browsers that are taller than they are wide when on screens with a resolution width of 1024 or lower.

If you didn't want the two media queries to overlap, you could add a minimum width onto the 760-pixel media query, such as:

```
@media screen and (min-width: 551px) and (max-width: 760px)
```

This media query would apply only to windows between 551–760 pixels, not to mobile devices under 551 pixels wide. This might be good or bad, depending on your particular project. In our case, it would mean repeating a lot of the rules from the 760-pixel media query in the 550-pixel one, since we want a lot of the styles to be the same in both. For instance, we want the intro paragraph to have only one column of text in both the 550-pixel layout and the 760-pixel layout. When these two media queries overlap, we only have to declare the one column in the 760-pixel media query, and then it will also apply to windows under 550 pixels.

In our example page, overlapping the media queries lets us reuse several styles and keep our CSS more streamlined. On other sites, however, you may want very different styles at each width, so it may make more sense to not let your media queries overlap. Keeping them separate may also be less confusing for you, as you don't have to keep track of the cascade. Again, there's no right or wrong answer here—it all depends on what you're trying to accomplish.

In this case, we're going to leave the 760-pixel media query as it is, and make sure the 550-pixel media query comes below it so that *both* apply to windows under 551 pixels wide.

REMOVING FLOATS

The primary change we need to make to the mobile design of the site is getting rid of the floats so that the entire page is one column. Most mobile web pages are a single column—there's simply not enough room for columns to sit side by side on those little screens.

Add the following rules to the third media query:

```
@media screen and (max-width: 550px) {
    #content-main, #content-secondary {
        float: none;
        width: 100%;
    }
    #about, #credits {
        float: none;
        width: 100%;
    }
    #credits { margin-top: 1.6em; }
}
```

Now the sidebar column displays under the main content column, and the "Credits" block in the footer displays under the "About" block (**Figure 6.15**). The top margin added to the credits div keeps the blocks in the footer spaced out from each other.

FIGURE 6.15 The layout is all one column now in extremely narrow mobile viewports.

REDUCING HEIGHTS

Another useful change to make to many mobile pages is to reduce the vertical space that elements take up, reducing the amount that users have to scroll down the long single column.

The text in the tagline and introductory paragraph doesn't need to be quite so large when viewed up close on a mobile device, so you can reduce both font sizes by creating new h1 and h1 + p rules:

```
h1 { font-size: 225%; }
h1 + p { font-size: 100%; }
```

Figure 6.16 shows the result of these CSS additions.

FIGURE 6.16 **Making the introductory text smaller reduces the need for so much scrolling in tiny mobile screens.**

Working our way further down the page, you'll see that the product icons look rather large in the context of such a narrow window, and the text beside them could use more room. Luckily, the Yummy icon set I've used for the illustrations came in three sizes: 128 pixels, 64 pixels, and 48 pixels. We can switch the background images to the 64-pixel size in our mobile media query:

```
.feature { padding-left: 70px; }
#feature-candy { background-image:
              url(images/icon_candy_64-trans.png); }
#feature-pastry { background-image:
              url(images/icon_pastry_64-trans.png); }
#feature-dessert { background-image:
              url(images/icon_dessert_64-trans.png); }
```

TIP: Instead of swapping in the different images, you could use background-size to resize the icons. This has the disadvantage of making the icons a little less sharp-edged, but the advantage of having only one set of images to load.

Now the featured products area takes up less overall height and looks more balanced (**Figure 6.17**).

FIGURE 6.17 Reducing the size of the icons in the featured products area makes them look more balanced against the blocks of text in narrow widths.

Next, check out the email newsletter subscription block. The text field within it takes up its full width, but there's now room to display the label text and button on the same line as the text field, at least on larger mobile screens. Add these rules to the media query:

```
#form-newsletter * { display: inline; }
#form-newsletter input[type=text] { width: auto; }
```

These changes tighten up the newsletter block's appearance (**Figure 6.18**). In portrait-oriented mobile screens, the subscribe button will drop down to a second line, but even then the form still makes better use of the space overall.

EMAIL NEWSLETTER
Sign up to get monthly recipes, exclusive offers and more.
Email:
subscribe

FIGURE 6.18 The form elements in the newsletter subscription block now all display on the same line in landscape-oriented mobile screens.

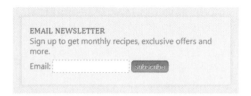

Finally, we can make a small change in the footer to slightly reduce its height. Float the `dt` elements within the credits `div`, since there's room to show the label text, like "Web Fonts," next to the description text, like "Nadia Serif from Kernest":

```
#credits dt {
   clear: left;
   float: left;
   margin: -.05em .2em 0 0;
}
```

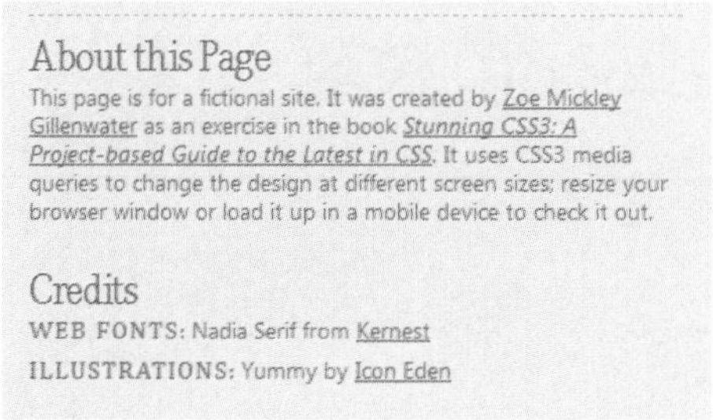
About this Page
This page is for a fictional site. It was created by Zoe Mickley Gillenwater as an exercise in the book Stunning CSS3: A Project-based Guide to the Latest in CSS. It uses CSS3 media queries to change the design at different screen sizes; resize your browser window or load it up in a mobile device to check it out.
Credits
WEB FONTS: Nadia Serif from Kernest
ILLUSTRATIONS: Yummy by Icon Eden

FIGURE 6.19 With each credit label and description on a single line, the Credits block in the footer takes up less space.

PREVENTING OVERLAPPING HEADER ELEMENTS

In small mobile screens, the possibility of page elements overlapping each other is of course increased. You can see this problem in the header of our example page. With the viewport at 550 pixels wide, the search form fits fine beside the logo, but at around 400 pixels they start to overlap. If the user has a larger text size, the overlap will happen even sooner.

To reduce the chance of overlap, reduce the width of the text field in the search form by adding this rule to the third media query:

```
#form-search input[type=text] { width: 100px; }
```

Next, add a fourth media query below the 550-pixel one. This media
query will target windows less than 401 pixels wide:

```
@media screen and (max-width: 400px) {
}
```

Add a rule within this media query to make the label in the search
form display as a block-level element so it will sit on a line above the
text field:

```
@media screen and (max-width: 400px) {
    #form-search label { display: block; }
}
```

Now the search form takes up less width at both 550 pixels wide and
400 pixels wide, and it's not likely to overlap the logo even in 320-
pixel wide mobile phone screens (**Figure 6.20**).

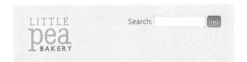 

FIGURE 6.20
The search form now
also takes up less space,
so it's less likely to overlap the logo in small
mobile screens such as
480 pixels wide (left)
and 320 pixels wide
(right).

Improving the Look on High-resolution Displays

The iPhone 4 has a new type of screen called a "retina display" that is
higher resolution than that on previous versions of the iPhone and
iPod Touch. Its resolution is 640 by 960, but it displays the same area
as older iPhones because it uses two *device* pixels for every one *CSS*
pixel. This means it doubles up the pixels it uses to display each pixel
you declare in your CSS—this is what makes it high resolution, and
this is why its device width is still 320 (half of 640).

For the most part, you'll want all versions of the iPhone to have the
same styles, but you may want to take advantage of the retina display
by feeding higher resolution images to the iPhone 4. For instance,
our three product icons look a little pixelated compared to the razor-
sharp text seen on a retina display.

To target the iPhone 4, you can set -webkit-min-device-pixel-ratio,
one of Webkit's proprietary media features, to 2:

```
@media screen and (-webkit-min-device-pixel-ratio: 2) {
}
```

NOTE: There's also a resolution media feature, which allows you to feed styles to devices of a minimum dpi, but it's not currently supported by Webkit-based browsers—including Mobile Safari on the iPhone 4. Other devices with high-resolution displays might support it, though, so test it on the device you're trying to target to see if it might be useful to you.

This makes the media query apply only when the phone's device-to-CSS pixel ratio is two to one—like on the iPhone 4. Right now, this is the only device the media query will apply to, but other Apple devices may have retina displays in the future. So to make this media query more future-proof, add another condition onto the media feature to make it apply only to the small screen of the iPhone 4:

```
@media screen and (-webkit-min-device-pixel-ratio: 2)
¬and (max-width: 480px) {
}
```

Now we can feed larger images to the iPhone 4, and then shrink them using the background-size property, to effectively squeeze more pixels into the same amount of space. Add these rules inside the new media query:

```
.feature {
    -webkit-background-size: 64px 64px;
    background-size: 64px 64px;
}
#feature-candy { background-image:
                    url(images/icon_candy_128-trans.png); }
#feature-pastry { background-image:
                    url(images/icon_pastry_128-trans.png); }
#feature-dessert { background-image:
                    url(images/icon_dessert_128-trans.png); }
```

These images are twice as big—128 pixels by 128 pixels—as the size we really want them to display at: 64 pixels by 64 pixels. When they're shrunk down to 64 pixels using background-size, a normal browser now has twice as many pixels as it needs to display those 64-pixels-worth of image. So when the iPhone 4 doubles each pixel, it already has two pixels there to display, instead of having to make a single pixel of the image twice as large, which would result in blurriness. The images now look sharp.

This is only one of the changes we could make on the iPhone 4. For more ideas on how to take advantage of its high-resolution display, see "Designing for the Retina Display (326ppi)" by Luke Wroblewski (www.lukew.com/ff/entry.asp?1142).

The Viewport meta Tag

If you save and test the page at this point in a desktop browser, it will work just as you expect it to as you narrow the window. But if you load it up on a smartphone like an iPhone or Android device, you may be surprised to find that none of the media queries are taking effect. The page will display with the normal styles, showing a two-column layout that's been zoomed out (**Figure 6.21**).

FIGURE 6.21 The page displays with a wide, two-column layout in many mobile devices, instead of using the styles from the third media query.

This is because many smartphones use a virtual viewport that's larger than the actual screen size in order to not destroy all those web pages out there that weren't designed for mobile by squeezing them into a tiny 320-pixel-wide viewport. The mobile web development expert Peter-Paul Koch calls this virtual viewport the "layout viewport" and the actual viewable area the "visual viewport."

NOTE: For an in-depth explanation of mobile viewports as well as the viewport meta tag, see Peter-Paul Koch's article "A tale of two viewports—part two" at www.quirksmode.org/mobile/viewports2.html.

When you load a page on a mobile phone that uses a layout viewport, the mobile browser will zoom out to the maximum level so that the entire layout viewport fits on screen. This makes everything appear tiny, but it ensures that your layout looks the same as it does on a typical desktop browser. Different mobile browsers use different widths for the layout viewport—Mobile Safari on the iPhone and iPod Touch uses 980 pixels, Android Webkit uses 800 pixels, Opera uses 850 pixels—but the point is that the mobile phones are pretending they have larger screens than they do, when sometimes you want them to fess up and show only the number of pixels they truly have.

Luckily, there's a specific meta tag whose whole purpose is to tell the mobile browsers that you've optimized your site for them and let you adjust the size and zoom level of the layout viewport.

HOW IT WORKS

This mobile-optimized tag is called the viewport meta tag, as you set the name attribute's value to viewport. It looks like this:

```
<meta name="viewport" content="">
```

Inside the content attribute, you include whatever instructions you want to provide about how to handle the viewport. Table 6.3 shows the possible properties you can include in the content attribute.

TABLE 6.3 content **attribute properties for the viewport** meta **tag**

PROPERTY	DESCRIPTION
width	Width of the viewport in pixels. You can set it to an actual number or to device-width.
height	Height of the viewport in pixels, set as a number or device-height.
initial-scale	Scale or zoom level of the viewport the first time it is displayed. A value of 1.0 makes the page display at its true size, neither zoomed out nor zoomed in.
minimum-scale	Minimum zoom level of the viewport. It controls how far the user is allowed to zoom out. A value of 1.0 prohibits being able to zoom out past the true size of the page.
maximum-scale	Maximum zoom level of the viewport. It controls how far the user is allowed to zoom in. A value of 1.0 prohibits being able to zoom in past the true size of the page.
user-scalable	Determines whether or not the user can zoom in and out. Set this to yes to allow scaling and no to prohibit scaling.

The viewport meta tag was invented by Apple and is not yet a standard. However, many mobile browsers beyond iPhones support it.

ADDING IT TO THE PAGE

Let's add a viewport meta tag to the bakery page now. Add the following tag to the head of the page:

```
<meta name="viewport" content="width=device-width">
```

This tells the mobile browser that you want it to make the size of the layout viewport equal to the device width, or the size of the screen. If you save your page and view it on an iPhone or similar device now, you will see that the mobile browser is showing only 320 pixels of width to display the layout in, allowing our media query to take effect (**Figure 6.22**).

FIGURE 6.22 **With the viewport** meta **tag added, the iPhone shows only 320 pixels across the screen, instead of zooming out to show 980.**

TESTING MEDIA QUERIES

As you develop your media queries, you'll find yourself spending a lot of time resizing your browser window back and forth to see if the styles you've written are working the way you expected. Let me share a few tips for how to make testing media queries a little quicker and pain-free.

First of all, the ProtoFluid web app (http://protofluid.com) is specifically designed for testing media queries. You put in a URL and then choose the device, such as iPhone or Motorola Droid, whose screen size you want to see it in. It pops up a window showing your page constrained to that width, and allows you to click a button to switch back and forth between orientations quickly. But be aware that it doesn't actually emulate these devices—it just creates a window the same size as their screen. What you see doesn't correctly represent the effect of the viewport `meta` tag, for instance. Also, ProtoFluid doesn't support `device-width` media queries; use `min-width` and `max-width` instead for testing purposes, and then switch to `min-device-width` or `max-device-width`, if you like, once you're done with testing.

Another method that I like to use for testing media queries is to preset a number of different viewport sizes in Firefox using the Web Developer extension (http://chrispederick.com/work/web-developer). In the Resize menu, you can add as many window or viewport sizes as you like. Add ones that match with common device screen sizes, such as 320 by 356 for the viewable area of an iPhone screen in portrait and 480 by 208 for the viewable area of iPhone landscape, as well as ones that match with the specific media query widths you've written into your style sheet. Then you can simply click a menu item to instantly resize your browser to those dimensions and see how things look. Again, this doesn't truly emulate the behavior of mobile devices, but it does allow you to easily test a number of different widths quickly.

However, if you rotate the iPhone to landscape orientation, the page still displays in 320 pixels, not 480. Mobile Safari simply zooms in on it instead of changing the size of the layout viewport, making the logo and other images a little blurry (**Figure 6.23**).

FIGURE 6.23
In landscape mode, the iPhone still shows only 320 pixels, zooming in so it fills the 480 pixels of width available.

This is because the reported device width on iPhones and iPod Touches is 320 pixels in both portrait and landscape, remember? To get Mobile Safari to make the layout viewport 480 pixels in landscape mode, you need to stop it from zooming in on the 320 pixels to fill the screen. Setting the `maximum-scale` value to `1.0` keeps the browser (and user) from being able to zoom in past the true size of the page, so add it to the `meta` tag:

```
<meta name="viewport" content="width=device-width,
¬maximum-scale=1.0">
```

NOTE: The iPad also sees and uses the viewport `meta` tag, even though its screen dimensions are more like a desktop than a mobile phone. Luckily, the way we've written our `meta` tag doesn't produce any unwanted results in the iPad—the layout displays at 768 pixels in portrait and 1024 in landscape, just as we would like.

Now when you view the page in landscape, Mobile Safari will keep the same zoom level of 100 percent, forcing it to expand the layout viewport to 480 pixels to fill the screen (**Figure 6.24**).

FIGURE 6.24 Changing the `maximum-scale` **of the viewport** `meta` **tag forces the iPhone to expand the layout to 480 pixels in landscape mode.**

Workarounds for Non-supporting Browsers

Browsers that don't support media queries, such as IE 8 and earlier and Firefox 3.1 and earlier, will simply display a regular page with the regular styles. Although the design will not look as good at extremely narrow and wide viewport sizes, the large majority of your users won't be using these sizes. You can add a `min-width` and `max-width` to the page to keep these browsers from ever seeing these extreme widths; override them in the media queries for browsers that don't need them.

This, of course, does nothing to help mobile devices. Luckily, most popular mobile devices support media queries (see www.quirksmode.org/mobile/browsers.html). Many of those that don't support media queries do support the `handheld` media type, however, so you could feed them their own mobile-optimized sheet this way. The article "Return of the Mobile Stylesheet" by Dominique Hazaël-Massieux at www.alistapart.com/articles/return-of-the-mobile-stylesheet explains a method for feeding a few different style sheets to mobile browsers based on whether or not they support the `handheld` media type and media queries.

If these workarounds won't cut it for your project, you can use JavaScript. The best script available is css3-mediaqueries-js by Wouter van der Graaf (http://code.google.com/p/css3-mediaqueries-js). All you have to do is link to the script—it automatically parses the media queries that exist in your CSS and makes them work in older browsers.

This script is included in the exercise files you downloaded for this chapter, so add a link to it in the head of the page:

```
<script src="scripts/css3-mediaqueries.js"></script>
```

Save the page and view it in a browser that doesn't support media queries natively, like IE 8. Resize your window and you will see that the layout now changes to use the media queries. It's as simple as that!

The only downside to using this script is that it adds another HTTP request, plus 16 kilobytes of data for users to download. Because of this, you may want to apply it only to the browsers that need it most—IE 6 through 8—by using conditional comments:

```
<!--[if lte IE 8]>
<script src="scripts/css3-mediaqueries.js"></script>
<![endif]-->
```

Although browsers such as Firefox 3.1 will now not be able to understand and use the media queries, your user base is not likely to contain many visitors using these browsers. In this case, I think it's probably better for a few non-IE- and non-media-query-supported visitors to miss out on the media queries than for all browsers to have to download the script.

The Finished Page

The bakery page now has a unique layout for several different window sizes, making it look good and work well on both large-screen desktop monitors as well as small-screen mobile devices (**Figure 6.25**).

NOTE: The exercise files contain the latest version of the script available at the time of this writing (the script is dated March 2010), but there may be a newer version by the time you read this, which you should use instead. Check at http://code.google.com/p/css3-mediaqueries-js.

NOTE: If you're using jQuery, there are a couple plugins that make media queries work; see www.protofunc.com/scripts/jquery/mediaqueries and www.csslab.cl/2009/07/22/jquery-browsersizr.

NOTE: The completed page showing all of these effects is named media-queries_final.html in the exercise files for this chapter.

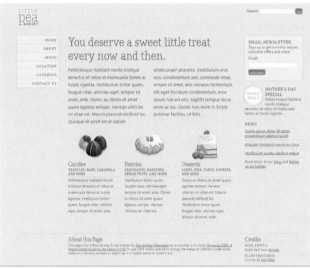

FIGURE 6.25 The bakery page in its four different sizes and designs.

7

Flexing Your
Layout Muscles

*Although we've been encouraged for many years to use CSS
to control the layout of our pages, the CSS 2.1 mechanisms
that can be used for layout are quite slim. Absolute positioning
is not used often by most developers since it's too rigid; floats
have been used extensively, but were never really meant for
full-page columnar layouts, and are limited in what effects
they can produce. CSS3 introduces a number of new layout
mechanisms that will make the building of multi-column
layouts much easier and also allow for creating complex
layout behaviors that simply can't be accomplished with the
properties and techniques of CSS 2.1. While these techniques
are still somewhat experimental, this chapter will get your
prepared for how layouts will be built in the future, as well
as introduce you to a few practical ways you can use the new
flexible box layout model now.*

WHAT YOU'LL LEARN

We'll be creating multi-column layouts for the entire page, as well as widgets on the page, using these pieces of CSS3:

+ The flexible box layout model

+ The box-sizing property

We'll also preview two of the upcoming layout systems in CSS3—template layout and grid positioning.

Changes on the Horizon

Throughout this book, we've focused on practical CSS3 techniques that can be used in your work right away as a progressive enhancement method. This final chapter, however, is going to cover many properties that have poor or even nonexistent browser support, and which are much more essential to the page, rather than being visual effects that older browsers can do without. However, I still think they're important to learn, as they offer powerful new ways to build web pages that will cause a huge shift in our web design and development process. Plus, there are ways to use them in a more limited manner now for effects that degrade well in non-supporting browsers.

So think of this final chapter as primarily a look ahead at how we'll be building sites a few years from now. By learning these new techniques now, you'll be able to gradually introduce them into your sites in small ways, and when they're finally ready for full-blown use, you'll be at the front of the pack.

> **NOTE:** The flexible box model doesn't replace the CSS 2.1 box model; it's an additional box model that works together with it.

The most fully developed, best supported, and thus practical of these new layout techniques is called the *flexible box layout model* (to which most of the chapter will be devoted). The flexible box layout model lets you specify whether boxes should be laid out horizontally or vertically, how they should be aligned with each other, and how they should share the available space. At first, this doesn't sound like such a big deal—don't existing CSS 2.1 properties let you do all this? For the most part, yes—but not with such ease and flexibility as the flexible box model allows.

Creating Multi-column Layouts Without Floats or Positioning

The flexible box layout model introduces a dedicated system for creating multi-column and multi-row layouts that works very differently than floats or absolute positioning. It's easiest to see how the flexible box model works with real examples, so download the exercise files for this chapter at www.stunningcss3.com, and open the file flexbox_start.html in your code editor.

This page is the same bakery page from Chapter 6, but I've removed the media queries just to keep things simple for this example, and I've gotten rid of the CSS rules that created side-by-side columns. Each of the divs stacks vertically down the page, as do all block-level elements by default (**Figure 7.1**). We can use flexible box layout to make them display horizontally instead.

FIGURE 7.1 **Without using** float, **the** divs **stack vertically down the page.**

The first step to making blocks sit next to each other horizontally is to set the `display` value of their container to `box`—a new value in CSS3 for the familiar old `display` property. A `div` named content is the container for the two main columns, the content-main and content-secondary `div`s; this wrapper `div` was not present in the page in Chapter 6, but I've added it here because it's necessary for using flexible box layout. In the styles in the `head` of the page, add a new rule for `#content` to match the following:

```
#content {
    display: -moz-box;
    display: -o-box;
    display: -webkit-box;
    display: box;
}
```

Setting `display` to `box` turns the `div` into what the W3C calls a *flexible box*, or often simply *box*, and tells the browser that you want to switch to the flexible box model for this `div` and its children. Firefox and Webkit-based browsers—the only browsers that currently support the flexible box layout model—support the values `-moz-box` and `-webkit-box`, respectively. Right now, no browser supports the non-prefixed box value, and Opera doesn't yet support `-o-box`, but we've added these properties for future compatibility.

EXTRA WRAPPER divs

The fact that I had to add an extra wrapper `div` around the content-main and content-secondary `div`s illustrates one of the disadvantages inherent in the flexible box model: it requires extra nesting of `div`s that float-based layouts often don't need. You always have to have that outer `div` to set to `display: box` before you can turn the inner `div` into columns. A few extra wrapper `div`s is not a huge problem, especially given the advantages of simplified CSS and broadened layout options that the flexible box model offers, but it's worth mentioning—I believe in full disclosure here!

IE 9 COMPATIBILITY

The IE 9 platform preview available at the time of this writing supports flexible box layout if you use the -ms- prefix on the properties and values, but the current IE 9 beta—which is newer than the platform preview—does not support it, with or without the prefix. Apparently Microsoft decided to remove the functionality when it created the beta. Whether or not the final version of IE 9 will have it added back in, and whether or not it will use the prefix, is unclear. You can test the -ms- properties and values to see if IE 9 does support it by the time you're reading this. Or, if you want to be extra safe, you can just go ahead and add them all on preemptively now.

Next, tell the browser that you want to lay out the child elements horizontally by using the box-orient property, along with the browser-specific equivalents:

```
#content {
    display: -moz-box;
    display: -o-box;
    display: -webkit-box;
    display: box;
    -moz-box-orient: horizontal;
    -o-box-orient: horizontal;
    -webkit-box-orient: horizontal;
    box-orient: horizontal;
}
```

When you set display to box, the browser automatically sets box-orient to inline-axis, which, in languages like English that run horizontally, does the same thing as a value of horizontal does: it lays out the blocks side by side instead of top to bottom. So, technically, we don't need to include the box-orient property here—the boxes would be horizontal without it. But I've included it here in the interest of clarity, so you can see how to use this new property.

Adding this rule makes the page change dramatically in appearance; the content-main and content-secondary divs are now sitting side by side, but you can hardly tell it because each has grown to a ridiculous width—so wide, in fact, that you can't even see any of the secondary content in the viewport in this example. Instead, you see an extensive horizontal scrollbar in the browser (**Figure 7.2**).

FIGURE 7.2 The two content divs are now placed side by side, but overflow tremendously off the right side of the viewport.

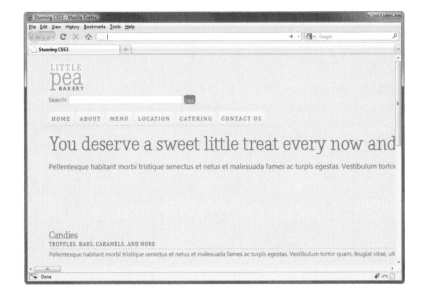

This happens because children of flexible boxes are made as wide as needed for their content; this is called *intrinsic* sizing, similar to how floats without widths are sized. The longest sentence or widest image in the div determines its width. In many cases, this would be a desirable thing, but not in the case of our content divs. To overcome this, you can either give each div a width or max-width, or you can make one or both of the divs flexible using the box-flex property.

Making Blocks Flex

The box-flex property doesn't actually stop the child divs from being sized intrinsically, but it does force the content within them to wrap so they don't push their container wider than 100 percent width. It makes the divs adjust their width flexibly to the width of their container. If the total of the children's intrinsic widths is less than the width of the container, the children increase in width to fill the extra space. If the total of the intrinsic widths is more than the width of the container, the children decrease in width.

The amount they increase or decrease by is a proportion of their intrinsic widths, not an absolute value. Flexible blocks also flex in proportion to each other. For instance, a block with a box-flex value of 2 is twice as flexible as a block with a box-flex value of 1—the extra space would be doled out to the blocks in a two-to-one ratio.

This is easiest to see with real examples. **Figure 7.3** shows a gray 800-pixel-wide box holding two inflexible divs at their intrinsic sizes; at the text size shown, the yellow div is 99 pixels wide and the pink div is 493 pixels wide. That leaves 208 extra pixels of space inside the box. If you set the box-flex value to 1 on both divs, they would divide up the 208 pixels of extra space in a one-to-one ratio— in other words, they'd split it evenly (**Figure 7.4**). But if you gave the pink div box-flex: 2, it would get twice as much of the extra space as the yellow div gets (**Figure 7.5**).

FIGURE 7.3 The yellow and pink divs are both sized only as large as their content, leaving extra space within their gray container div.

FIGURE 7.4 Both divs have 104 pixels of space added on to them.

FIGURE 7.5 Out of the 208 extra pixels, the pink div gets 139 pixels added on to it, while the yellow one gets only 69 pixels added, since their box-flex values are in a two-to-one ratio.

It works the same way when the blocks are too wide for their parent box—the overage of space just gets *subtracted* from each block in the ratio set by the box-flex values. For instance, in **Figures 7.6** and **7.7**, the widths of the containing boxes have been reduced to 500 pixels wide, less than the total of the intrinsic widths of the child divs. In Figure 7.6, both children divs have box-flex: 1, so both are shrunk by 46 pixels. In Figure 7.7, the pink div has box-flex: 2, so it gets shrunk twice as much as the yellow div.

NOTE: The amount that blocks get stretched or shrunk due to box-flex is constrained by the blocks' maximum and minimum widths, whether explicit or intrinsic, so sometimes the width values you end up with might not be exactly what you expect.

FIGURE 7.6 Both divs have 46 pixels subtracted from their widths in order to fit in the 500-pixel-wide box.

FIGURE 7.7 The pink div has 61 pixels subtracted from it, while the yellow one has only 31 pixels subtracted, since their box-flex values are in a two-to-one ratio.

In our page, let's first try making both the content-main and content-secondary divs equally flexible by setting box-flex to 1 in the existing #content-main and #content-secondary rules:

```
#content-main {
    -moz-box-flex: 1;
    -o-box-flex: 1;
    -webkit-box-flex: 1;
    box-flex: 1;
    margin-bottom: 40px;
}
#content-secondary {
    -moz-box-flex: 1;
    -o-box-flex: 1;
    -webkit-box-flex: 1;
    box-flex: 1;
    margin-bottom: 40px;
}
```

Now both divs are constrained within the wrapper div (**Figure 7.8**). But Firefox and Webkit-based browsers decide differently how large to make each content div; Figure 7.8 shows the layout in Firefox, and

Figure 7.9 shows it in Chrome, both at the same viewport width. I don't know which of these is correct—or even if either is technically wrong, as the W3C spec may not provide enough detail on how the browser should determine an element's intrinsic size.

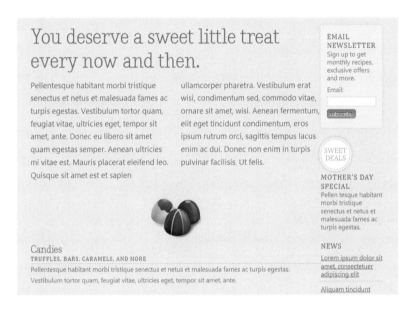

FIGURE 7.8 The two content columns being sized intrinsically by Firefox.

FIGURE 7.9 The two content columns being sized intrinsically by Chrome; note how much larger the sidebar is than in Firefox.

NOTE: If the boxes were stacked vertically instead of horizontally, the box-flex value would affect their height, not their width. It controls the flexibility of the space along the same axis on which the boxes are laid out.

Regardless, it's clear that in this case, setting both of the content divs to be flexible is not going to work for our design. Instead, let's give the sidebar an explicit width, as well as a left margin to create some space between it and the main content column:

```
#content-secondary {
    width: 16em;
    margin: 0 0 40px 40px;
}
```

Now the sidebar will always be 16 ems wide and the main content column will flex to fill whatever space is left after the sidebar and its margins have been accounted for (**Figure 7.10**). This works even if the overall layout isn't liquid to adjust to the viewport; if the wrapper div was set to 960 pixels wide, for instance, the sidebar would take up 16 ems of that, and then the main content column would take up the remaining number of pixels. The "flex" part of the box-flex property refers to the block's ability to flex in order to fill whatever space is available in its parent box—even if that parent is fixed-width—not necessarily to flex to fill the viewport.

NOTE: The page with all the changes to this point is named flex-box_1.html in the exercise files for this chapter.

FIGURE 7.10 The sidebar is now 16 ems wide, leaving the rest of the width for the main content column.

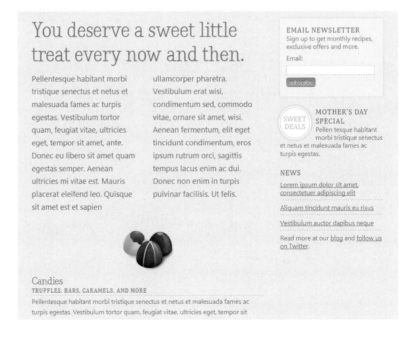

You deserve a sweet little treat every now and then.

Pellentesque habitant morbi tristique senectus et netus et malesuada fames ac turpis egestas. Vestibulum tortor quam, feugiat vitae, ultricies eget, tempor sit amet, ante. Donec eu libero sit amet quam egestas semper. Aenean ultricies mi vitae est. Mauris placerat eleifend leo. Quisque sit amet est et sapien

ullamcorper pharetra. Vestibulum erat wisi, condimentum sed, commodo vitae, ornare sit amet, wisi. Aenean fermentum, elit eget tincidunt condimentum, eros ipsum rutrum orci, sagittis tempus lacus enim ac dui. Donec non enim in turpis pulvinar facilisis. Ut felis.

EMAIL NEWSLETTER
Sign up to get monthly recipes, exclusive offers and more.

Email:

subscribe

SWEET DEALS

MOTHER'S DAY SPECIAL
Pellen tesque habitant morbi tristique senectus et netus et malesuada fames ac turpis egestas.

NEWS
Lorem ipsum dolor sit amet, consectetuer adipiscing elit

Aliquam tincidunt mauris eu risus

Vestibulum auctor dapibus neque

Read more at our blog and follow us on Twitter.

Candies
TRUFFLES, BARS, CARAMELS, AND MORE
Pellentesque habitant morbi tristique senectus et netus et malesuada fames ac turpis egestas. Vestibulum tortor quam, feugiat vitae, ultricies eget, tempor sit

Adding Columns

This layout illustrates one of the advantages of the flexible box model: you can easily combine elements of different units side by side. The main content column is in percentages (implicitly), the margin in pixels, and the sidebar in ems. This type of hybrid layout is possible without flexible box layout, but it's more difficult and messy.

Using flexible box layout, on the other hand, made creating this two-column hybrid layout pretty simple. Here's all it took:

1. Set the `display` of the container of the columns to `box`.

2. Set the `box-orient` of the container to `horizontal`.

3. Give the sidebar a width.

4. Make the main content column fill the rest of the space using `box-flex`.

If you had more columns, you could give those widths as well, or make them flex to the space available using `box-flex`. You wouldn't need to readjust all the widths and margins to make room for the extra columns—everything adjusts automatically.

To see this in action, let's add another column to the footer. First, we need to put the existing two `div`s in the footer into the same two-column layout as the two content `div`s are in. Add the `display` and `box-orient` properties to the existing `#footer` rule:

```
#footer {
    display: -moz-box;
    display: -o-box;
    display: -webkit-box;
    display: box;
    -moz-box-orient: horizontal;
    -o-box-orient: horizontal;
    -webkit-box-orient: horizontal;
    box-orient: horizontal;
    padding: 10px 0;
    border-top: 1px dashed #3C9;
}
```

Next, add these new rules for the divs within the footer:

```
#about {
    -moz-box-flex: 1;
    -o-box-flex: 1;
    -webkit-box-flex: 1;
    box-flex: 1;
}
#credits {
    width: 10em;
    margin: 0 0 40px 40px;
}
```

And just like that, we have a two-column layout in the footer. Changing it into a three-column layout is just as simple. First, add the third div in between the about and credits divs. Copy and paste the following HTML from the file flex-box_2.html from the exercise files for this chapter:

```
<div id="learn-more">
    <h2>Learn More</h2>
    <p><a href="http://www.w3.org/TR/css3-mediaqueries/"
    >Media queries</a> are a way of tailoring the site
    design to the characteristics of each user's display,
    using regular CSS embedded in your main style sheet.
    </p>
</div>
```

Now, add a rule for the learn-more div, setting its width and margins:

```
#learn-more {
    width: 10em;
    margin: 0 0 40px 40px;
}
```

Without making any other changes to the CSS, the footer now has a three-column layout instead of two (**Figure 7.11**). We didn't need to adjust the widths or margins of the about or credits divs; since the about div had been set to flex, it automatically shrank to make room for the new third column. Again, this would happen just the same if the wrapper were a fixed pixel width instead of a liquid width that adjusts to the viewport.

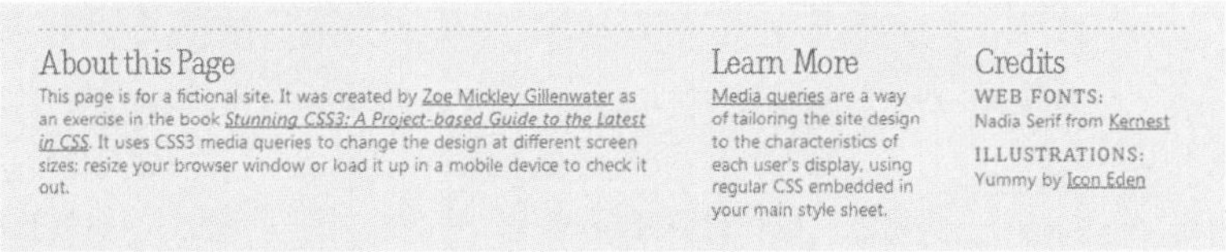

FIGURE 7.11 The about div automatically flexes to decrease in width to make room for the new learn-more div.

About this Page

This page is for a fictional site. It was created by Zoe Mickley Gillenwater as an exercise in the book *Stunning CSS3: A Project-based Guide to the Latest in CSS*. It uses CSS3 media queries to change the design at different screen sizes: resize your browser window or load it up in a mobile device to check it out.

Learn More

Media queries are a way of tailoring the site design to the characteristics of each user's display, using regular CSS embedded in your main style sheet.

Credits

WEB FONTS:
Nadia Serif from Kernest

ILLUSTRATIONS:
Yummy by Icon Eden

This ability to add and remove columns easily without having to change dimensions of surrounding elements can make your CSS cleaner and easier to develop in a number of real scenarios. For instance, your site may have a news sidebar that shows on only certain pages, such as the home page, Newsroom, and About Us sections of the site. The two-column pages and the three-column pages that include the news sidebar can all be coded identically, save for the addition of the news div in the HTML, because the other divs in the page will automatically adjust to make room for it if it's there. You *don't* have to create separate CSS rules for the two- and three-column versions of all the divs in the page, like this:.

```
body.two-col #content { width: 75%; }
body.three-col #content { width: 60%; }
body.two-col #nav { width: 25%; }
body.three-col #nav { width: 20%; }
```

Reordering Columns

Another benefit of using flexible box layout is that it's easy to visually reorder columns without having to touch the HTML. There are a couple properties that will help you do this.

The simpler of these properties is the box-direction property. If you want the sidebar to be on the left instead of the right, for instance, set box-direction to reverse in the #content rule, and change the left margin on the sidebar to a right margin:

```
#content {
    display: -moz-box;
    display: -o-box;
    display: -webkit-box;
    display: box;
    -moz-box-orient: horizontal;
    -o-box-orient: horizontal;
    -webkit-box-orient: horizontal;
    box-orient: horizontal;
    -moz-box-direction: reverse;
    -o-box-direction: reverse;
    -webkit-box-direction: reverse;
    box-direction: reverse;
}
#content-secondary {
    width: 16em;
    margin: 0 40px 40px 0;
}
```

This makes the browser lay out the divs horizontally, starting on the right side instead of the left. Since the content-main div comes first in the HTML, the browser starts off with it, placing it on the right side, and then puts the content-secondary div to its left (**Figure 7.12**). If the divs were stacked vertically instead of horizontally, setting box-direction to reverse would make them stack from bottom to top instead of top to bottom.

FIGURE 7.12 Setting box-direction to reverse places the first div in the HTML, the content-main div, on the right side of the page.

For more control over where each block is placed, you can use the box-ordinal-group property to assign a placement order. The blocks with a box-ordinal-group value of 1 are placed first, then the ones with a value of 2, and so forth. This means that if you wanted the learn-more div in the footer to be placed on the far left instead of in the middle, you set the box-ordinal-group values on the three footer children divs accordingly:

```
#about {
    -moz-box-flex: 1;
    -o-box-flex: 1;
    -webkit-box-flex: 1;
    box-flex: 1;
    -moz-box-ordinal-group: 2;
    -o-box-ordinal-group: 2;
    -webkit-box-ordinal-group: 2;
    box-ordinal-group: 2;
}
```

```
#credits {
    -moz-box-ordinal-group: 2;
    -o-box-ordinal-group: 2;
    -webkit-box-ordinal-group: 2;
    box-ordinal-group: 2;
    width: 10em;
    margin: 0 0 40px 40px;
}
#learn-more {
    -moz-box-ordinal-group: 1;
    -o-box-ordinal-group: 1;
    -webkit-box-ordinal-group: 1;
    box-ordinal-group: 1;
    width: 10em;
    margin: 0 0 40px 40px;
}
```

Also, switch the learn-more div's left margin over to the right:

```
#learn-more {
    -moz-box-ordinal-group: 1;
    -o-box-ordinal-group: 1;
    -webkit-box-ordinal-group: 1;
    box-ordinal-group: 1;
    width: 10em;
    margin: 0 40px 40px 0;
}
```

PROBLEMS IN REVERSE

Be careful when setting box-direction to reverse—this can reverse
more than just the stacking order of the boxes. For instance, content
may overflow to the left instead of the expected right. It can make other
properties, such as box-align and box-pack, which control placement and alignment of blocks (more on these later), contradict their
normal behavior. If you're ripping your hair out trying to figure out why
a block is doing the opposite of what you're telling it to, check to see if
you've reversed its direction—that might be the culprit. Test it well!

Since the learn-more div now has a lower box-ordinal-group value
than its sibling divs, the browser places it first. And because we've
told it to place the boxes from left to right (the box-orient is horizontal and the box-direction is implicitly normal on the footer), that
puts the learn-more div on the far left (**Figure 7.13**). The browser then

NOTE: The page
with all the changes
to this point is named
flex-box_2.html in the
exercise files for this
chapter.

places the about and credits `div`s to the right. Since these `div`s both have the same `box-ordinal-group` value, the browser decides which of the two to place first by looking at the source order: boxes that come first in the source get placed first, as you're used to with normal boxes in the flow of the page.

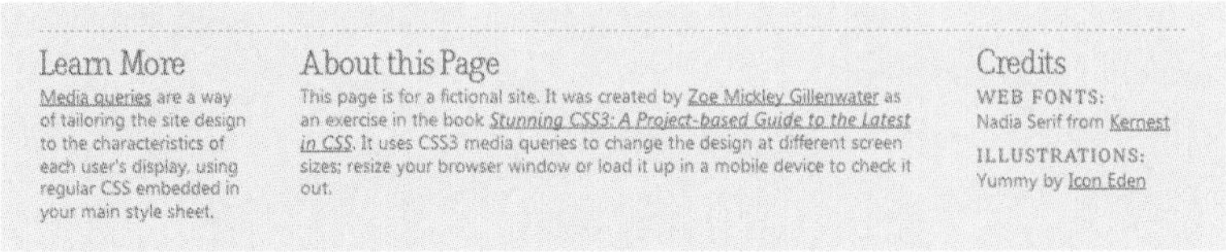

FIGURE 7.13 Even though the learn-more `div` comes in between the about and credits `div`s in the HTML, its `box-ordinal-group` value lets the browser place it on the far-left side of the page.

Being able to control the visual placement of blocks in a layout without regard for the source order is incredibly powerful. It lets you put the most important content first in the HTML, even if you don't want that content to display first visually, which helps the page degrade well in assistive technology, linearize well in devices without CSS support, and perform better in search engines.

Equal-height Columns

Another nice benefit of flexible box layout—though a more trivial one—is that creating equal-height columns is dead easy.

Many designers from the pre-CSS days (like me) got used to being able to easily create equal-height columns using tables. Cells in the same table row automatically expand to the same height, but individual `div`s that just so happen to display side by side have no reason to do this. In a quest to get `div`-based columns in a layout to appear to be equal in height, designers and developers came up with many clever but hacky CSS solutions. These equal-height column techniques might involve one or more extra wrapper `div`s, background images (even when all you wanted was a solid background color, or no background at all but just a border), and relatively complicated CSS.

Using flexible box layout for equal-height columns still requires a wrapper `div`, but it doesn't take any images (helping your pages load faster by saving HTTP requests), and it uses very simple CSS. All you have to do is set the `box-align` property to `stretch` on the flexible box, which is the parent of the columns. This is the default value of the `box-align` property, so you can see it working in our example page simply by setting background colors on the two main content columns:

```
#content-main {
    -moz-box-flex: 1;
    -o-box-flex: 1;
    -webkit-box-flex: 1;
    box-flex: 1;
    margin-bottom: 40px;
    background: #dcdcdc;
}
#content-secondary {
    width: 16em;
    margin: 0 40px 40px 0;
    background: #fcc;
}
```

Save the page and view it in Firefox, Safari, or Chrome. The pink background of the sidebar stretches down to the end of the gray background of the much-longer main content column (**Figure 7.14**).

FIGURE 7.14 **The two content** divs **stretch to the same height, because the children of boxes are given a** box-align **value of** stretch **by default.**

Again, this happens because boxes by default have box-align set to stretch; we'd get the same effect if we added it explicitly to the #content rule, like this:

```
#content {
    display: -moz-box;
    display: -o-box;
    display: -webkit-box;
    display: box;
    -moz-box-orient: horizontal;
    -o-box-orient: horizontal;
    -webkit-box-orient: horizontal;
    box-orient: horizontal;
    -moz-box-direction: reverse;
    -o-box-direction: reverse;
    -webkit-box-direction: reverse;
    box-direction: reverse;
    -moz-box-align: stretch;
    -o-box-align: stretch;
    -webkit-box-align: stretch;
    box-align: stretch;
}
```

The box-align property controls how a box's children are aligned relative to each other perpendicularly to the box's orientation. So if the box's children are being laid out horizontally, as in our example, box-align controls the vertical alignment; if our blocks were stacked vertically, box-align would control their horizontal alignment.

The possible values for box-align are described in **Table 7.1**. Note that the definitions for start and end are the opposite for reverse-direction boxes; for instance, horizontal blocks that are reversed and have a box-align value of start should be aligned on the bottom, not the top as usual. However, browsers don't currently follow this.

TABLE 7.1 box-align **values**

VALUE	HORIZONTAL CHILDREN	VERTICAL CHILDREN
start	Aligned at the top	Aligned on the left
end	Aligned on the bottom	Aligned on the right
center	Vertically centered (equal space on its top and bottom)	Horizontally centered (equal space on its left and right)
baseline	The first text line of each block are aligned on the baselines of the text, and then the highest child is placed against the top edge of the box	Same as center*
stretch	Stretched vertically to fill the height of the box	Stretched horizontally to fill the width of the box

* Firefox treats a value of baseline for vertical blocks the same as start, not the same as center.

Vertical and Horizontal Centering

The box-align property not only makes equal-height columns possible, but it also means that vertical centering—one of the hardest
effects to accomplish with CSS 2.1—is now an easy feat, even when
both the parent box and child block have unknown heights. In addition, another new property named box-pack makes horizontal centering in traditionally tricky situations really simple too.

Let's try out both types of centering in the header area of our page.
I've changed the HTML markup for this area slightly from the page
used in Chapter 6: now the header div wraps around the logo image
and search form, and the nav-main div is separate.

VERTICALLY CENTERING THE LOGO AND SEARCH FORM

Having a wrapper around only the logo and form makes it possible to
vertically center these two elements in relation to each other.

First, make the header div into a flexible box by setting its display to box:

```
#header {
    display: -moz-box;
    display: -o-box;
    display: -webkit-box;
    display: box;
    padding: 20px 0;
}
```

As explained earlier, children of flexible boxes will display horizontally
by default, without setting the box-orient property, so this CSS change
alone puts the logo and search form on the same line (**Figure 7.15**).

FIGURE 7.15 Now that
the logo and the search
form are children of a
flexible box, they sit side
by side.

To get the search form to display on the right side of the screen instead of up against the logo, you need to tell it to stretch to fill the rest of the space left over after the logo. You also need to set text-align to right to move the content within the form to its right side. Add a new rule for #form-search to do both of these things:

```
#form-search {
    -moz-box-flex: 1;
    -o-box-flex: 1;
    -webkit-box-flex: 1;
    box-flex: 1;
    text-align: right;
}
```

Now the search form is over on the right where we want it in Safari and Chrome (**Figure 7.16**). But in Firefox, it hasn't budged. This is because Firefox is sizing the header div intrinsically, making it only as wide as its content. This behavior is correct for *children* of boxes, but Firefox should not be doing it to the box itself. But it's easy to fix—just set the width of the header div to 100 percent:

```
#header {
    display: -moz-box;
    display: -o-box;
    display: -webkit-box;
    display: box;
    width: 100%;
    padding: 20px 0;
}
```

FIGURE 7.16 **In Webkit-based browsers, the search form now flexes to fill all the space to the right of the logo, and the content within the form is aligned to the right.**

This makes Firefox stop shrinkwrapping the header and instead stretch it out to fill the full width of the wrapper div. Now the search form is on the right side of the screen in Firefox as well as in Webkit-based browsers.

Now that the logo and form are in the right spots horizontally, let's move them to the vertical spots we want. All you have to do is set box-align to center on the header div:

```
#header {
    display: -moz-box;
    display: -o-box;
    display: -webkit-box;
    display: box;
    -moz-box-align: center;
    -o-box-align: center;
    -webkit-box-align: center;
    box-align: center;
    width: 100%;
    padding: 20px 0;
}
```

And with that, the logo and search form are aligned in the middle with each other and vertically centered within the header div (**Figure 7.17**). No matter how large the font size for the form grows, or if the elements of it wrap onto two lines, it will always adjust and stay vertically centered.

FIGURE 7.17 Setting box-align to center on the header div vertically centers the logo and search form.

HORIZONTALLY CENTERING THE NAV BAR

Now we can turn our attention to the next item on the page, the nav bar. To center it horizontally in the wrapper div, setting box-align to center won't work—remember that it applies only to the vertical space around horizontal boxes (and vice versa for vertical boxes). We need a property that affects the extra space in the same axis as the blocks—in this case, horizontal.

DISAPPEARING BOXES AND BLOCKS

If you're using the flexible box model on just an element or two rather than a whole page layout, it's quite possible that you'd have the `float` or `overflow` properties applied to an element that also has a `display` value of box, or is the child of a flexible box. If this is the case, you're going to run into trouble.

Safari and Chrome have a bug that makes boxes and children of boxes with the `float` property on them disappear. While `float` is not allowed on the children of boxes, it shouldn't make anything fail to show up—the property should just be ignored. Firefox has a similar bug that makes boxes disappear when they have `overflow` set on them, rather than `float`.

Both of these bugs make combining flexible box layout with older layout methods (in order to deliver fallbacks to older browsers) much more difficult. For instance, in the nav bar in our example page, the `li` elements are each floated, which makes the links line up horizontally in all browsers. If you wanted the `ul` element to contain its floated children, you might use one of the common float-containment methods of either floating the `ul` element or setting `overflow: auto` or `overflow: hidden` on it. But since the `ul` element is the child of a flexible box, floating it would make it disappear in Webkit browsers, and setting `overflow` would make it disappear in Firefox.

This is exactly what the `box-pack` property does. We can use it to move the `ul` element into the center of the nav-main `div`. To do so, first turn the nav-main `div` into a box and set its `box-pack` value to `center`. Make these changes to the existing `#nav-main` rule:

```
#nav-main {
    display: -moz-box;
    display: -o-box;
    display: -webkit-box;
    display: box;
    -moz-box-pack: center;
    -o-box-pack: center;
    -webkit-box-pack: center;
    box-pack: center;
    overflow: auto;
    margin: 0 0 20px 0;
}
```

Next, you need to make a couple changes for Firefox's sake. Add `width: 100%` to make the `div` stretch to fill its container. Also, remove the `overflow: auto` declaration to fix a Firefox bug that would cause the nav-main `div` to disappear (see "Disappearing boxes and blocks" above for more explanation):

```
#nav-main {
    display: -moz-box;
    display: -o-box;
    display: -webkit-box;
    display: box;
    -moz-box-pack: center;
    -o-box-pack: center;
    -webkit-box-pack: center;
    box-pack: center;
    width: 100%;
    margin: 0 0 20px 0;
}
```

If you save your page and view it in Firefox, Safari, or Chrome now, you'll see that the nav bar is indeed horizontally centered within the page (**Figure 7.18**). Setting box-pack to center tells the browser to take whatever extra horizontal space is left over within the nav-main div and divide it equally on either side of the ul block within it.

NOTE: The completed page showing all of these effects is named flex-box_final.html in the exercise files for this chapter.

FIGURE 7.18 Setting box-pack **to** center **on the nav-main** div **horizontally centers the nav bar.**

WRAPPING A BOX'S CHILDREN

By default, the children of a flexible box will not wrap onto multiple lines if there isn't enough room to display them all on one line—they'll just overflow. This is exactly opposite to how floats work. Although floats' ability to wrap onto multiple lines is sometimes frustrating, overall it's actually a good thing. For instance, the li elements in the nav bar are each floated, so that when the window is too narrow to display them all side by side, they wrap, allowing all to stay in view at all times. If the ul element were instead a flexible box with horizontally-oriented children, the li elements would not wrap, but would stubbornly remain on the same line in even very narrow windows or with very large font sizes.

In cases like this, where you do want wrapping to occur, you can set the box-lines property to multiple on the box. Unfortunately, it's not supported by any browser yet. So, for now, don't use flexible box layout on anything where wrapping is essential.

All of the possible values for box-pack are described in Table 7.2. Remember, as with box-align, the definitions for start and end are the opposite for reverse-direction boxes. Firefox does follow this, but Webkit-based browsers do not.

TABLE 7.2 box-pack **values**

VALUE	HORIZONTAL CHILDREN	VERTICAL CHILDREN
start	Placed on the left side of the box	Placed at the top of the box
end	Placed on the right side of the box	Placed at the bottom of the box
center	Horizontally centered (equal space on left and right)	Vertically centered (equal space on top and bottom)
justify*	Space divided evenly in between each child, with no extra space placed before the first child or after the last child. If only one child, same as start.	Same

* The justify value of the box-pack property is not supported by Firefox; it's simply treated the same as start.

Reality Check: What Works Now

Unfortunately, most of the work we've done on this layout is just an illustration of what's possible—not a demonstration of how you should actually use flexible box layout today. In IE, Opera, and other browsers that don't support it, the layout looks like a broken mess (**Figure 7.19**). This is not like using border-radius and having rounded corners not show up in IE; here, the CSS3 properties we're using affect the layout of the whole page and are more than simple decorative effects.

The latest version of Modernizr can detect whether the browser supports the flexible box model, so we could use it to feed non-supporting browsers alternate layout styles using floats or other techniques. Of course, this would usually defeat the purpose of using the flexible box model to create the layout to begin with—if you have to spend the time creating a fallback float-based layout that will work everywhere, why take extra time to create a flexible-box-based layout too?

FIGURE 7.19 The layout is broken in browsers that don't support flexible box layout, such as IE 8.

But don't despair! There *are* some practical uses of flexible box layout today. In the previous section, I showed how it can be used to create full-page multi-column layouts because it illustrates most of the flexible box properties nicely, and because it demonstrates how we all might be building layouts in the future. But there are ways you can use it in a more limited manner right now.

For instance, centering the horizontal nav bar was a cinch using the flexible box model, and it degrades well in non-supporting browsers. Because I didn't use flexible box layout to make the individual links line up horizontally, but just to center the ul as a whole, IE and Opera still see a horizontal list of links—it's just left-aligned instead of centered. In many cases, this would be a perfectly acceptable fallback for non-supporting browsers, and it would keep you from having to resort to other, more complicated methods of horizontally centering a float-based nav bar.

In addition to centering a horizontal nav bar, let me show you a couple more examples of practical uses of flexible box layout.

Flexible Form Layout

One great way to use flexible box layout is to lay out and align form elements easily. As an example of this, open the exercise file form_start.html in a browser. This is the same page used in Chapter 6, with all the floats restored, so that the layout works in all browsers.

In the media query for viewports of 550 pixels and narrower, the label, text field, and button of the email newsletter subscription form lay out in a single line (**Figure 7.20**). However, the form doesn't stretch to fill up the entire width of the box it's in. It would be nice if the text field adjusted in width to fill up the remaining space left over from the label and button. This is possible to do without flexible box layout, but it involves nesting a number of divs and using complicated absolute positioning rules (see http://friedcellcollective.net/outbreak/2009/10/04/fluid-searchbox).

FIGURE 7.20 The text field is a fixed width— it looks fine now, but doesn't stretch to fill up the entire width available to it.

EMAIL NEWSLETTER
Sign up to get monthly recipes, exclusive offers and more.

Email: [   ] subscribe

But using flexible box layout makes the text-field-stretching effect easy to accomplish. First, find the `max-width: 550px` media query near the bottom of the `style` element in the head of the page. Delete the following two rules within it:

```
#form-newsletter * { display: inline; }
#form-newsletter input[type=text] { width: auto; }
```

We're deleting these rules to start out with a blank slate, so you can see how the new flexible box layout rules affect the styling of the email newsletter form without anything else interfering.

Next, turn the form into a flexible box; this will make its children lay out horizontally by default. You also need to set its width to 100 percent to make it stretch to fill the whole block it's in. Do this in a new rule for #form-newsletter inside the media query:

```
#form-newsletter {
    display: -moz-box;
    display: -o-box;
    display: -webkit-box;
    display: box;
    width: 100%;
}
```

Next, add a small amount of margin in between each of the elements in the form:

```
#form-newsletter * {
    margin-right: 3px;
}
#form-newsletter :last-child {
    margin-right: 0;
}
```

So far, the form looks pretty much as it did before—like it does in Figure 7.20—the text field is still not stretching to fill the available space. That's because all the elements of the form are being sized intrinsically right now. That's perfect for the label and the button—we want them both to be as wide as needed for their text and no wider— but we haven't told the browser we want the text field to flex. Do that now by adding the following new rule within the media query:

```
#form-newsletter input[type=text] {
    -moz-box-flex: 1;
    -o-box-flex: 1;
    -webkit-box-flex: 1;
    box-flex: 1;
}
```

Save the page and view it in Firefox, Safari, or Chrome. Narrow your window under 550 pixels to activate the media query, and then check out the newsletter subscription form. Narrow your window further and watch how the text field always fills the available space between the label text and the subscribe button (**Figure 7.21**). Even if this box were set to a fixed pixel size, if the user has a larger or smaller text size than the default, changing the overall size of the label and button, the text field will also adjust to whatever space is left.

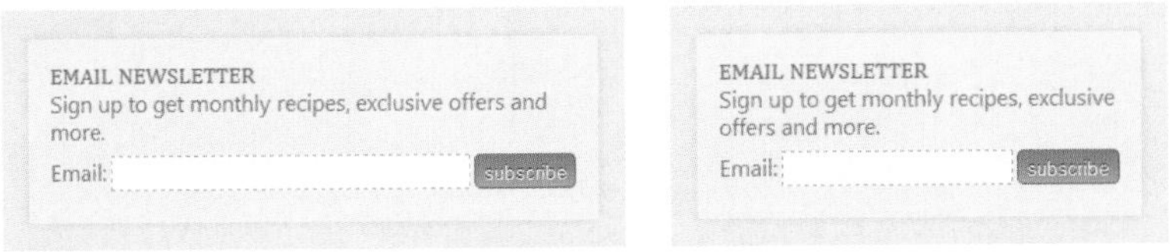

FIGURE 7.21 The text field now stretches to fill the whole space between the label and button, no matter how wide or narrow the newsletter box is.

This effect works great for search fields in headers. You can have label text, a text field, a submit button, and even a link to an advanced search, all lined up on one line, with the text field adjusting to whatever space is available. Form elements can also sometimes be hard to align as you would like, but box-align and box-pack can really simplify that task.

FALLBACK STYLES FOR NON-SUPPORTING BROWSERS

The subscription form now looks better in Firefox and Webkit-based browsers, but it looks a little worse in Opera and IE 9—browsers that *do* support media queries but don't support flexible box layout. Each element in the form is on its own line (**Figure 7.22**).

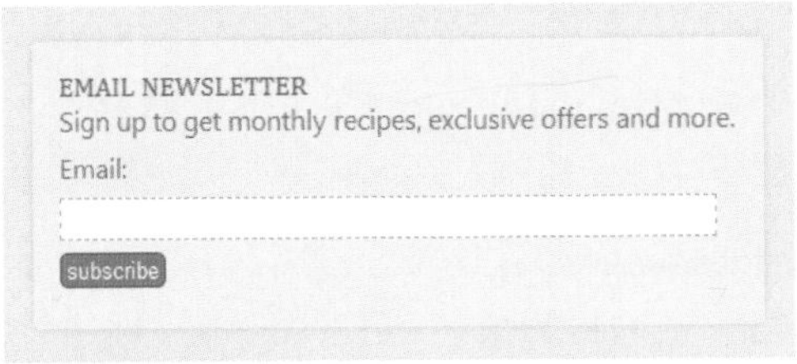

FIGURE 7.22 In browsers that don't support flexible box layout (like Opera 10.6, shown here), each element of the form is on its own line instead of sitting side by side.

Even though we can't feed these non-supporting browsers their own non-flexible-box styles, unseen by Firefox and Webkit, we can—in this case—provide fallback styles seen by all browsers that we then override for Firefox and Webkit without the non-supporting browsers knowing it.

To get the form elements back on one line in browsers that don't support flexible box layout, add `width: auto` to the #form-newsletter input[type=text] rule, and `display: inline` to the #form-newsletter * rule:

```
#form-newsletter * {
    display: inline;
    margin-right: 3px;
}
#form-newsletter input[type=text] {
    -moz-box-flex: 1;
    -o-box-flex: 1;
    -webkit-box-flex: 1;
    box-flex: 1;
    width: auto;
}
```

This restores the styles we previously had on these elements for all browsers, putting the form back on one line in Opera and IE 9. Yes, we could have left them there all along, but removing them and then adding them gives you a clearer view of the before and after.

The only problem with setting the form elements to display as inline elements instead of blocks is that this overrides the flexible box model, removing the flexibility of the text field. To get it back, keep `display: inline` in the #form-newsletter * rule, but add `display: box`, plus the browser-specific equivalents, below it:

```
#form-newsletter * {
    display: inline;
    display: -moz-box;
    display: -o-box;
    display: -webkit-box;
    display: box;
    margin-right: 3px;
}
```

Setting `display` to `box` overrides the earlier `inline` value, restoring the flexible box model and the flexibility of the text field. Browsers that don't understand the flexible box model won't understand the `box` value for the `display` property, so they ignore the subsequent `display` declarations, and therefore stick with the first one, which sets the elements to `inline`.

With these styles, users of browsers that don't support the flexible box model see the same layout for the subscription form as shown in Figure 7.20—the same styles we used in Chapter 6 for everyone—while

NOTE: The completed page is named form_final.html in the exercise files for this chapter.

users of browsers that do support the flexible box model see an enhanced version of the form, as shown in Figure 7.21. Although the scarcity of browser support may keep you from using the flexible box model to control the layout of your entire page, there's no reason why you can't use it right now in instances like this as a nice little progressive enhancement technique.

Sticky Footers

Another way you can use flexible layout right now without harming non-supporting browsers is to create a *sticky footer* effect. A sticky footer is the common name for having the footer of a page stick to the bottom of the viewport when the content isn't long enough to push it down (**Figure 7.23**). This can be accomplished without CSS3, but once again, it's more complicated. (See www.cssstickyfooter.com/using-sticky-footer-code.html for one way to do it, plus links to a number of other versions.)

FIGURE 7.23 In the left page, the footer appears at the bottom of the viewport. In the right page, the footer appears right after the content above it ends.

The key to creating a sticky footer using the flexible box model is to use box-flex to make the div *before* the footer flexible. This will make that div stretch to fill whatever space is left in the viewport after the height of the other divs has been accounted for. If there's no extra space—in other words, if the page is already longer than the viewport—the div before the footer will just be its normal height, and the footer will appear immediately after it, as usual.

To try this out yourself, open the file sticky-footer_start.html in your code editor. This is the same page from Chapter 6, but I've added a div named content around the content-main and content-secondary divs. I've also removed a bunch of content to make the page very short so you can see that the footer currently displays immediately after the content div, with extra space in the viewport appearing under the footer (**Figure 7.24**).

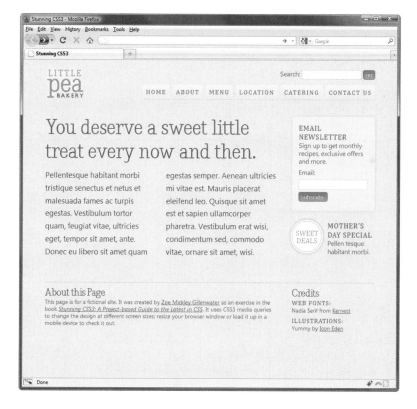

FIGURE 7.24 The footer displays right after the content div, not at the bottom of the viewport.

Since we want the entire layout to be at least as tall as the viewport at all times, we need to first set the body and html elements to stretch to be as tall as the viewport, even if they don't contain much content.

Create a rule for the html element, setting its height to 100 percent, and add height: 100% to the existing body rule as well:

```
html {
    height: 100%;
}
body {
    height: 100%;
    margin: 0;
    padding: 0;
    background: url(images/background.jpg);
    color: #666;
    font-family: "Segoe UI", Segoe, Calibri, Arial,
    ¬ sans-serif;
    font-size: 100%;
    line-height: 1.6;
}
```

Next, turn the wrapper div into a flexible box using the display property, and tell it to display its children vertically using the box-orient property. And set its minimum height to 100 percent, so that it will always be at least as tall as the viewport:

```
#wrapper {
    display: -moz-box;
    display: -o-box;
    display: -webkit-box;
    display: box;
    -moz-box-orient: vertical;
    -o-box-orient: vertical;
    -webkit-box-orient: vertical;
    box-orient: vertical;
    min-height: 100%;
    margin: 0 6%;
}
```

This makes the three children divs of the wrapper—named header, content, and footer—stack vertically. This is already their normal behavior, so adding these properties doesn't change the appearance in any browsers, whether or not they support the flexible box model. But we have to make the wrapper div into a flexible box in order to make any of its children flex.

The child div that we want to flex is the content divs, so add a new rule for it, setting box-flex to 1:

```
#content {
    -moz-box-flex: 1;
    -o-box-flex: 1;
    -webkit-box-flex: 1;
    box-flex: 1;
}
```

Now, after the intrinsic height of the header and footer have been accounted for, whatever extra height is left inside the wrapper div goes to the content div, so that the combined heights of the three divs always equals at least the height of the viewport. Thus, the footer sits at the bottom of the viewport instead of right underneath the content div (**Figure 7.25**).

FIGURE 7.25 Now the footer sits at the bottom of the viewport, with any extra space placed between it and the content div.

Browsers that don't support the flexible box model simply ignore this rule and see the page as it was before (and as almost all pages online behave): the footer appears right under the content div. Users of these browsers have no reason to know that they're seeing something a little different than others. The sticky footer is just another decorative bonus for users of the most advanced browsers.

NOTE: The completed page is named sticky-footer_final.html in the exercise files for this chapter.

THE LOWDOWN ON THE FLEXIBLE BOX LAYOUT MODEL

The Flexible Box Layout module is found at www.w3.org/TR/css3-flexbox. The flexible box model is a new system of properties for creating layouts that provides more control over alignment and use of space than the layout-related properties of CSS 2.1.

To invoke the flexible box model, you set the `display` property of a wrapper element to `box`, a new value in CSS3. You then control the child blocks of the flexible box using a series of new properties (shown in **Table 7.4**).

Other than the examples already given in this chapter, you might want to use flexible box layout for:

- Putting the most important content block first in the HTML but not placing it visually first in the layout, using `box-direction` or `box-ordinal-group`

- Moving a featured blog post or product to the top of the page, even if it's not first in the HTML, using `box-ordinal-group`

- Creating a full-width horizontal nav, with each button stretching, using `box-flex`

- A nav bar where the hovered-over or current item takes up the remaining space to become larger than other links; see www.ie7nomore.com/fun/flexiblenav.

- Image galleries, with different-height thumbnails vertically centered in each row

- Video player controls where a slider takes up the remaining space after buttons are accounted for; see http://clubajax.org/css3-layouts-the-flexible-box-model-basics.

- Vertically centering a content image next to its descriptive block of text

Most of these examples are not practical to use right now, given the level of browser support and bugs, but if you're building an app for a particular browser, such as Safari on iOS, they may be worth trying now.

TABLE 7.3 Flexible box model browser support

IE	FIREFOX	OPERA	SAFARI	CHROME
No	Partial with -moz-	No	Partial with -webkit-	Partial with -webkit-

TABLE 7.4 Flexible box model properties

PROPERTY	ALLOWS YOU TO:
box-orient	Stack the blocks vertically or horizontally
box-direction	Reverse the default top-to-bottom or left-to-right stacking order
box-ordinal-group	Number the blocks in the order you want them to appear, providing more control over stacking order than box-direction alone
box-flex	Make blocks flex to fill up available space left over after other blocks have been accounted for
box-flex-group	Group flexible blocks using numbers, so that when there's extra space, the browser will first adjust the widths of all the blocks in the first flex group, and then move on to the second if there's still extra space, etc.
box-align	Control the alignment and placement of blocks along the axis perpendicular to the one they're on, including stretching to fill the available space to create equal-height or equal-width blocks
box-pack	Control the alignment and placement of blocks along the same axis that they're on
box-lines	Let the box wrap its children if they don't all fit on a single line, similar to how floats will drop down instead of overflow

Alternatives to the Flexible Box Model

Flexible box layout is not the only new layout tool in CSS3. There are other layout systems and properties in the works, with varying levels of browser support. We'll start with the best-supported, versatile box-sizing property, and then talk about what we can look forward to.

The box-sizing Property

In the traditional W3C box model of CSS 2.1, the value you declare for width or height controls the width or height of the content area only, and then the padding and border are added onto it. This is called the content-box model, and if you've worked with CSS for a while, you're probably used to it and don't really think much about it. But it can be inconvenient to work with at times, such as when you want to set a box's width and padding in different units of measurement from each other, like percentages for the width and pixels for the padding.

For instance, what if we wanted to give each of the three featured product boxes in our bakery page a background color and use padding in pixels to move the content in the boxes away from the edges of the color? And what if we also wanted to give each box a border in pixels?

To see what would happen in this scenario, open the file box-sizing_ start.html from the exercise files for this chapter. It's the same page from Chapter 6, with the media queries removed just to keep things simple.

Find the existing .feature rule on line 116, about halfway down the style element in the head of the page. Modify the padding value to add padding to the sides and bottom of each box:

```
.feature {
    float: left;
    width: 30%;
    margin: 0 4.5% 0 0;
    padding: 130px 15px 5px 15px;
    background-repeat: no-repeat;
    background-position: top center;
}
```

Next, add a background color and border:

```
.feature {
    float: left;
    width: 30%;
    margin: 0 4.5% 0 0;
    padding: 130px 15px 5px 15px;
    border: 1px dashed #3C9;
    background-color: hsla(0,0%,100%,.3);
    background-repeat: no-repeat;
    background-position: top center;
}
```

Save your page and view it in a browser. The third box will have dropped down onto a new line (**Figure 7.26**). That's because the total space each box takes up is 30 percent plus two pixels for the side borders plus 30 pixels for the side padding. When you add on the 4.5 percent margin on the first and second boxes, the total space the three boxes take up is now greater than 100 percent. How much greater than 100 percent we don't know—it will be different at each viewport size—but the point is that combining pixels and percentages makes it impossible to know what width to set each box to in order to make them all fit.

tempor sit amet, ante. Donec eu libero sit amet quam egestas semper. Aenean ultricies mi vitae est. Mauris placerat eleifend leo. Quisque sit amet est et sapien

ipsum rutrum orci, sagittis tempus lacus enim ac dui. Donec non enim in turpis pulvinar facilisis. Ut felis.

Candies
TRUFFLES, BARS, CARAMELS, AND MORE
Pellentesque habitant morbi tristique senectus et netus et malesuada fames ac turpis egestas. Vestibulum tortor quam, feugiat vitae, ultricies eget, tempor sit amet, ante.

Pastries
CROISSANTS, DANISHES, CREAM PUFFS, AND MORE
Vestibulum tortor quam, feugiat vitae, ultricies eget, tempor sit amet, ante. Donec eu libero sit amet quam egestas semper. Aenean ultricies mi vitae est.

Desserts
CAKES, PIES, TARTS, COOKIES, AND MORE
Donec eu libero sit amet quam egestas semper. Aenean ultricies mi vitae est. Mauris placerat eleifend leo. Vestibulum tortor quam, feugiat vitae, ultricies eget, tempor sit amet, ante.

DEALS Pellen tesque habitant morbi tristique senectus et netus et malesuada fames ac turpis egestas.

NEWS
Lorem ipsum dolor sit amet, consectetuer adipiscing elit

Aliquam tincidunt mauris eu risus

Vestibulum auctor dapibus neque

Read more at our blog and follow us on Twitter.

FIGURE 7.26
The Desserts box has dropped onto a new line because the addition of padding and borders onto each box doesn't leave room for it above.

To try to fix this, you could decrease the width of each box. Try setting it to 25 percent instead of 30, and you'll see that the three boxes now fit on one line at some window sizes—but on narrower ones, the last box still drops down (**Figure 7.27**). Plus, on very wide windows, there's an extra gap to the right of the third box. They no longer perfectly fill up the row at all times.

Instead of changing the width of the boxes, another way to work around this would be to nest another div inside each feature box and apply the border and padding to this inner div instead. That way, each outer box would still take up exactly 30 percent, with the border and padding nested inside, effectively subtracted from that 30 percent. Nesting a few extra divs in this page wouldn't be that big a deal, but in complicated designs, the number of extra divs can really add up, which increases both your development time and the file size of the HTML and CSS.

FIGURE 7.27 Decreasing the width of each individual box makes all boxes fit across in larger viewports, but not in narrower ones.

The more efficient, CSS3 way to handle this is to leave the HTML alone and set the new `box-sizing` property to `border-box` instead of the default `content-box`. When a box is using the border-box box model, the browser will subtract the padding and border from the width of the box instead of adding it (**Figure 7.28**). You always know that the total space the box takes up equals the `width` value you've declared.

FIGURE 7.28
The difference between `content-box` **and** `border-box` **is whether the** `width` **determines the size of the content area or the entire box from border to border.**

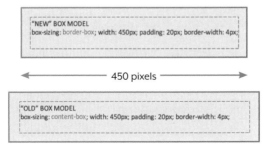

MORE COMPLEX WIDTH CALCULATIONS

Another piece of CSS3 that would come in handy in our mixed-units example page is the calc function. It can be used as a value wherever length units are allowed, such as with the width and margin properties, to specify an equation that computes a length. For instance, on our bakery page, we could set each feature box's width value to calc(30% - 32px).

The really cool and powerful thing about calc is that you can use much more complicated equations than the one I just provided, allowing it to handle much more than box-sizing can. The downside is that you have to hard-code the values into the equation, so if you later change padding, for instance, you have to also remember to change it in the calc function.

Unfortunately, as of this writing, no browser supports calc. The upcoming Firefox 4 will, along with the min and max functions, but these functions are not yet in the beta versions that are publicly available. See http://hacks.mozilla.org/2010/06/css3-calc for more information on Firefox's implementation as well as examples for how to use calc in general. The official W3C description is at www.w3.org/TR/css3-values/#calc.

With the width value back at 30%, add the box-sizing property, plus the -moz- and -webkit- versions, to the .feature rule:

```
.feature {
    float: left;
    -moz-box-sizing: border-box;
    -webkit-box-sizing: border-box;
    box-sizing: border-box;
    width: 30%;
    margin: 0 4.5% 0 0;
    padding: 130px 15px 5px 15px;
    border: 1px dashed #3C9;
    background-color: hsla(0,0%,100%,.3);
    background-repeat: no-repeat;
    background-position: top center;
}
```

The `-moz-` version is used by Firefox, the `-webkit-` version by Safari and Chrome, and the non-prefixed version by Opera and IE 8 and later. Now the total space each box takes up is still 30 percent, and the border and padding are inside this width, making the content area of each box 30 percent minus 32 pixels. This allows all three boxes to fit on the same line at all times (**Figure 7.29**).

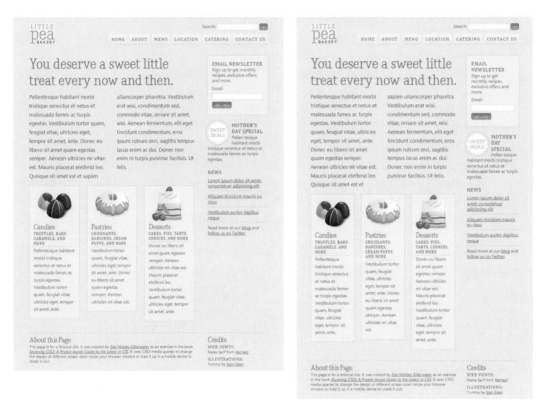

FIGURE 7.29 With `box-sizing` set to border-box, **all three boxes fit on the same line at all window sizes.**

TABLE 7.5 `box-sizing` **browser support**

IE	FIREFOX	OPERA	SAFARI	CHROME
Yes, 8+	Yes with -moz-	Yes	Yes with -webkit-	Yes with -webkit-

THE LOWDOWN ON THE box-sizing PROPERTY

The box-sizing property is part of the Basic User Interface module found at www.w3.org/TR/css3-ui. It allows you to switch the box model between content-box, where the padding and border of a box are added onto its declared width and height, and border-box, where the padding and border are subtracted from its width and height.

Firefox supports a third value, padding-box, that subtracts the padding but not the borders from the width and height. It's not part of the W3C specification and doesn't look like it will be added.

The box-sizing property is good for:

◆ Mixing units of measurements within a single box, so that you can determine what total space it takes up and make room for it alongside other boxes.

◆ Making a box stretch to 100 percent to fill its parent, while still sporting padding and borders.

WORKAROUNDS FOR IE 7 AND EARLIER

IE 7 and earlier versions do not support box-sizing, which, like flexible box layout, produces an effect that's more essential than purely decorative. Thus, you'll probably want to provide a workaround. In our case, the easiest workaround is to set the padding in percentages instead of pixels and reduce the width of each box by the same amount. Add the following new rule:

```
.ie6 .feature, .ie7 .feature {
    width: 25.5%;
    padding: 130px 2% 5px 2%;
}
```

This effectively maintains each box at 30 percent wide—two percent padding on each side plus 25 percent width equals 29.5, which leaves a little extra wiggle room for those pixel-sized borders. While percentage-sized padding may not be ideal, it looks only slightly different than pixel-sized padding, and it's certainly better than having the third box dropped to a new line!

NOTE: The completed page is named box-sizing_final.html in the exercise files for this chapter.

An alternative workaround is to put IE into quirks mode, which uses the same sort of box model as border-box provides. But I wouldn't recommend it. For one thing, it's much harder to put IE 7 into quirks mode than earlier versions. It basically requires you to use an old or ill-formed DOCTYPE, which harms all browsers. Plus, once it's in quirks mode, you would need to make sure you were using the border-box model throughout your entire site; otherwise, some boxes will look correct in IE 7 and earlier and others will look broken.

Your final option for working around the lack of box-sizing support is to use a script. Dean Edwards' IE7 script (http://code.google.com/p/ie7-js) makes box-sizing work in IE, but only if you use the IE8.js or IE9.js version of the script. The downside to using a script, of course, is that it doesn't work if JavaScript is not enabled. Again, the box-sizing property is more essential to the overall layout and look of the page, so relying on JavaScript may be a little risky in this case.

Future Layout Systems

Flexible box layout is not the only new layout system in CSS3. There are currently two other layout systems, called *template layout* and *grid positioning*. Both are in the early stages of development (especially grid positioning); no browser supports them or plans to do so soon. However, it's worth briefly describing each so you can get a glimpse of what may be coming down the road.

TEMPLATE LAYOUT

CSS3 template layout (previously called "advanced layout") allows you to place content into "slots" in the page layout. You define these slots with letters placed into a grid, like ASCII art, in the display property. For instance, here's what a grid could look like:

```
body {
    display: "aaa"
             "bcc";
             "ddd";
}
```

Then, you assign divs to sit in each of those lettered slots, like so:

```
#header { position: a; }
#content { position: b; }
#sidebar { position: c; }
#footer { position: d; }
```

It can get a lot more complicated than this, of course—we haven't assigned widths to any of the slots, heights to any of the rows, or gaps between elements, for instance. But the point is that you can move any div placed anywhere in the HTML to any spot visually on the page, and you can easily make elements span multiple columns. Some people love this flexibility and simplicity; others passionately hate the whole idea behind CSS3 template layout.

Either way, you can learn more about it at www.w3.org/TR/css3-layout. If you want to play around with it now, Alexis Deveria has made a jQuery plugin to make it work using JavaScript; see http://code.google.com/p/css-template-layout.

GRID POSITIONING

CSS3 grid positioning also allows you to create grids, naturally, but not with a series of letters. Instead, you use the grid-columns and grid-rows properties to explicitly declare a grid. You still use floating or absolute positioning to move the elements around the page, but you can place them in relation to the grid you've created using the new gr unit, a grid unit equal to the width of one of your columns, as well as the new float-offset property.

The first draft of the grid-positioning module (www.w3.org/TR/css3-grid) came out in September 2007, and it hasn't been updated since then, so its status is not very clear. The W3C may consolidate the template and grid modules together, partially or completely. Even if they don't consolidate them, it remains to be seen if or how they can be used together, as well as how they interact with flexible box layout. It's all pretty murky right now.

Browser
Support

The following table repeats all the browser support information given throughout the chapters for the covered CSS3 properties, selectors, and functionality. In a few cases, there were notes provided alongside the original tables to provide supplemental information; those notes have been removed from this appendix.

TABLE A.1 Browser support for CSS3 properties, selectors, and functionality

CSS3 FUNCTIONALITY	COVERED IN CHAPTER	IE	FIREFOX	OPERA	SAFARI	CHROME
@font-face	3	Yes	Yes, 3.5+	Yes, 10+	Yes	Yes
:nth-child()	5	Yes, 9+	Yes, 3.5+	Yes	Yes	Yes
:nth-of-type()	5	Yes, 9+	Yes, 3.5+	Yes	Yes	Yes
:target	5	Yes, 9+	Yes	Partial	Yes	Yes
2D transforms	2	No	Yes with -moz-, 3.5+	Yes with -o-, 10.5+	Yes with -webkit-	Yes with -webkit-
3D transforms	2	No	No	No	Yes with -webkit-, 5+	No
animation	5	No	No	No	Yes with -webkit-	Yes with -webkit-
Attribute selectors	4	Yes, 7+	Yes	Yes	Yes	Yes
background-clip	3	Yes, 9+	Yes, 4+; Partial, 1+, with -moz-	Yes	Yes, 3+, with -webkit-; Partial, 5+	Yes
background-size		Yes, 9+	Yes, 4+; 3.6 with -moz-	Yes	Yes, 5+; 3+ with -webkit-	Yes
border-image	3	No	Partial with -moz-, 3.5+	Partial, 10.5+	Partial with -webkit-	Partial
border-radius	2	Yes, 9+	Yes with -moz-	Yes	Yes, 5+; 4+ with -webkit-	Yes
box-shadow	2	Partial, 9+	Yes with -moz-, 3.5+	Yes, 10.5+	Yes with -webkit-	Yes with -webkit-
box-sizing	7	Yes, 8+	Yes with -moz-	Yes	Yes with -webkit-	Yes with -webkit-
Flexible box model	7	No	Partial with -moz-	No	Partial with -webkit-	Partial with -webkit-
Gradients	2	No	Yes, 3.6+, with -moz-	No	Yes, with -webkit-	Yes, with -webkit-
Media queries	6	Partial, 9+	Partial, 3.5+	Partial	Partial	Partial
Multi-columns	6	No	Partial	No	Partial	Partial
Multiple background images	3	Yes, 9+	Yes, 3.6+	Yes, 10.5+	Yes	Yes
RGBA/HSLA	2	Yes, 9+	Yes	Yes	Yes	Yes
text-shadow	2	No	Yes	Yes	Yes	Yes
transition	5	No	Yes with -moz-, 4+	Yes with -o-, 10.5+	Yes with -webkit-	Yes with -webkit-
word-wrap	2	Yes, 5.5+	Yes, 3.5+	Yes	Yes	Yes

Conclusion

Thanks for sticking with me on this journey through engaging visual effects, attractive typography, powerful selectors, and effective usability enhancements. You've learned how to make pages that offer as rich and enjoyable an experience as possible to all your visitors, while using efficient, cutting-edge, and standards-compliant CSS techniques.

I hope that you'll use the new techniques you've learned to experiment, have fun, and improve your work. As I've said before, CSS3 is still evolving and we web designers are still learning how to use it to its full extent. When you create something cool with it, please share! Email me through the form on www.stunningcss3.com, or share with the web design community on Twitter using the hash tag #stunningcss3. Let's all learn from each other how we can make the web more stunning.

Index

Credits

FIGURES

FIGURE 1.1 www.w3.org

FIGURES 1.3–1.7 www.hsrc.unc.edu

FIGURES 1.8 and **1.9** www.twitter.com

FIGURE 2.8 www.digitalmediaminute.com/reference/entity

FIGURE 2.26 www.useragentman.com/IETransformsTranslator

FIGURES 3.27 and **3.28** www.fontsquirrel.com

FIGURE 5.8 http://en.wikipedia.org

FIGURE 7.23 www.cssstickyfooter.com

RESOURCES IN THE EXERCISE FILES

The water stain images used in the exercise files for Chapters 3, 4, and 5 were created with Photoshop brushes by Obsidian Dawn (www.obsidiandawn.com/water-stains-photoshop-gimp-brushes).

The Prelude font provided in the exercise files for Chapters 3, 4, and 5 is from Font Squirrel (www.fontsquirrel.com).

The icons provided in the exercise files for Chapters 4 and 5 are part of the famfamfam Silk icon set designed by Mark James (www.famfamfam.com/lab/icons/silk).

The Modernizr script (modernizr-1.6.min.js) provided in the exercise files for Chapter 5 was created by Faruk Ateş and Paul Irish (www.modernizr.com).

The css3-mediaqueries-js script (css3-mediaqueries.js) provided in the exercise files for Chapter 6 was created by Wouter van der Graaf (http://code.google.com/p/css3-mediaqueries-js).

The illustrations used in the exercise pages for Chapters 6 and 7 are part of the Yummy icon set designed by Icon Eden (www.iconeden.com/icon/yummy-free-icons.html).

The Nadia Serif font provided in the exercise files for Chapters 6 and 7 is from Kernest (www.kernest.com).

My thanks to all of the developers and designers who created these assets and allowed me to use them in this book.

Meet Creative Edge.

A new resource of unlimited books, videos and tutorials for creatives from the world's leading experts.

Creative Edge is your one stop for inspiration, answers to technical questions and ways to stay at the top of your game so you can focus on what you do best—being creative.

All for only $24.99 per month for access—any day any time you need it.

peachpit.com/creativeedge